The Anthropology of Pregnancy Loss

The Anthropology of Pregnancy Loss

Comparative Studies in Miscarriage, Stillbirth and Neonatal Death

Edited by
Rosanne Cecil

Berg
Oxford • Washington, D.C.

First published in 1996 by
Berg
Editorial offices:
150 Cowley Road, Oxford, OX4 1JJ, UK
13950 Park Center Road, Herndon, VA 22071, USA

Berg is the imprint of Oxford International Publishers Ltd.

Library of Congress Cataloging-in-Publication Data

A catalogue record for this book is available from the Library of Congress.

British Library Cataloguing-in-Publication Data

A catalogue record for this book is available from the British Library.

ISBN 1 85973 120 1 (Cloth)
1 85973 125 2 (Paper)

Typeset by JS Typesetting, Wellingborough, Northants.
Printed in the United Kingdom by WBC Book Manufacturers, Bridgend, Mid Glamorgan.

Contents

Part II Other Studies

Acknowledgements

Many people have contributed in different ways to the production of this book. In particular I must thank my colleagues in the Department of Social Anthropology at the Queen's University of Belfast, especially Hastings Donnan, Declan Quigley and Elizabeth Tonkin, as well as Simon Harrison at the University of Ulster. My thanks also go to my husband, Julian Leslie, who has, as always, given generously of his time and advice. Finally, I would like to thank the contributing authors who have received the comments and suggestions of a novice editor with great courtesy and goodwill.

Rosanne Cecil
Belfast

Notes on Contributors

Rosanne Cecil is a Research Fellow in the Department of Social Anthropology, the Queen's University of Belfast (Northern Ireland). She has undertaken work into miscarriage and other aspects of women's reproductive health. She previously carried out research into sectarianism, kinship and gender in Northern Ireland. Her publications include (with John Offer and Fred St Leger) *Informal Welfare: A Sociological Study of Care in Northern Ireland*, Aldershot, Gower, 1987. Her main research interests are in medical anthropology, dietary practices and beliefs, and religious practice and discourse.

Beverley Chalmers is an Associate Professor and Clinical Scientist at the University of Toronto, Perinatal Clinical Epidemiology Unit (Canada). Her areas of interest lie in the field of health psychology, particularly maternal and child health, and multi-cultural health psychology and health promotion. Formerly at the University of Witwatersrand (South Africa), she is the author of over a hundred publications, including *African Birth: Childbirth in Cultural Transition*, Sandton, Berev Publications, 1990, and *Pregnancy and Parenthood*, Sandton, Berev Publications, 1990.

Michael A. DeLuca is a doctoral student in anthropology at the State University of New York, Binghampton (USA). His research interests include growth and development, human ecology, and the biological and health implications of sedentism among formerly nomadic peoples. His current research focus is reproductive ecology and intra-uterine mortality among the Turkana population of northwestern Kenya.

Mark Jackson is a Research Associate and Lecturer at the Wellcome Unit for the History of Medicine in the University of Manchester (England). He is the author of *New-born Child Murder: Women, Illegitimacy and the Courts in Eighteenth-Century England*, Manchester, Manchester University Press, 1996. His current research interests include the social history of mental deficiency in the late nineteenth and early twentieth centuries (on which subject he has several recent and forthcoming public-ations), and a new project on the history of immunology in the twentieth century.

Patricia Jeffery is Professor in the Department of Sociology, University of Edinburgh (Scotland). Her interests include gender and development, especially childbearing, women's reproductive rights, social demography and population policies in South Asia. Her publications include *Migrants and Refugees: Muslim and Christian Pakistani Families in Bristol*, Cambridge, Cambridge University Press, 1976; *Frogs in a Well: Indian Women in Purdah*, London, Zed Press, 1979, and (with Roger Jeffery and Andrew Lyon) *Labour Pains and Labour Power: Women and Childbearing in India*, London, Zed Books, 1989. She and Roger Jeffery are co-authors of two other books, *Don't Marry me to a Plowman! Village Women in North India*, Boulder, Colorado, Westview Press, 1996 and *Population and Politics: Gender, Class and Ethnicity in Rural North India*, Cambridge, Cambridge University Press, forthcoming.

Roger Jeffery is Senior Lecturer in the Department of Sociology, University of Edinburgh (Scotland). His interests include social demography, agrarian change and forest management. Apart from his joint publications with Patricia Jeffery, his publications include *The Politics of Health in India*, Berkeley, Los Angeles, and London, University of California Press, 1988, several articles on health policy in India and Pakistan, and a collection (co-edited with Alaka Basu) entitled *Girl's Schooling, Women's Autonomy and Fertility Change in South Asia*, New Delhi, Newbury Park, California and London, Sage, 1996.

Linda L. Layne, a cultural anthropologist, is Alma and H. Erwin Hale '30 Teaching Professor of Humanities and Social Sciences in the Department of Science and Technology Studies, Rensselaer Polytechnic Institute, New York (USA). She is the author of *Home and Homeland: The Dialogics of Tribal and National Identities in Jordan*, Princeton, New Jersey, Princeton University Press, 1994, and *Motherhood Lost: Cultural Constructions of Miscarriage and Stillbirth in America*, New York, Routledge, forthcoming. She is the editor of *Elections in the Middle East*, Boulder, Colorado, Westview Press, 1987. Her current research interests include new reproductive technologies, the intersections of biomedical, religious and popular discourses, representations of nature, technoscience and everyday life in the USA and the Arab world.

Paul W. Leslie is an anthropologist with interests in human ecology and demography. He pursued his graduate training at Pennsylvania State University and is currently Associate Professor of Anthropology and Fellow, Carolina Population Center, University of North Carolina at

Chapel Hill (USA). He has conducted research in the Caribbean and East Africa, most recently focusing on the ecology of reproduction among the Turkana of northwest Kenya. He is the author of a number of works on demography and human biology, reproductive ecology, and the Turkana of northwest Kenya.

Olayinka M. Njikam Savage, an anthropologist, is Senior Lecturer in the Department of Sociology, University of Douala (Cameroon). She is a Technical Adviser of the Cameroon National Family Planning Association, CAMNAFAW. Her research interests include socio-cultural aspects of fertility control and management, infertility (including fetal wastage), assisted reproduction and breast-feeding. She is the author of a number of works, including *Some Socio-cultural and Behavioural Aspects of Sexually Transmitted Diseases (STD) and Infertility in Cameroon*, Cameroon, University Annals of Medical Science, 1991.

Elisa Janine Sobo is a Lecturer in the Department of Anthropology at the University of Durham, England. Her recent book *One Blood: The Jamaican Body*, Albany, State University of New York Press, 1993, concerns traditional Jamaican ethnophysiological and ethnomedical beliefs and practices. The Jamaican research has also led to a number of publications in journals and edited collections. In addition to the Caribbean research Dr Sobo is active in the field of HIV/AIDS studies. A book concerning her research with inner-city African Americans, *Women, Relationships and AIDS Risk Denial* is forthcoming, and articles on this subject have appeared in a number of journals. Dr Sobo has taught anthropology in the USA at New Mexico State University, Case Western Reserve University and the University of Arizona.

J.A.R. Wembah-Rashid is a socio-cultural anthropologist and museologist with research interests in economic development, medical and applied anthropology, contemporary Eastern African art and crafts and gender, refugees and biodiversity. He obtained his Ph.D from the University of Illinois at Urbana-Champaign in 1983 and is currently Senior Research Fellow at the Institute of African Studies, the University of Nairobi (Kenya). He is the author of *Introducing Tanzania through the National Museum*, Dar es Salaam, National Museums of Tanzania, 1974, and *The Ethno-History of the Matrilineal Peoples of Southeast Tanzania*, Vienna, E. Stiglmyr, 1975.

Anna Winkvist is a Research Associate in the Department of Epidemiology and Public Health, Umea University (Sweden). Her work focuses on the health of women and children from both anthropological and epidemiological perspectives. The research described in this volume was undertaken while working at the Division of Nutritional Sciences as well as at the Program on International Development and Women, Cornell University, New York (USA). Other work by Dr Winkvist includes nutritional and ethnographic studies of low-income women in Punjab, Pakistan.

Introduction: An Insignificant Event? Literary and Anthropological Perspectives on Pregnancy Loss

Rosanne Cecil

Introduction

The loss of a pregnancy through miscarriage, stillbirth, abortion, or the birth of a non-viable child is a subject which raises a number of questions of anthropological interest. It has not, however, hitherto been the focus of much anthropological investigation. This may seem rather surprising when one considers that pregnancy loss is linked so closely on the one hand to reproduction and birth, a subject which has, particularly in recent years, been an area of anthropological concern, and on the other hand to death and thus to the anthropological interest in funerary rites and rituals. Pregnancy loss also touches upon the very question of what is human: When does life begin? What is human and what is not? These are surely questions of fundamental concern to every society.

It may seem self-evident that a pregnancy loss cannot have the social impact of either a birth or a death. It does not result in the creation of a new person who is to be incorporated into society, neither is it the loss of one who has been a recognized part of the existing social order. Yet only an examination of miscarriages and other pregnancy losses from a comparative perspective can determine whether this is necessarily the case. How a miscarriage is viewed, experienced and managed, and how (and indeed, if) it is spoken of and expressed, may rest upon a wide range of social and cultural factors. A fundamental issue is likely to be the stage (pre- or post-partum) at which the fetus/baby is attributed with human status; this may vary widely across different cultures and at different periods in history. It is an issue addressed in a number of the chapters which follow, for the focus of this collection is on involuntary pregnancy loss and how it is experienced, managed and understood in culturally and historically diverse situations. The distinctions between different *types* of pregnancy loss are not always clear cut. It could be argued that abortion for many, if not all, women is no more a choice, in terms of social, financial and familial constraints, than is miscarriage (see, for example, Hey, 1989). Termination for fetal abnormality closes still further the gap between the voluntary and the involuntary (see the work of Rapp, 1988, 1991). While the focus of this book is upon involuntary loss, in particular miscarriage, it is inevitable that at times the full range of pregnancy losses is addressed.

When I first began to undertake research into pregnancy loss (specifically into miscarriage), I found that work in the area was conducted almost exclusively by psychologists and medical practitioners, although social scientists such as Lovell (1983), Oakley, McPherson and Roberts (1984) and Reinharz (1988) had also published work on the subject. What seemed to be lacking was a body of anthropological work based on ethnographic study in a range of different cultures. Very little anthropological work seemed to have been undertaken into pregnancy loss. When I began to review the literature I found a number of studies which made some reference to pregnancy loss, though in very few of these was it central to the narrative.

The dearth of ethnographic writing on pregnancy loss is not perhaps surprising, for many aspects of women's lives have escaped thorough documentation. This may in part reflect the interests of ethnographers in the past as well as, perhaps, their more restricted access to women informants. What is likely to be more significant is women's attitudes to their pregnancy losses and their willingness and ability to talk about them. If a woman's primary role is considered to be the bearing of children, then the loss of a pregnancy or the birth of a non-viable baby will be considered a failure. What is more, the loss of a pregnancy is frequently accompanied by a considerable amount of physical pain, blood and mess. It is an embarrassing failure and one that may not be easy to talk about. As the actual experience of pregnancy, childbirth and pregnancy loss can only be known by women, one issue is the relationship between gender and language use (discussed by Ardener (1975a, 1975b), Philips, Steele and Tanz (1987) and Cameron (1990) among many others). There may not, quite literally, be the words to discuss and describe the event. Leclerc has written of the difficulty or impossibility of writing about pregnancy and childbirth: 'Who could tell me, could I ever express (and what words would I use) . . .' (1990, p. 76). The feelings concerning simultaneous birth and death, the death of one who never was, may be virtually impossible to convey.

Pregnancy Loss in Literature

Some indication of the significance which a pregnancy loss has for a culture can be gleaned from considering how miscarriages and other losses are dealt with in its literature and poetry. If ethnographies may be viewed as works of fiction (see Clifford and Marcus, 1986), conversely, fiction may offer insights of anthropological interest by expressing and reflecting some of the dominant interests and concerns of a society. In both types of narrative, the subject matter will be that which the writer chooses to focus upon. What is given expression through the mouths of informants/characters is necessarily largely what is of interest to the writer; and what is of interest to the writer will have its roots, not only within his or her personal biography, but also within the hegemonic ideology of the day. 'Even the best ethnographic texts – serious, true fictions – are systems, or economies, of truth. Power and history work through them . . .' (Clifford, 1986, p. 7)

Before considering how pregnancy loss has been addressed within social anthropology, an attempt is made here to assess how pregnancy loss is presented within the literature of Western (mainly British) writers, that is, that literature with which I am most familiar. Within this restricted field, I have ranged rather widely in terms of time periods, the gender of the writers and the form of the writing (prose and poetry). While a more systematic study would take these differences into account, this brief review merely endeavours to illustrate that, with a few exceptions, pregnancy loss has rarely been portrayed in any detail within literature.

Leroy (1988) suggests that the theme of the loss of a child as a punishment for wrong-doing, which occurs in a number of fairy tales and legends, indicates that this is 'a persistent part of human thinking about reproduction' (p. 96). That is: 'Bad actions lead to the loss of a child, or the loss of a child is the punishment for some transgressions or failure' (p. 96). Thus, for example, in the tale of Rapunzel a man steals lettuce for his pregnant wife from a witch's garden. When he is caught by the witch, she lets him have the lettuce but demands to be given the child in return, when it is born.

While a number of fairy tales tell of the loss of a child or, even more frequently, the longing of a childless couple for a baby, there is no portrayal of pregnancy loss as such. However, the tale of Tom Thumb tells the strange story of a tiny child who is born at three months gestation (that is, around the time at which a miscarriage is most likely to occur) and proceeds to have a number of adventures. The magician Merlin tells the wife of 'Thomas of the mountaine', who was persuaded by her husband to go to him to be cured of her barrenness:

> Ere thrice the Moone her brightnes change,
> A shapelesse child by wonder strange,
> Shall come abortiue from thy wombe,
> No bigger than thy Husbands Thumbe:
> And as desire hath him begot,
> He shall haue life, but substance not;
> No blood, nor bones in him shall grow,
> Not seene, but when he pleaseth so:
> His shapelesse shadow shall be such,
> You'l heare him speake, but not him touch:
> And till the world to ending come,
> There shall be Tales told of Tom Thumbe.
> (quoted in Opie and Opie, 1974, p. 42)

In this tale a child, who is miraculously born alive at an early stage of his mother's pregnancy, embarks upon a series of fantastic adventures which would not have been possible for a fully grown (full-term) child.

In the literature of the nineteenth century, references to the loss of infants and young children are not uncommon. References to miscarriage or a stillbirth are less so and, if made at all, are dealt with fairly briefly as, for example, in the work of George Eliot and Thomas Hardy. In Eliot's *Middlemarch*, the miscarriage of Rosamond is mentioned as if in passing and is of no significance to the subsequent events in the narrative. The miscarriage which occurs in Hardy's *Jude the Obscure* follows immediately upon the violent death of three young children. The main female character, Sue, the mother of two of the children and the stepmother of the third, is so shocked and distressed by their deaths that she goes into premature labour and loses her baby. The impact of this additional tragedy is largely subsumed by the horror of the first three deaths. In Hardy's *The Mayor of Casterbridge*, the impact of the miscarriage of Lucetta is presented as being of little significance in itself; the main tragedy lies in the consequent death of the would-be mother.

Portrayals of pregnancy loss have tended to present miscarriage as an event which occurs within wedlock, abortion as one which occurs out of it. Rosamond Lehmann's novel *The Weather in the Streets* (published in 1936), while conforming to this pattern, is interesting in its presentation of abortion and miscarriage and of the distress associated with both types of pregnancy loss. The abortion of the pregnancy of the central character, Olivia, stands in juxtaposition to the miscarriage of the wife of Olivia's lover. Although the wife is barely portrayed in the book, it is nevertheless her miscarriage and her subsequent long-term physical and emotional weakness which hangs as the backdrop to the affair of the two main characters. Olivia's pregnancy and abortion occur, with ironic timing, at the point when her lover's wife achieves a second and presumably successful pregnancy.

The 'social realism' of some later twentieth-century novels resulted in the portrayal of a number of hitherto largely hidden aspects of everyday life, including miscarriage, as in Stan Barstow's book *A Kind of Loving* (1960). In this novel, miscarriage is viewed from the man's perspective. The miscarriage of his new wife is for him an irony rather than a tragedy, for it was only her pregnancy that led to their hasty marriage. (This situation is also portrayed, although only as a minor theme, in Susan Hill's *Air and Angels* (1991).) Irony seems particularly to be associated with miscarriage when it is a male perspective on pregnancy and pregnancy loss that is presented, as, for example, in Nina Bawden's *George Beneath a Paper Moon* (first published in 1974). Yet in Lynne Reid Banks' tale of a pregnant and unmarried woman (1960), irony is again employed in the portrayal of the threatened miscarriage of what had been an unwanted pregnancy.

Some feminist writers, in their endeavour to explore and portray the complexity and detail of women's lives, have written extensively about reproductive issues, including miscarriage. Two short stories which focus on miscarriage (Dick, 1988; Maitland, 1993) deal also with the feelings of ambivalence and guilt that pregnancy and pregnancy loss may engender.

In *Three Women,* the poet Sylvia Plath explicitly locates miscarriage within the context of the other reproductive choices or constraints which women face. A woman who successfully gives birth, a woman who miscarries and a woman who gives birth but gives her baby up for adoption speak in turn about their situation. The cry of the miscarrying woman, 'I lose life after life. The dark earth drinks them', expresses grief and despair. In Plath's *Parliament Hill Fields*, the hidden nature of an early miscarriage is expressed: 'Your absence is inconspicuous/ Nobody can tell what I lack'.

A more thorough search of poetry and literature would undoubtedly reveal further references to miscarriage and other pregnancy losses. Nevertheless, it is unlikely that it would uncover reams of detailed and explicit descriptions of the widespread yet so private event that is pregnancy loss. Rather, it is likely that the review presented here, brief and piecemeal as it is, is not untypical of the way in which pregnancy losses are dealt with in literature. Where a pregnancy loss is mentioned, it tends to be given little prominence within the text and is rarely portrayed as an event of any great significance to either the narrative or the characters involved. To a very large extent, pregnancy loss appears not to have been considered to be a subject worthy of literary attention. It could, of course, be said that many aspects of life are not portrayed in any detail, if at all, within literature. Nevertheless, the lack of attention given to an event which is a devastating experience for many women does merit consideration. It suggests, at least, that the impact which pregnancy loss may have upon a woman (and, in some cases, her partner) is not recognized and shared by the rest of society, despite the fact that (or perhaps because) it is a very common event. There is no consensus within society as to the significance of the fetus, and thus to its loss. Through comparative studies of other cultural systems we can investigate whether there are societies whose members share a perspective on the nature of pregnancy and of pregnancy loss, as well as examining those where diverse views are held by different sections of society.

Pregnancy Loss and Social Anthropology

In contrast to anthropology, a considerable amount of work into pregnancy loss has been undertaken within psychology in recent years. Psychological models and psychometric tests have been used to examine and measure depression and anxiety (Tharpar and Tharpar, 1992; Prettyman, Cordle and Cook, 1993). A strong focus has been upon women's experiences of the miscarriage event, thus grieving characteristics (Leppert and Pahlka, 1984), women's views of GP care (Friedman, 1989), hospital care (Jackman, McGee and Turner, 1991) and the long-term impact of pregnancy loss (Robinson, Stirtzinger, Stewart and Ralevski, 1994; Cordle and Prettyman, 1994; Statham and Green, 1994) have been investigated.

Such studies are, in part, responsible for the growing awareness of pregnancy loss as an event of considerable significance and the recognition that it may be the cause of much distress for women and their partners. The majority of the studies have been undertaken in Western Europe and North America. Comparisons of women's experiences in a range of different cultures have not hitherto been available. Furthermore, with the exception of Chalmers and Meyer (1992a, 1992b), attention has not been given to ethnic and cultural differences *within* any one study area.

Pregnancy loss has not, however, been totally ignored by anthropologists. There are several works in which at least a passing reference is made to miscarriage, stillbirth or the birth of an abnormal child. In addition, it is possible, from the many anthropological studies which have focused on pregnancy and childbirth, to draw a picture of the meaning and significance which infants and small children, if not the fetus, have for a culture. As these studies did not focus on miscarriage and other pregnancy losses it is perhaps inevitable that many of the references pertinent to pregnancy loss seem frustratingly slight, vague or incomplete. For example, Evans-Pritchard, writing of the Nuer, observed that:

> People do not mourn for a small child, for 'a small child is not a person (*ran*). When he tethers the cattle and herds the goats he is a person'. [. . .] A man will not say that he has a son till the child is about six years of age. A small child is buried by old women and without sacrifice. (1956, p. 146)

This tantalizing statement leaves us wishing to know more about the nature of personhood among the Nuer: we might wish to know whether the statement applies equally to female children; whether women view their infants in a similar fashion; how older children view the loss of their young siblings; and so on.

Scheper-Hughes (1991, p. 1145), writing of infant and child deaths in Brazil, noted that:

> Concern about child survival, when 30-40% mortality in the first year of life is not uncommon, leads to certain seemingly paradoxical practices and to various individual and collective defenses. For instance, maternal attachment and bonding are much more gradual processes. [. . .] Mothers may be slow to personalize the infant, to give it a name or . . . to baptize the child . . .. The process of anthropomorphisation becomes delayed until the mother is more certain that the infant will survive.

In Nigeria, in the context of a high infant and child mortality rate, some children, are considered to be 'born to die'; these are known as *abiku* (Maclean, 1971). In a family in which a child has died, the next child to be born will be scrutinized for signs of being *abiku*. If the child is *abiku* it is considered to be the 'same child' as its dead sibling; it will thus only wish to spend a short time on earth before it leaves to join its spirit companions. Its mother will attempt to persuade it to stay, 'calling it pathetically by special names such as "*Malome* – Do not go again"; "*Banjoko* – Sit down and stay with us"; and "*Duro oro ike* – Wait and see how you will be petted".'(ibid., p. 51) Very young children are not regarded as possessing a fully independent existence apart from their mothers, and their death is not mourned by most adults in the family, although the mother 'bewails their passing with wild, abandoned weeping' (p. 51). For the *abiku*, however, not even the mother may mourn.

In certain circumstances in some societies, such as those described by Maclean and Sheper-Hughes, infants and small children are not recognized as fully 'human' or as true members of the society. It thus seems likely that the unborn child would not be viewed as such either, and that consequently, pregnancy losses would be attributed with little significance. Yet without investigation we do not know whether this would be the case in these and other societies: possibly, in some circumstances, the potential which the unborn child offers is viewed more favourably than the sickly wasting toddler already in existence. The gender of a child lost during pregnancy, and of any existing child, might also be crucial in determining reactions to the loss.

Those studies which do discuss miscarriage itself tend to do so rather sparingly. An early study, undertaken during the late 1920s and early 1930s among the Kgatla of the Bechuanaland Protectorate (now Botswana; Schapera, 1940), is an exception. It is unusual for not only was the issue of miscarriage addressed directly, but considerable detail was given of the emic view of fetal development:

> During the first two or three months of pregnancy . . . 'the womb shakes about; it mixes up with the bloods of the man and the woman, so that they become thick, like cheese, and form the seed' . . .. By the fourth month the 'bloods' have coalesced completely, and the foetus has taken form. At this stage it is said to look like a lizard, with nothing to indicate that it is human. In the fifth month it acquires human characteristics . . . there-after it grows steadily in size. (Schapera, 1940, p. 217)

However, this knowledge was limited, according to Schapera, to older women who had experience of dealing with miscarriages. The Kgatla believed that miscarriages were caused by sorcery or the breach of a taboo by the pregnant woman, although they were also said by some to be due to a husband's infidelity during his wife's pregnancy. After a miscarriage a doctor was called to give the woman medicine to clean her stomach and to restore her blood to its former purity. Both she and her husband were considered to have 'hot blood' and had to observe a number of restrictions until the woman menstruated again.

Whether or not pregnancy is something which is made publicly known or not, and at what stage, will have a bearing upon the way in which miscarriage is managed. Among the Ngoni of Nyasaland (now Malawi), a pregnant woman concealed her condition from her husband for as long as possible; she was also forbidden to inform her mother-in-law herself of her pregnancy (Read, 1959). If a pregnant woman suffered from 'a shaking inside' and feared a miscarriage, she would stay in her hut and, saying that she had a headache, would ask her husband to call for her friend, who would inform her mother-in-law. A doctor would then be called, who would bring medicines 'to make the inside not shake'(p. 50). According to Read a Ngoni woman feared that her husband's relatives would be critical of her family if she had a miscarriage, for not giving her enough food before her marriage to make her strong and healthy in child-bearing.

Some of the difficulties of undertaking research into the subject of pregnancy loss are evident from Ardener's study of marital stability and fertility among the Bakweri (1962). He found that the distinction between miscarriage and stillbirth he required for his study was not always maintained by the women, nor was that between a stillbirth and an infant death. He also observed that the subject of pregnancy loss was clearly painful for the women.

Margaret Mead is one early anthropologist who mentions miscarriage (Mead and Newton, 1967). Perhaps her own experiences of miscarriage, recorded in her autobiography (1973), led her to an awareness of miscarriage which was evident among only a few anthropologists of her generation.

With the development of interest in feminism within anthropology in the 1970s and 1980s, studies which focused on a range of aspects of women's lives emerged. Those that discuss pregnancy loss, in passing at least, include the work of Llewelyn-Davies (1978), Shostak (1981), Homans (1982), Holmes Williamson (1983), Reynolds Whyte (1990) and Caplan (1992).

The responsibility for ensuring a healthy pregnancy and for minimizing the risk of a pregnancy loss clearly fell to women in many of the societies studied. The Masai told Llewelyn-Davies that 'women may cause their children to be stillborn or deformed if they ignore certain food and sexual prohibitions during pregnancy' (Llewelyn-Davies, 1978, p. 209). Holmes Williamson (1983), in her paper on conception beliefs among the Kwoma of Papua New Guinea, observed that the Kwoma consider that twin pregnancies are liable to miscarry, which is 'considered unfortunate and a ground for divorce'. It is not stated whether the grounds for divorce in this situation lie equally with each partner. In addition to the risk of twin pregnancy, problems with a pregnancy may occur if a woman does not observe dietary restrictions. The expectant father also has a small number of restrictions to observe. If a woman miscarries or if the child is stillborn or dies soon after birth, the parents, 'are under no obligation to mourn the child or to replace it' (p. 22). No information is given about the emotional response of the parents to such an event. In her work on sex and death in western Kenya, Reynolds Whyte (1990) observes that miscarriage may be one consequence of the disorder which results from a certain type of inappropriate behaviour, namely *ishira*, a state of danger 'following immodesty between generations'. In the example given, a pregnant woman saw her daughter having intercourse with a young man. The woman was considered to be at risk of miscarrying unless the young man's family provided an animal 'to cleanse away the wrong'. Such *ishira* is more likely to be the result of a woman's than a man's wrong actions, and to afflict a woman, and her children, rather than a man. Thus a married woman who has sex with another man puts both herself and her children at risk, whereas a man's sexual behaviour was only rarely considered to cause trouble. Among her Swahili informants, Caplan (1992) reported that a mother blamed a seven-month stillbirth on supernatural means orchestrated by the father, from whom she wished to be divorced.

The other accounts draw out different aspects of pregnancy loss. The account recorded by Shostak (1981) of the life of Nisa, a !Kung woman, explores in detail Nisa's reproductive history, including pregnancy losses. It is unusual not just for the explicit and detailed nature of Nisa's story, but also for the inclusion of her memories, as an elderly woman, of her feelings about the events. Homans (1982) looked at experiences and beliefs concerning pregnancy and childbirth among Asian and white women in Britain and found a number of differing attitudes to pregnancy loss between the two groups. A small number of the white women, but none of the Asian women, expressed the view that they would rather miscarry than give birth to a 'deformed' child (1982, p. 244). Beliefs about prohibitions and restrictions during pregnancy in order to avoid a miscarriage overlapped in a number of cases (notably the restriction on not lifting heavy weights or undertaking heavy work) and differed in others, such as specific dietary restrictions.

From this brief review it is evident that pregnancy loss has not been ignored by anthropologists, for it has been alluded to, if rarely addressed directly, by a number of ethnographers. A recurring theme apparent in a number of the studies is the emphasis upon women's role in maintaining healthy pregnancies. Dietary and other prohibitions apply to a far greater extent to women than to men; for the good of her unborn child it seems that women's conduct needs to be controlled and constrained in a way that a man's does not. The experience and impact of pregnancy loss clearly needs to be examined within the light of existing knowledge about gender in any given society.

This book brings together work on pregnancy loss which has been undertaken in a diverse range of cultures by nine social anthropologists, a psychologist and an historian. The chapters are based primarily on recent and past fieldwork with the exception of the historical study, which draws upon English court records from the eighteenth century.

The book falls into two parts. Five ethnographic accounts of pregnancy loss from diverse societies comprise the first part. Patricia Jeffery and Roger Jeffery begin this part with an examination of the local understandings of the physiological process of becoming pregnant and maintaining a pregnancy in rural North India. The role of dietary practices, the sexual division of labour and the threat posed by evil spirits are discussed within the context of the degree of autonomy of women's lives. In the following chapter, Elisa Sobo draws out the importance of understanding kinship and inter-gender relations in rural Jamaica, where *false bellies* (pregnancies which end in miscarriage or with the birth of a malformed baby) may be due to a *hex* set on the woman by a jealous neighbour or to a ghost having fathered the child.

Anna Winkvist, drawing upon her work among the Abelam of Papua New Guinea, charts the practices involved in achieving successful reproduction and examines, in particular, the role of ritual specialists in promoting fertility and ensuring successful pregnancies. Pregnancy loss is discussed within the wider context of successful and unsuccessful reproduction. J.A.R. Wembah-Rashid discusses the beliefs held by the matrilineal societies of southeast Tanzania about the causes of miscarriage and stillbirth, where every effort is made to prevent such events from occurring, but little mourning takes place for those losses not considered (because of malformation or gestational age) to be human. In Cameroon the responsibility of ensuring successful reproduction lies largely with women. In the last chapter of this part, Olayinka Njikam Savage discusses and draws out the implications of this for maternal and infant health.

The chapters in Part II encompass perspectives which diverge slightly from 'mainstream' anthropological and ethnographic accounts. The first chapter, by Michael DeLuca and Paul Leslie, looks at the data on interpopulation variation in pregnancy loss, drawing upon their own work among the nomadic and settled Turkana of Kenya. Linda Layne's chapter is a study of pregnancy loss support groups in the USA, in particular their newsletters and publications, and focuses upon the use of irony in the expression of parental bereavement and grief. The contribution from psychologist Beverly Chalmers is a comparison between the pregnancy loss experiences of women from different cultural groups within South Africa. Her results, indicating the cultural diversity of the experiences of pregnancy loss, are discussed with reference to implications for clinical management.

The last two chapters move into the realm of history. The recent history of rural women in Northern Ireland is the context of my study into recollections of experiences of miscarriage and infant death. The final contribution, from historian Mark Jackson, is an exploration of the various popular, medical, legal and political meanings attached to menstrual blood loss and pregnancy loss in eighteenth-century England.

References

Ardener, E., *Divorce and Fertility: An African Study*, Oxford, Oxford University Press, 1962

——, 'Belief and the Problem of Women', in S. Ardener (ed.) *Perceiving Women*, London, J.M. Dent and Sons Ltd., 1975a

——, 'The 'Problem' Revisited', in S. Ardener (ed.) *Perceiving Women*, London, J.M. Dent and Sons Ltd., 1975b

Barstow, S., *A Kind of Loving*, London, Michael Joseph, 1960

Bawden, N., *George Beneath a Paper Moon*, London, Virago, 1994 [1974]

Cameron, D., *The Feminist Critique of Language*, London, Routledge, 1990

Caplan, P., 'Spirits and Sex: A Swahili Informant and his Diary', in J. Okely and H. Callaway (eds), *Anthropology and Autobiography*, (ASA Monograph 29), London, Routledge, 1992

Chalmers, B. and Meyer, D., 'A Cross-cultural View of the Psychosocial Management of Miscarriage' *Journal of Psychosomatic Obstetrics and Gynaecology*, vol. 13, no. 3, 1992a, pp. 163–76

——, 'A Cross-cultural View of the Emotional Experience of Miscarriage', *Journal of Psychosomatic Obstetrics and Gynaecology*, vol. 13, no. 3, 1992b, pp. 177–86

Clifford, J., 'Introduction: Partial Truths', in J. Clifford and G.E. Marcus (eds), *Writing Culture*, Berkeley, University of California Press, 1986

——, and Marcus, G.E., *Writing Culture*, Berkeley, University of California Press, 1986

Cordle, C.J. and Prettyman, R.J., 'A Two-Year Follow-up of Women who have Experienced Early Miscarriage', *Journal of Reproductive and Infant Psychology*, vol. 12, no. 1, 1994, pp. 37–44

Dick, L., 'Envy', in A. Fell (ed.), *The Seven Deadly Sins*, London, Serpent's Tail, 1988

Eliot, G., *Middlemarch: A Study of Provincial Life*, Edinburgh and London, William Blackwood and Sons, 1875

Evans-Pritchard, E.E., *Nuer Religion*, Oxford, Clarendon Press, 1956

Friedman, T., 'Women's Experiences of General Practitioner Management of Miscarriage', *Journal of the Royal College of General Practitioners*, vol. 39, 1989, pp. 456–8

Hardy, T., *Jude the Obscure*, London, Macmillan, 1974 [1896]

——, *The Mayor of Casterbridge*, Oxford, Oxford University Press, 1987 [1886]

Hey, V., 'A Feminist Exploration', in V. Hey, C. Itzin, L. Saunders and M. Speakman (eds), *Hidden Loss: Miscarriage and Ectopic*

Pregnancy, London, The Woman's Press, 1989
Hill, S., *Air and Angels*, London, Mandarin, 1991
Holmes Williamson, M., 'Sex Relations and Gender Relations: Understanding Kwoma conception', *Mankind*, vol. 14, no. 1, 1983, pp. 13–23
Homans, H., 'Pregnancy and Birth as Rites of Passage for Two Groups of Women in Britain', in C. MacCormack (ed.), *Ethnography of Fertility and Birth*, London, Academic Press, 1982
Jackman, C., McGee, H.M. and Turner, M., 'The Experience and Psychological Impact of Early Miscarriage', *Irish Journal of Psychology*, vol. 12, 1991, pp. 108–20
Leclerc, A., 'A Woman's Word', in D. Cameron (ed.), *The Feminist Critique of Language*, London, Routledge, 1990
Lehmann, R., *The Weather in the Streets*, London, Virago, 1981 [1936]
Leppert, P.C. and Pahlka, B.S., 'Grieving Characteristics after Spontaneous Abortion: A Management Approach', *Obstetrics and Gynaecology* vol. 64, 1984, pp. 119–22
Leroy, M., *Miscarriage*, London, Macmillan Optima, 1988
Llewelyn-Davies, M., 'Two Contexts of Solidarity', in P. Caplan and J. M. Bujra (eds), *Women United, Women Divided*, London, Tavistock Publications, 1978
Lovell, A., 'Some Questions of Identity: Late Miscarriage, Stillbirth and Perinatal Loss', *Social Science and Medicine*, Vol. 17, no. 11, 1983, pp. 755–61
Maclean, U., *Magical Medicine*, Harmondsworth, Penguin Books, 1971
Maitland, S., 'Blessed Are Those That Mourn', in S. Maitland, *Women Fly When Men aren't Watching*, London, Virago, 1993
Mead, M., *Blackberry Winter: My Earlier Years*, London, Angus and Robertson, 1973
——, and Newton, N., 'Cultural Patterning of Perinatal Behaviour', in S. Richardson and A. Guttmacher (eds), *Childbearing: Its Social and Psychological Aspects*, Baltimore, Williams and Wilkins, 1967
Oakley, A., McPherson, A. and Roberts, H., *Miscarriage*, Glasgow, Fontana, 1984
Opie, I. and Opie, P., *The Classic Fairy Tales*, Oxford, Oxford University Press, 1974
Philips, S.U., Steele, S. and Tanz, C., (eds), *Language, Gender and Sex in Comparative Perspectives*, Cambridge, Cambridge University Press, 1987
Plath, S., 'Parliament Hill Fields', in T. Hughes (ed.), *Sylvia Plath: Collected Poems*, London, Faber and Faber, 1981
——, 'Three Women: A Poem For Three Voices', in T. Hughes (ed.), *Sylvia Plath: Collected Poems*, London, Faber and Faber, 1981

Prettyman, R.J., Cordle, C.J. and Cook, G.D., 'A Three-Month Follow-up of Psychological Morbidity After Early Miscarriage', *British Journal of Medical Psychology*, vol. 66, 1993, pp. 363–72

Rapp, R., 'The Power of "Positive" Diagnosis: Medical and Maternal Discourses on Amniocentesis', in K. Michaelson (ed.), *Anthropological Perspectives in Childbirth in America*, South Hadley MA, Bergin and Garvey, 1988

——, 'Constructing Amniocentesis: Maternal and Medical Discourses', in F. Ginsburg and A. Tsing (eds), *Uncertain Terms: Negotiating Gender in America*, Boston, Beacon Press, 1991

Read, M., *Children of their Fathers: Growing up among the Ngoni of Nyasaland*, London, Methuen and Co., 1959

Reid Banks, L., *The L-Shaped Room*, Harmondsworth, Penguin Books 1960

Reinharz, S., 'Controlling Women's lives: A Cross-cultural Interpretation of Miscarriage Accounts', *Research in the Sociology of Health Care*, vol. 7, 1988, pp. 3–37

Reynolds White, S., 'The Widow's Dream: Sex and Death in Western Kenya', in M. Jackson and I. Karp (eds), *Personhood and Agency: The Experience of Self and Other in African Culture*, Washington, Smithsonian Institution Press, 1990

Robinson, G.E., Stirtzinger, R., Stewart, D.E. and Ralevski, E., 'Psychological Reactions in Women Followed for One Year After Miscarriage', *Journal of Reproductive and Infant Psychology*, vol. 12, no. 1, 1994, pp. 31–6

Schapera, I., *Married Life in an African Tribe*, London, Faber and Faber, 1940

Scheper-Hughes, N., 'Social Indifference to Child Death', *Lancet*, vol. 337, 1991

Shostak, M., *Nisa: The Life and Words of a !Kung Woman*, Cambridge, Harvard University Press, 1981

Statham, H. and Green, J.M., 'The Effects of Miscarriage and Other "Unsuccessful" Pregnancies on Feelings Early in a Subsequent Pregnancy', *Journal of Reproductive and Infant Psychology*, vol. 12 no. 1, 1994, pp. 45–54

Tharpar, A.K. and Tharpar, A., 'Psychological Sequelae of Miscarriage: A Controlled Study Using the General Health Questionnaire and the Hospital Anxiety and Depression Scale', *British Journal of General Practice*, vol. 42, 1992, pp. 94–6

Part I

Ethnographies

—1—

Delayed Periods and Falling Babies: The Ethnophysiology and Politics of Pregnancy Loss in Rural North India

Patricia Jeffery and *Roger Jeffery*

Throughout rural north India, a child-bearing career is an essential part of an adult woman's life. Fertility is very important to men and women alike. Perhaps the most compelling reason for this is the necessity of having a new generation of workers who will support their parents in old age. Not to want children is unthinkable. Infertility or the failure to bear children who survive is usually calamitous for a woman, since these are acceptable reasons for a man to repudiate his wife or take a second woman into his home. Moreover, most village women are poorly nourished. This means that pregnancy is a risky business, both for the mother and the baby. Indeed, the generally high fertility rates, the low birth weights and the high rates of infant and maternal deaths that are prevalent in the region are indicative (at least in part) of this situation. Thus, a high incidence of pregnancy loss would not be in the least surprising, and we might expect pregnancy loss to be a major concern for women, their families and the local medical services.

During our research on women's experiences of child-bearing in rural Bijnor District, in North India, we asked women to recount all their pregnancies, asking specifically about 'delayed periods', 'falling babies', and 'babies born dead' or described as dying after just a couple of breaths.[1] Certainly, local understandings of pregnancy and the factors that can contribute to its untimely or unsuccessful end were matters that concerned women. Yet, the numbers of mishaps reported were far below any expectations based on Western medical views of pregnancy loss.[2] Taking those figures that relate to the period 1980 to 1989, for instance, the ever-married women in the four villages where we worked reported 1366 conceptions. Of these, we were told of just forty-five that ended before time, mainly in the middle and last trimesters (about 33 per 1000 conceptions). There were another forty-one babies delivered in the last trimester who were born dead or died almost immediately (about 30 per 1000 conceptions).

In order to tease out the ramifications of such low levels of reported pregnancy loss, we need to explore the wider setting in which pregnancy and pregnancy loss are diagnosed and experienced. In the Bijnor case, this includes local understandings of pregnancy as both a condition that normally requires no formal medical intervention and as a 'matter of shame' that should not be publicized. In contrast to the medicalization of pregnancy and pregnancy loss in the West, for instance, women in Bijnor experience scarcely any antenatal medical care.

Issues beyond the immediate confines of the health services also have crucial implications for how pregnancy loss is handled. In particular, the situation of the child-bearing woman in her in-laws' home impacts on her daily life, including her experiences of pregnancy and pregnancy loss. Briefly, child-bearing women in Bijnor are usually married in their teens to a man of their parents' choice, and generally in a village some distance from their natal village. A married woman is entitled to be supported by her husband and his relatives, though she herself is a vital (though usually unpaid) worker for the family. Her own lack of independent income, whether from employment or from ownership of productive resources such as land, places her in a position of relative weakness within her husband's household.

Being somewhat distant from her parents compromises her ability to obtain support from that quarter. And this is most acutely the case in relation to her child-bearing experiences, for it is inappropriate for a daughter to have close contact with her natal kin during pregnancy, childbirth and the immediate post-partum period. Crucially, these features of women's daily lives underpin the local demographic regime, which is characterized by high levels of fertility and child mortality. Only within this broader context can we unravel women's experiences of pregnancy loss in rural Bijnor.[3]

Conception and Ethno-embryology

Pregnancies are usually understood within a framework provided by the ethno-physiological theories of becoming and remaining pregnant to full term and their associated 'country' or 'home' remedies. Such taken-for-granted understandings of bodily processes and how they relate to diet and life-style can provide a route into understanding how a woman comes to know that she is pregnant and, by the same token, that her pregnancy has terminated before its due time.

Sexuality and reproduction are closely linked with a pair of opposites commonly used in local medical models, *garmi* (heat, activity, stimulation) and *thand* (coldness, calmness, pacification).[4] The effect (*tāsir*) of climate, people's temperaments, individuals' bodies, medicines and foods can all be described in these terms. Good health both requires and reflects a balance between these qualities, a balance unique to each individual and one which can be upset by their diet or the climate. A naturally *garm* (hot, active) person (as displayed in hot temper or skin rashes) suffers during hot weather or after taking *garm* food, but a *thandā* (cold, tranquil) person is less severely affected. In terms of this framework, an ailment may indicate an internal imbalance: diagnosis discerns its cause, and dietary and other avoidances (*parhez*) are prescribed to remedy the problem.

Women often described the female body as a black hole (*kāli-kothri*) in which the belly or abdomen (*pet*) is a conglomeration of tubes (*nas* or *nali*, the nerves, intestines and blood vessels). Women were generally unclear about how the tubes interconnect with one another and are linked to the liver, kidneys, stomach and other organs such as the uterus (*bachā-dāni* or baby-receptacle). Most women referred to one uterus which is normally closed by the cervix (*munh*, mouth or orifice). The vagina (*bachā-kā-rāstā* or baby's path) and rectum are thought to connect with the tubes inside, but most women were unclear about urination.

For a girl, puberty marks the start of fluctuations in her bodily state. Heat gradually accumulates in her body until it precipitates a menstrual flow which prevents the heat concentrating in her head and making her crazed. Since blood is hot, women are anxious if menstruation is delayed or light, although an excessively heavy menstrual flow is considered weakening. Menstrual blood is also regarded as defiling, and a complete and rapid 'cleansing' (*safāi*) is necessary to prevent the poison from accumulating dangerously in the body. A menstruating woman is unclean until her cleansing bath after the flow ends.[5] Physical maturity is also linked with sexual 'heat' or passion, and parents are generally keen to marry their adolescent daughters quickly for fear that they will engage in inappropriate sexual relationships.

At puberty, a boy's body begins to produce semen (*pāni*, or water), a highly concentrated distillation from blood.[6] Semen is even hotter than blood, and accumulating semen could result in excessive heat and (if it goes to the head) madness. This can be averted through moderately frequent sexual intercourse.[7] People use a variety of terms when talking about sexual intercourse, some suggesting that intercourse is like farming, referring to work or even ploughing. Semen contains the seeds (*bij*) that a man plants in his wife and which develop into a baby. Like crops, the children belong to whoever ploughs and owns the field.

During sexual intercourse, the heat generated opens the woman's cervix and permits the man's seeds to enter the fertile environment that her uterus provides. A woman is considered capable of conceiving at any time in the menstrual cycle, provided that she is hot enough to receive sexual advances and to nourish a man's seeds. The woman who is too cold will be infertile (*bānj*), the word also used to describe a barren field.[8] If conception occurs, the cervix is believed to close to prevent another conception, and it should open again only during labour to permit the baby to pass along the vagina. Just as the soil nourishes the seed planted in it, so too is the pregnant woman's role essentially a nurturant one, in which the growing baby is enabled to grow and is prevented from drying out by the 'dirty' or defiling blood (*gandā khun*) that would otherwise flow if the mother continued to menstruate.[9]

The diagnosis of both pregnancy and pregnancy loss, however, does not take place in a medicalized setting. Of the various practitioners (Government and private), none is engaged in any substantial outreach or systematic surveillance of the local populace for any condition, including pregnancy. Formally, the ANMs (Auxiliary Nurse-Midwives) posted in clinics in most sizeable villages should give pregnant women regular medical checks, distribute iron and folic acid tablets (to combat anaemia, which is presumed universal), monitor fetal development (for example, by weighing the mother), give a course of free injections of tetanus toxoid (to avert neonatal tetanus caused by cutting the cord with an infected instrument), identify women at risk, and attend such women's deliveries or refer them to the Government women's hospital in Bijnor. However, the Government antenatal service relies on women seeking out their advice, and many women do not consult the ANM at all during pregnancy. Those who do are unlikely to seek confirmation that they are pregnant. The ANM should also maintain a network of traditional birth attendants (*dāi*s) to identify pregnant women and register them with her. Some *dāi*s claimed that they could diagnose pregnancy after two missed periods, for an internal examination indicates if the cervix is closed or if the amenorrhoea has some other cause. But, in fact, women seldom consult *dāi*s during pregnancy either, and they do not systematically receive medical care from them. Pregnancies, then, are not officially registered through the medical services or the traditional birth attendants.[10]

In practice, the diagnosis of pregnancy depends on the woman herself, perhaps along with another woman in her husband's village such as his mother or the wife of his brother or paternal cousin. The cessation of menstruation is considered to be a key sign of pregnancy, connected with which the woman becomes increasingly hot because of the accumulating menstrual blood. Thus the pregnant woman will almost certainly experience some symptoms of heat, such as skin rashes or nausea and vomiting.[11] Generally, women note the start of their menstruation according to a lunar calendar and, if their next period does not begin, they say that 'one month is completed'.[12] Using this calculation, women consider that pregnancies should last between nine and ten lunar months.

Pregnancy and Shame

Even though a woman's child-bearing abilities are an important element in her in-laws' expectations of her, pregnancy is not something about which she should be openly proud. Moreover, despite the importance of fertility, pregnancy is not formally marked through any celebratory and supportive customs.[13]

Shame or embarrassment (*sharm*) are important components of many aspects of women's lives.[14] In the course of their child-bearing, women undergo several physiological processes which are regarded as shameful, and many of them also as polluting. Pregnancy is considered a 'matter of shame' (*sharm-ki-bāt*) because it draws attention to the pregnant woman's sexual activity, but it is not polluting. In general, though, pregnancy is couched around in circumlocutions. While women do talk about a pregnancy taking up residence (*garbh rahnā*) or becoming with-pregnancy (*garbh-se*), with-belly (*pet-se*) or heavy-legged (*pānw bhāri honā*), there are also several popular euphemisms. Older women delight in embarrassing recently married women by asking if they have acquired any 'earnings' (*kamāi*) yet. People also talk of expectation, of waiting for the purpose to emerge, or, more graphically, of something suspicious (*dāl-me kuch kālā*, literally, something black in the pulses).

The young married woman herself, however, is unlikely to make an explicit statement that she believes she is pregnant. Rather, the pregnant woman should display more 'shame' than usual in the way she dresses and moves. Her mother-in-law may guess that she is pregnant only by noting when she last had the purifying bath signifying the end of menstruation, though some women regularly interrogate their daughters-in-law to check if they are menstruating normally.

Ethno-physiology of Pregnancy Loss and its Prevention

Although women reported fewer pregnancy losses than we expected, they were indeed concerned about the possibility of pregnancy loss. While harbouring the baby during pregnancy, the pregnant woman is like a field nourishing her husband's seeds. Consequently, her general bodily state and her behaviour affect not only her own well-being but also the baby's development and the chances that the pregnancy will culminate in the timely birth of a strong and healthy baby. In order to prevent a sickly baby or one that is deformed prudent women should take various precautions.[15] Similarly, women are concerned to avoid deliveries 'before the appointed moment' (*samāy-se pehle*) because a baby needs to remain in its mother's belly for the correct time in order to be strong enough to survive.[16] Consequently, some strategic changes (especially in diet and work) are considered desirable for the pregnant woman's daily life.

Premature labour is believed to occur for several reasons. Of these, excessive heat is considered particularly important. Women who are normally very hot (for instance, whose menstrual periods are heavy) are especially prone to have babies fall. Among other things, heat implies over-stimulated tubes in the belly in general and it can mean that the cervix dilates and uterine contractions begin. Indeed, this is exactly what must happen at the end of a full-term pregnancy. But excessive heat is to be avoided at other times, especially in early pregnancy, before the fetus is properly established. The woman who is too cold, however, will fail to conceive at all. One who is somewhat hotter will conceive a girl, for which she may well be blamed.[17] In order to conceive a boy, a woman should be hotter still. But a male fetus is itself considered more hot than a female one, and male babies are believed to be much more likely to miscarry precipitately if the women herself becomes excessively hot.[18]

The developing fetus grows and takes its strength from the mother's retained menstrual blood. To ensure that this process proceeds satisfactorily, the woman should eat well and include items in her diet that are locally considered to be 'strengthening' because they build up blood.[19] Essential though that blood is, however, it is also hot. Thus, its accumulation can result in the unpleasant symptoms characteristic of heat and even untimely uterine contractions. According to some *dāi*s this is especially so in early pregnancy when the fetus is not yet established. Ideally, then, the pregnant woman's diet contains items with both cooling and strength-providing properties. Milk and fruit are especially valued. Hot items such as tea, unrefined sugar, spices and certain pulses should be avoided altogether or taken only in moderation. The hottest foods (especially eggs and meat) pose no serious problem, since they are insignificant in village women's diets. In addition, the pregnant woman should avoid eating items that are 'windy' (*bādi* or flatulence-generating), even if they are cold, because they may distend her tubes and cause the baby to fall. Rather, she should take foods that are considered light and easily digested (*halkā*).[20] In addition, the heating effects of sexual intercourse cause cervical dilatation, and a pregnant woman should not attend another's delivery for fear of absorbing the heat of the labouring woman's contractions and going into untimely labour herself. While a woman can usually avoid attending a delivery, she may have greater difficulty in avoiding sexual intercourse with her husband, as we suggest below.

Concerns about overheating during pregnancy are also evidenced in views about illness and its treatment. Fevers such as malaria and typhoid, and hot medicines (such as anti-malaria drugs, aspirins and many other allopathic medicines), might make a woman so hot that her cervix dilates and uterine contractions begin. By the same token, many women refuse to have the tetanus toxoid injections given in the last trimester.[21] In line with this logic, treatments for infertility may entail the consumption of hot items for the woman too cold to conceive, while an abortion can be induced and a slow labour accelerated in the same way.

Considerations of heat and cold are not the only pertinent issues for pregnancy loss, however. The pregnant woman ideally avoids heavy lifting work. Her mobility should also be somewhat limited, partly to conceal the pregnancy from others because it is a matter of shame, partly to protect the woman from jolts while travelling by bus or cart. Her pregnancy may also be put at risk if she falls heavily. All these events can strain or twist her tubes and precipitate untimely uterine contractions. Rather than that, she should avoid strenuous work and take more rest than usual. Women also say that frequent pregnancies can weaken the uterus so that it cannot retain a baby, and some women also cited wife-beating as a reason why their pregnancy had failed to go to full term. Furthermore, going anywhere outside domestic space, especially places away from human habitation, can make a woman vulnerable to attack by evil spirits. Indeed, because such restraints are not always practicable, many women regularly wear amulets to protect themselves. This will be considered particularly important if a woman's previous pregnancy resulted in a weak or deformed baby or a stillbirth, even though her own health was apparently good.

Any of these factors can operate late in a woman's pregnancy. Several women reported going into labour in the second or third trimesters because they had lifted a heavy load or had been affected by evil spirits. In all such cases, the women talked unequivocally about 'pregnancy' (*garbh*) and the delivery of a baby who was either dead at birth (*marā huā*) or who died 'having taken a few breaths' (*ek-do sāns le kar mar gayā*).

A particular feature of local understandings of fetal development, however, influences women's perceptions of pregnancy loss earlier in pregnancy. Women generally note the dates of their menstrual periods and talk initially of 'delayed periods' (*dyn charhnā*, or the days being in arrears) and not of pregnancy. Vaginal bleeding at that point would be considered a late period rather than a pregnancy that has ended in miscarriage. Women will say, 'there was no pregnancy', merely a 'blob of flesh' (*mās-kā-pindā*, *māns-kā-golā*, *golā-kā-pindā*) that broke up into blood clots and caused bleeding. At that stage, there are no limbs or organs, and no baby (*bachā*). It is only after nearly three months have elapsed from the start of the last menstrual period that women talk of pregnancy. At this stage they refer to the baby as such (*bachā*) and consider that it has 'adhered' ('rooted' or 'flourished', using *jamnā*, a verb that also connotes germination in plants). This is the time when the life or spirit (*jān*) enters the baby, its body parts begin developing and its sex is settled.[22] Thereafter, vaginal bleeding is called a 'baby falling' or the 'belly falling' (*bachā girnā*, *pet girnā*).[23]

This distinction between a 'delayed period' (when a 'blob of flesh' is discarded) and the 'falling of a baby' is crucial for assessing the frequency of pregnancy loss. Our records almost certainly undercount pregnancy loss as understood in the Western medical model, simply because many 'pregnancies' are described locally as 'the days being in arrears' and not as pregnancy at all. This undercounting is probably compounded because women occasionally conceive during post-partum amenorrhoea and do not immediately realize they are pregnant: a child conceived in this fashion is called a *lamrā bachā*. If such a conception ends in pregnancy loss during the first trimester or so, the woman may not even be aware that she was ever pregnant. Moreover, even those pregnancy losses locally understood as such are probably undercounted because women tend to have lengthy and complex maternity careers from their mid-teens nearly to the menopause, and they probably forget at least some early pregnancy losses. For all that we reiterated that we wanted to hear about all their pregnancies, several women got part way through their maternity history before recalling an earlier 'baby falling'.

To all this, we can add another feature of the physiological processes entailed in reproduction. If pregnancy is rendered inconspicuous by the embarrassment that surrounds it, women will try to conceal pregnancy loss because it (like menstruation and childbirth) also entails pollution and defilement from the 'dirty' menstrual blood which is retained during pregnancy but is so suddenly lost when a baby falls.[24]

Arresting a Falling Baby

Babies, of course, do sometimes threaten to fall. The pregnant woman who suffers abdominal pains and vaginal bleeding may resort to domestic remedies to arrest the process, taking cool and easily digested foods such as rice with *mung-ki-dāl* (a kind of pulse) and avoiding hot ones, refraining from sexual intercourse, resting from heavy work until the symptoms abate, or lying on a bed with the foot raised by a pair of bricks. Some *dāi*s offer country medicines containing cold ingredients such as dried water-lily seed and dried water chestnut pounded together with a local medicine called *kamar-kas* and drunk with cold milk. But women rarely call on *dāi*s, let alone government or private medical practitioners.

Even after such efforts, some babies cannot be stopped from falling. The only remedy is for the woman to consume hot foods, so that she is completely cleansed of the 'dirty' menstrual blood.[25] Once pregnant again, she may take precautions, such as avoiding hot foods, to prevent a repetition. Often it is concluded that the woman has been possessed by evil spirits (*asar, bhut, hawā* or *satāo*) or attacked by the evil eye (*nazar*) of someone envious of her pregnancy. While it is believed that no medicine could have prevented the loss of the baby, her next pregnancy can be put at less risk by wearing amulets. She will also probably avoid graveyards and cremation grounds (where there is 'dirty' air), and wooded areas, the favourite haunts of evil spirits. Some women, however, consider that such attacks by spirits can just as easily occur at home as well.[26]

The Child-bearing Woman and Domestic Politics

The frequency of reported pregnancy loss, then, is probably much lower than would be expected within the Western medical model. In particular, the diagnosis of pregnancy is not medicalized, and local medical models distinguish between the 'delayed period' and the 'falling baby'. Only the latter is considered to have been a pregnancy. These understandings are part of a system of ethno-medical knowledge within which people comprehend the physiological processes, normal and abnormal alike, that are entailed in child-bearing. Within this framework, women can articulate precautions or remedies that should be taken by the pregnant woman or the women whose baby threatens to fall. In practice, however, a woman is unlikely to implement the desirable changes in diet, rest and general activities to ensure the satisfactory outcome of her pregnancy.

By itself, then, the ethno-physiological knowledge about pregnancy outlined above can give us no more than a limited understanding of why pregnancy loss, as locally defined, is dealt with as it is. To go further, we must also examine the position of relative powerlessness in which the typical child-bearing woman is located in her husband's household.[27]

Basically, child-bearing women are rarely in a position to determine their diets. They do not control much independent income and they must depend on what their in-laws permit them to eat. Few women reported any changes at all in their diets during pregnancy, whether an increase in food intake, the rigid adherence to cold foods or the avoidance of windy ones. Fruits tend to be costly, and few families can sacrifice other foodstuffs to allow a pregnant woman to eat fruit. And should a woman buy fruit with the small sums of money saved from her parents' gifts, she will be chided for treating herself well and failing to share with other people. Moreover, in most homes, milk is not regularly available throughout the year, even in those households with their own milch animals. Milk is also expensive to purchase. Poor households with milch animals generally depend on the income from selling the milk, and do not regularly consume it themselves. Even in wealthier households, though, pregnant women rarely obtain a special diet during pregnancy, since that would imply putting their wishes before the needs of other household members. In practice, dietary 'avoidances' (*parhez*) usually apply only to the post-partum period, when the woman takes hot foods to ensure that she is properly 'cleansed' and protected from 'cold'.[28]

Pregnant women are especially keen to stop their heaviest tasks, such as making dung-cakes, fetching head-loads of fodder, chopping fodder or carrying buckets of water. Yet they are rarely able to do so. Although women's work is generally devalued, the young married woman is not only a bearer of children but also an important worker for her in-laws. Her work is regulated by them, and few households can continue to function if women relinquish their work, even temporarily. Pregnant women generally continue with their normal duties, later in pregnancy maybe sitting down to work or working in snatches, carrying lighter head-loads of dung and dumping it in the midden instead of crouching making dung-cakes. The pregnant woman still living jointly with her mother-in-law may be an exception to this, but relief is offered only late in her pregnancy and is likely to be only partial.[29]

Additionally, her husband will probably insist on having sexual intercourse with his pregnant wife. As several women put it, 'men are more concerned with their own pleasures than with the health of their wife and baby'.

Normal pregnancy is not considered to need medical surveillance or interventions, but even in abnormal pregnancies specialist medical advice is likely to be sought only if domestic remedies seem to be failing badly. Many women reported having health problems while pregnant, but symptoms regarded as 'little-little troubles' are unlikely to entitle a woman to either rest or medical care. As one woman put it, 'illness in pregnancy is an affectation of the rich'.

Even in serious situations, medical care is rarely sought in a hurry. The pregnant woman herself is not well placed to take the initiative. She is unlikely to command the resources to pay for medicines. If she claims special entitlement to medical care she will seem to be setting herself above others in her husband's household, while taking action on her own account would leave her open to blame if anything went wrong. Her in-laws must first concede that her condition constitutes a medical problem that is sufficiently serious to warrant the financial cost of medicines and the time lost because other household members abandon their work to accompany her to a clinic or hospital. Further, several considerations specific to pregnancy tend to inhibit women's access to medical care even more than usual. It is considered unwise to treat some ailments during pregnancy, since allopathic medicines are often hot. In any case, people often say, many conditions have been precipitated by the pregnancy itself and will right themselves after delivery, without needing to waste scarce money on treatments. The shame of pregnancy, too, inhibits people from seeking medical treatment, especially for conditions that are directly associated with the pregnancy.[30]

The major exception is the woman who has repeatedly had babies fall. She may be taken to a medical practitioner, who may advise cooling foods to be consumed along with specially prepared cold medicines. She is likely to be granted more rest, and, even without medical advice, her diet may be monitored to ensure that she takes cooling items and systematically avoids hot foods until the baby is properly rooted. For reasons of 'shame', most pregnant women are unlikely to visit their natal kin, at least once the pregnancy is conspicuous. The woman with a history of pregnancy loss may, however, stay at her parents' home for some months to enjoy a respite from life in her husband's village (more rest, better diet and no sexual intercourse) and to escape whatever evil influence had caused her babies to fall.

However, the woman who experiences the falling of a baby as part of an otherwise successful maternity career will probably find that her loss is not singled out for special attention. She may be allowed to rest briefly, but will soon be on her feet again and contributing to the household's work. She is most unlikely to be provided with strengthening (and generally more expensive) foods to compensate for the blood loss, although she will probably be encouraged to select hot items from the family's normal repertoire of foodstuffs to ensure that she is completely cleansed of the 'dirty' blood. There will be no attempt to ensure that she does not conceive again quickly, and she is most unlikely to visit her parents in order to have rest and food to speed her recovery.

Overall, then, much as a woman's fertility is vital in her marital career and much as people express concerns about pregnancies that do not reach full-term, the pregnant woman typically lacks control over her diet, her work and rest, and her access to medical care. Pregnancy usually entitles her neither to substantial changes in her daily regime nor to special treatment. The ideal precautions to prevent pregnancy loss would involve additional work for other people and probably their sacrifice of food too. The position of the pregnant woman in her husband's village is not conducive to obtaining such allowances. Basically, she should fulfil her responsibilities without disrupting other people's routines. The compelling day-to-day requirements of household maintenance in a labour-intensive economy mean that maternity leave is problematic, even after a normal full-term birth, let alone in the event of a 'falling baby'.

The maternity careers reported by women also reflect women's lack of control over key aspects of their lives. Their frequent requests to us for contraceptive and abortion remedies were compelling testimony to the obstacles women face in trying to plan their maternity careers.[31] In some measure, as we suggested above, the lengthy and complex experiences of child-bearing probably contribute to the low levels of reported pregnancy loss. Indeed, women with several pregnancies to recount often became muddled about birth orders and would revise their accounts during the telling, or admit to being unable to provide details of a child's season of birth. None of this is especially surprising, for medical records and births are not systematically recorded officially, and low literacy rates mean that people generally cannot keep domestic records for themselves.

Crucially, though, child-bearing women are poorly placed to obtain care not only for themselves but also for their children. Much of their confusion over their maternity histories is linked to the high levels of child deaths. Collecting maternity histories was often distressing for all concerned, as women talked about loved children who had died suddenly from fever, or a protracted illness no one had been able to cure, or because the family could not afford medical treatment. Even though child mortality rates have declined strikingly since the mid-1960s, most women have experienced the death of at least one child. Taking the figures from the four villages just for 1980–9, about one in six of the babies born live died before their fifth birthday. The women reported 1279 live births, of which 136 resulted in the deaths of infants (i.e. under one year) (in other words, about 106 per 1000 live births). There were also seventy-nine deaths of children under five (approaching 62 per 1000 live births), a figure that does not include children born after 1985 who may eventually have died before their fifth birthday. The masculine sex ratio of reported births suggests that other deaths (that is, mainly of girls) might have occurred, but were not reported to us.[32]

Some elderly women, left with more dead than surviving offspring, were reduced to tears as they talked. By contrast, 'falling babies' and those who were 'dead at birth' or died immediately were usually mentioned with a marked lack of emotion and only after considerable prompting. Yet, if the deaths of toddlers and children are the focus of women's grief in a way that pregnancy-loss is not, mothers so bereaved have little opportunity to mourn their loss openly or at length. Condolence visits from relatives in other villages generally entail admonishments for the woman deemed to be making too much of her loss, comments to the effect that everyone else has experienced the death of a baby or child, and exhortations not to weep. And once the funeral rites are over, the bereaved mother must straightaway return to caring for her remaining children and doing her other normal duties for the well-being of the household as a whole.[33] In comparison, pregnancy losses are trivialized and rendered non-events, unmarked by any rituals, special treatment for the woman, or condolence visits from female relatives.[34]

Basically, then, an understanding of the meanings of pregnancy loss in rural north India cannot rest simply on a descriptive account of ethnomedical theories of the physiological processes associated with pregnancy. These theories must themselves be comprehended in broader social and political terms, of which the situation of child-bearing women in their husband's home is central. In other words, issues of domestic organization and gender politics are crucial ingredients of the way that pregnancy loss is perceived and handled. In essence, the marginalization of pregnancy loss in rural Bijnor reflects a context characterized by high levels of fertility and child mortality, where women have little influence over their own child-bearing careers, their work and diet during pregnancy, and their children's chances of survival.

Notes

1. The research from which this account is drawn was conducted in rural Bijnor District, in western Uttar Pradesh. In 1982–3 and 1985 we were based in two adjacent villages (one Hindu and one Muslim), our research focusing on women's experiences of child-bearing. In

1990–1, we worked in the two original villages and in two additional villages in the area, exploring the relationships between women's 'autonomy' and fertility. Our research was funded by the Social Science Research Council/Economic and Social Research Council (UK) and the Hayter Fund at Edinburgh University in 1982–3 and 1985, and by the Overseas Development Administration in 1990–1. We are grateful to the ESRC and ODA for their support. The views expressed in this paper are those of the authors and should not be attributed to the funding bodies. We are also grateful for comments on our work over the years from numerous colleagues.

2. A recent discussion of spontaneous abortion (Mishell, 1993) supports the view that our figures significantly undercount pregnancy loss in Bijnor.
3. These points are elaborated in P. Jeffery, R. Jeffery and A. Lyon, 1989.
4. Translating these terms as 'hot' and 'cold' does not fully capture the meanings of the Hindi words. The contrast they enshrine is not the only one relevant here, though it is particularly central. Some foods are considered to have a *bādi* influence, usually translated as windy or flatulence-creating; others are *halkā* or light and easily digested. Several other sources discuss various aspects of 'hot'/'cold' categories. See, for example, Kurin, 1982, 1984, 1988; Lambert, 1992; Nichter, 1986; Pastner, 1988; Rizvi, 1986; Zimmerman, 1988.
5. Women in this polluted condition should not perform religious duties or visit temples or mosques. Hindu women should not cook for other people while they are menstruating, although this cannot be expected of women who are the solitary adult woman in their household. For more general discussions of menstrual taboos and their implications, see also Hershman, 1974; Thompson, 1985; Yalman, 1963; Young and Bacdayan, 1965. For more details on post-partum pollution in Bijnor, see P. Jeffery et al., 1989, Ch. 6.
6. See, for example, Carstairs, 1957; McGilvray, 1982.
7. A sexually passionate man is *garm*; an impotent man is *thandā*. A man with nocturnal emissions is a *garmi-ki-mariz*, or suffering from heat which would decline if he had sexual intercourse. Excessively frequent intercourse drains the semen and is weakening, especially for the elderly.
8. Few women said that a woman produces a seed that merges with the man's seed to produce a baby, although some of the traditional birth attendants (*dāi*) (mainly those who had Government training) did say that women produce seeds and have a fertile period in the menstrual cycle. The farming analogy is discussed by Dube, 1986. Taylor, Sharma, Parker, Reinke and Faruqee (1983, p. 73) report that in Punjab the analogy of the field is common, but that the fertility of the uterus

declines midway between menstrual periods because the cervix slowly closes after menstruation.

9. Early in pregnancy, some of this blood also congeals into breast milk, which remains in the breast and becomes heavy or solidified and yellow in colour ('like pus'). Breast-feeding in pregnancy is not usually considered to be harmful for the developing fetus, but it is considered unsuitable for the breast-feeding toddler. Nevertheless, many women continue to breast-feed during pregnancy. We discuss this and the initiation of breast-feeding for the neonate in Jeffery et al., 1989, especially Chs 4 and 6.
10. We have discussed the health services available to rural women and especially the lowly position of the village *dāi* in north India and how her role is essentially limited to the delivery in P. Jeffery and R. Jeffery, 1993 and in Jeffery et al., 1989.
11. Although sexual intercourse makes the woman more hot and she becomes increasingly hot during pregnancy, the greater blood loss after childbirth is much more effective than menstruation in averting over-heating. Indeed, child-bearing is often a recommended solution for hysteria.
12. Hindus and Muslims follow twelve-month lunar calendars, particularly for setting the dates of religious festivals. Hindu months begin with the full moon, Muslim months with the new moon. Lunar months last twenty-nine or thirty days and lunar years are therefore about ten days shorter than the solar year. The Hindu calendar inserts an extra month every three years to bring it back into line with the seasons, but the Muslim calendar does not and it shifts through the seasons. Hindus and Muslims also use the Western solar calendar used by the Government for public events such as schooling etc.
13. South Indian practice is rather different. See, for example, Ferro-Luzzi, 1973. The contrasts are discussed by Wadley, 1980. Lewis, 1958, p. 47, discusses a pregnancy ritual in a village near Delhi, and Thompson, 1984, discusses pregnancy rites in a central Indian village.
14. The word *sharm* is widely used in the northern areas of South Asia to connote the embarrassment, bashfulness and shame that are experienced in different contexts and expressed through (for instance) different forms of body language. There is a huge literature discussing the connections between *sharm* and honour in South Asia (and more broadly through the Middle East as well). For South Asia, see, for instance, Mandelbaum, 1988; P. Jeffery, 1979; Papanek and Minault (eds), 1982; Sharma, 1978. Thompson, 1981, makes the useful distinction between 'good' and 'bad' *sharm*, or appropriately demure bashfulness in contrast to the dishonouring

sharm that is heaped on someone who has misbehaved.

15. When weak or deformed full-term babies are born, the mother may be blamed for her own carelessness (such as standing in a doorway during a solar eclipse) or some bodily inadequacy (such as weak blood that fails to nourish the baby sufficiently), or the mishap may be put down to the influence of evil spirits, even if the woman took precautions such as wearing an amulet during her pregnancy.
16. Women are not concerned about post-maturity and overly-long pregnancies, however.
17. 'Son preferences' are not the focus of this paper, but they are an important aspect of women's child-bearing experiences. Under circumstances where daughters are married out, generally with a dowry, while sons remain with their parents and ideally care for them in old age, a preference for sons is a general feature of rural north India (and other northern parts of South Asia). It is associated with less celebration when a girl is born as well as with sex-skewing in child mortality rates that can be attributed to differential feeding and access to health care. There is now a great deal of material discussing the topic. See, for instance, Das Gupta, 1987; Jeffery et al., 1989, Chs 6–8; Miller, 1981. In the context of pregnancy loss, it is pertinent to note that son preferences have become associated with the use of amniocentesis and the selective abortion of female fetuses, known in India as 'female feticide'. Again, there are several sources that address this in detail, among them Ramanamma and Bhambawala, 1980; Bardhan, 1982; Balasubrahmanyan, 1982; Dube, 1983; R. Jeffery, P. Jeffery and A. Lyon, 1984. A more recent account is in Booth, Verma and Bedi, 1994. As we remark below (note 22), son preferences are also linked to local remedies to obtain sons.
18. Associated with this, it is generally assumed that a male baby will more readily abort, for instance in response to the consumption of 'hot' foods or medicines, while a female baby is likely to be resistant to abortion attempts.
19. See Jeffery et al., 1989, Ch. 4, for more details. Eating to excess is considered likely either to cramp the baby or to result in a very large baby. A similar fear of large babies who are hard to deliver is reported in Nichter and Nichter, 1983; their paper also outlines a similar relationship between heat and pregnancy to that described here.
20. See note 3 above.
21. Tetanus toxoid injections are a key aspect of government antenatal services in rural north India. The Auxiliary Nurse-Midwife (ANM) is supposed to provide them to all the pregnant women who need

them in the catchment area of the health facility at which she is based, but ANMs rarely engage in outreach work, and coverage levels often fall far short of complete. For instance, we worked in four villages in 1990–1. In one Hindu-dominated village there was almost complete coverage among women of the dominant Hindu landowning caste group but much lower levels among the other caste groups and Muslims. In a second Hindu village the coverage was around two-thirds, while coverage in the two Muslim dominated villages was well under 10 per cent.

22. See Jeffery et al., 1989, pp. 191–3, for further discussion of the determination of a baby's sex and the *seh palat* medicines that may be used along with dietary restrictions on cold and windy items to obtain a boy. These remedies are well known in north India. For other discussions of how the baby's sex is determined, see Mani, 1981; McGilvray, 1982.
23. The word *girnā* means to fall. Its causative form *girānā* is the word used when describing an induced abortion, as in *bachā girānā* (to cause a baby to fall).
24. Jeffery et al., 1989, Chs 5–7, contains more details on childbirth pollution, the role of the *dāi* in removing it and the restrictions on the newly delivered mother because of it. Pollution beliefs are also associated with menstruation and with death.
25. Some *dāi*s claim to send the woman for a 'cleansing' or *safāi*, in this case dilatation and curettage. *Safāi* is also used for induced abortion, as well as for the cleansings that take place after menstruation and childbirth. Women themselves rarely mentioned dilatation and curettage as part of the repertoire for dealing with pregnancy loss.
26. Some *dāi*s, however, rejected such explanations, saying that women simply require medical treatment or that their conditions are due to God's will.
27. This is a theme that runs through Jeffery et al., 1989. See also R. and P. Jeffery, 1993; and P. and R. Jeffery, 1994.
28. For more details of dietary avoidances in pregnancy and the post-partum period, see Jeffery et al., 1989, Chs 4 and 6. The apparent absence of food avoidances during pregnancy in south India are discussed by Ferro-Luzzi, 1973, and in relation to the post-partum period by Ferro-Luzzi, 1974. For a discussion of the situation elsewhere in Uttar Pradesh see Luschinsky, 1962, p. 62. Writing about coastal Malaysian villagers, Laderman, 1983, p. 92, also notes that women usually fail to observe food avoidances in pregnancy.
29. For more details of the 'leave' obtained by child-bearing women in Bijnor, see Jeffery et al., 1989, Chs 4 and 7.

30. While medicalized surveillance during pregnancy has many limitations and may be oppressive, its virtually total absence in Bijnor makes any protection it can provide effectively unavailable to most child-bearing women there. Given the lack of outreach by medical services, there are no effective procedures to guarantee the timely diagnosis of medical problems relating to pregnancy.
31. We discuss this in more detail in Jeffery et al., 1989, especially Ch. 8.
32. These child mortality figures also display a marked skewing by sex, which we and others have discussed elsewhere. See Bardhan, 1982; Das Gupta, 1987; Dyson and Moore, 1983; Jeffery et al., 1989, Chs 6–8; Miller, 1981. The sex ratio at birth in our data was significantly more masculine than would be expected, indicating that the levels of female child mortality were probably higher that the reported deaths of girls would suggest.
33. See Scheper-Hughes, 1992, for a graphic account of how people in an urban slum in Brazil deal with child death.
34. It is important to note that pregnancy loss may be interpreted differently at different times in a child-bearing career: young childless women may experience it as a serious 'loss', whereas for multiparous women it may come as a relief. We cannot draw any clear conclusions on this because we are dealing with such small numbers.

References

Balasubrahmanyan, V., 'Women, Medicine and the Male Utopia', *Economic and Political Weekly*, vol. 17, 1982, p. 1725

Bardhan, P., 'Little Girls and Death in India', *Economic and Political Weekly*, vol. 17, 1982, pp. 1448–50

Booth, B.E., Verma, M. and Bedi, R.S., 'Fetal Sex Determination in Infants in Punjab, India: Correlations and Implications', *British Medical Journal*, vol. 309, 1994, pp. 1259–61

Carstairs, M., *The Twice-Born*, London, Hogarth Press, 1957

Das Gupta, M., 'Selective Discrimination against Female Children in Rural Punjab, India', *Population and Development Review*, vol. 13, 1987, pp. 77–100

Dube, L., 'Misadventures in Amniocentesis', *Economic and Political Weekly*, vol. 18, 1983, pp. 279–80

——, 'Seed and Earth: The Symbolism of Biological Reproduction and Sexual Relations of Production', in L. Dube, E. Leacock and S. Ardener (eds), *Visibility and Power: Essays on Women in Society and Development*, New Delhi, Oxford University Press, 1986

Dyson, T. and Moore, M., 'On Kinship Structure, Female Autonomy and Demographic Behaviour in India', *Population and Development Review*, vol. 9, no. 1, 1983, pp. 35–60

Ferro-Luzzi, G.E., 'Food Avoidances of Pregnant Women in Tamilnad', *Ecology of Food and Nutrition*, vol. 2, 1973, pp. 259–66

——, 'Food Avoidances During the Puerperium and Lactation in Tamilnad', *Ecology of Food and Nutrition*, vol. 3, 1974, pp. 7–15

Hershman, P., 'Hair, Sex and Dirt', *Man*, vol. 9, 1974, pp. 274–98

Jeffery, P., *Frogs in a Well: Indian Women in Purdah*, London, Zed Press, and Delhi, Vikas, 1979

——, and Jeffery, R., 'Traditional Birth Attendants in Rural North India', in S. Lindenbaum and M. Lock (eds), *Knowledge, Power and Practice in Medicine and Everyday Life*, Berkeley and London, University of California Press, 1993

——, and Jeffery, R., 'Killing my Heart's Desire: Education and Female Autonomy in Rural North India', in N. Kumar (ed.), *Women as Subjects: South Asian Histories*, Charlottesville, University Press of Virginia and Calcutta, Stree, 1994

——, Jeffery, R. and Lyon, A., *Labour Pains and Labour Power: Women and Childbearing in India*, London, Zed Books, and Delhi, Manohar, 1989

Jeffery, R. and Jeffery, P., 'A Woman Belongs to her Husband: Female Autonomy, Women's Work and Childbearing in Bijnor', in A. Clark (ed.), *Gender and Political Economy: Explorations of South Asian Systems*, Oxford, New York and Delhi, Oxford University Press, 1993

——, Jeffery, P. and Lyon, A., 'Female Infanticide and Amniocentesis', *Social Science and Medicine*, vol. 19, no. 11, 1984, pp. 1207–12

Kurin, R., 'Hot and Cold: Towards an Indigenous Model of Group Identity and Strategy in Pakistani Society', in S. Pastner and L. Flam (eds), *Anthropology in Pakistan: Recent Socio-cultural and Archaeological Perspectives*, Ithaca, South Asia Program, Cornell University, 1982

——, 'Morality, Personhood, and the Exemplary Life: Popular Conceptions of Muslims in Paradise', in B. Metcalf (ed.), *Moral Conduct and Authority: The Place of Adab in South Asian Islam*, Berkeley, Los Angeles and London, University of California Press, 1984

——, 'The Culture of Ethnicity in Pakistan', in K. Ewing (ed.), *Shari'at and Ambiguity in South Asian Islam*, Berkeley, Los Angeles and

London, University of California Press, 1988

Laderman, C., *Wives and Midwives: Childbirth and Nutrition in Rural Malaysia*, Berkeley and London, University of California Press, 1983

Lambert, H., 'The Cultural Logic of Indian Medicine: Prognosis and Etiology in Rajasthani Popular Therapeutics', *Social Science and Medicine*, vol. 34, no. 10, 1992, pp. 1069–76

Lewis, O., *Village Life in Northern India*, New York, Random House, 1958

Luschinsky, M.S., 'The Life of Women in a Village of North India', unpublished Ph.D. thesis, Cornell University, 1962

Mandelbaum, D.G., *Women's Seclusion and Men's Honor: Sex Roles in North India, Bangladesh and Pakistan*, Tucson, University of Arizona Press, 1988

Mani, S.B., 'From Marriage to Child Conception: An Ethnomedical Study in Rural Tamil Nadu', in G.R. Gupta (ed.), *The Social and Cultural Context of Medicine in India*, Delhi, Vikas, 1981

McGilvray, D.B., 'Sexual Powers and Fertility in Sri Lanka: Batticaloa Tamils and Moors', in C.P. MacCormack (ed.), *Ethnography of Fertility and Birth*, London and New York, Academic Press, 1982

Miller, B., *The Endangered Sex*, Ithaca, Cornell University Press, 1981

Mishell, D.R., 'Recurrent Abortion', *Journal of Reproductive Medicine*, vol. 38, no. 3, 1993, pp. 250–9

Nichter, M., 'Modes of Food Classification and Diet-Health Contingency: A South Indian Case Study', in R.S. Khare and M.S.A. Rao (eds), *Food, Society and Culture: Aspects in South Asian Food Systems*, Durham NC, Duke University Press, 1986

——, and Nichter, M., 'The Ethnophysiology and Folk Dietetics of Pregnancy', *Human Organisation*, vol. 42, no. 3, 1983, pp. 235–46

Papanek, H. and Minault, G., (eds), *Separate Worlds: Studies of Purdah in South Asia*, New Delhi, Chanakya Publications, 1982

Pastner, S.L., '*Sardar, Hakom, Pir*: Leadership Patterns among the Pakistani Baluch', in K. Ewing (ed.), *Shari'at and Ambiguity in South Asian Islam*, Berkeley, Los Angeles and London, University of California Press, 1988

Ramanamma, A. and Bhambawala, U., 'The Mania for Sons', *Social Science and Medicine*, vol. 14B, 1980, pp. 107–10

Rizvi, N., 'Food Categories in Bangladesh and Its Relationship to Food Beliefs and Practices of Vulnerable Groups', in R.S. Khare and M.S.A. Rao (eds), *Food, Society and Culture: Aspects in South Asian Food Systems*, Durham NC, Duke University Press, 1986

Scheper-Hughes, N., *Death without Weeping: The Violence of Everyday Life in Brazil*, Berkeley, Los Angeles and Oxford, University of

California Press, 1992

Sharma, U., 'Women and their Affines: The Veil as a Symbol of Separation', *Man*, vol. 13, 1978, pp. 218–33

Taylor, C.E., Sharma, R.S.S., Parker, R.L., Reinke, W.A. and Faruqee, R., *Child and Maternal Health Services in Rural India: The Narangwal Experiment*, Baltimore and London, Johns Hopkins University Press, 1983

Thompson, C.S., 'A Sense of *Sharm*: Its Implications for the Position of Women in Central India', *South Asta Research*, vol. 1, no. 2, 1981, pp. 39–53

——, 'Ritual States in the Life-Cycles of Hindu Women in a Village of Central India', unpublished Ph.D. thesis, University of London, 1984

——, 'The Power to Pollute and the Power to Preserve', *Social Science and Medicine*, vol. 21, no. 6, 1985, pp. 701–11

Wadley, S.S., 'The Paradoxical Powers of Tamil Women', in S.S. Wadley (ed.), *The Powers of Tamil Women*, Syracuse, Maxwell School, Syracuse University Press, 1980

Yalman, N., 'On the Purity of Women in the Castes of Ceylon and Malabar', *Journal of the Royal Anthropological Institute*, vol. 93, 1963, pp. 25–58

Young, F. and Bacdayan, A., 'Menstrual Taboos and Social Rigidity', *Ethnology*, vol. 4, 1965, pp. 225–40

Zimmerman, F., *The Jungle and the Aroma of Meats*, Berkeley and London, University of California Press, 1988

—2—

Cultural Explanations for Pregnancy Loss in Rural Jamaica

Elisa Janine Sobo

Introduction

Anthropological investigations of reproduction and associated concerns such as sexual behaviour have become almost common in the past twenty years, partly because of the large shift in attitudes about such matters. Contributions to the growing literature include works specifically focused on birth (Kay, 1982; Jordan, 1993), menstruation (Buckley and Gottlieb, 1988; Sobo, 1992), and fertility regulation techniques (Newman, 1985; Nichter and Nichter, 1987; Sobo, 1993a). While abortion or planned pregnancy termination has received increased attention recently (Luker, 1984; Ginsburg, 1989; Rylko-Bauer, 1996; Sobo, 1996), unintentional pregnancy termination or loss has not. This is so even in the literature on the Caribbean, in which reproduction has long been a salient topic.

Jamaica, a British colony until 1962, has been the subject of considerable research. Many early ethnographic reports on Jamaica contain general information on procreation and family matters (e.g. Beckwith, 1929; Hurston, [1938] 1990). Academic interest in the family gained institutional support in the 1940s, after a Royal Commission appointed by Jamaica's colonizers issued a report lamenting the apparent disorganization of family life and the high birth-rate among the masses. Research began to focus directly on conjugal arrangements and fertility patterns (e.g. Clarke, 1957; Blake, 1961; Powell, Hewitt, and Wooming, 1978; Roberts and Sinclair, 1978). Influenced by British scholarly tastes, these works are mainly sociological (although psychoanalytic arguments are found in Kerr, [1952] 1963 and Brody, 1981); they contain little information about the cultural aspects of family planning and less about the ethnophysiological notions that impact on procreation.

Several studies published in the 1980s refer to the ethnophysiology of reproduction as it relates to family-planning effectiveness (Brody, 1981; MacCormack, 1985; MacCormack and Draper, 1987). But, with the exceptions of Laguerre (1987), who examines African-Caribbean health-related understandings and practices, and Sobo (1993b), who explores Jamaican ethnophysiological and ethnomedical knowledge (see also Sobo, 1992, 1993a, 1994, 1996), only rudimentary ethnophysiological and ethnomedical descriptions are found in the literature. In this chapter I explore traditional rural Jamaican ethnophysiological notions about miscarriage in depth and describe in detail the ethnomedical knowledge and practices that pertain to it.

My findings highlight the disjunction between emic (indigenous) and etic (scientific) understandings of embodied or physical conditions. It is well known that the criteria for being deemed human, viable, or a valuable addition to the family differ cross-culturally, affecting post-partum abortion or infanticide and child-neglect practices (e.g. Korbin, 1987; Morgan, 1989; Scheper-Hughes, 1992). Similarly, the criteria for categorizing an embodied happening as conception, an abortion, a miscarriage, or even a birth differ (Sobo, 1993b, 1996). This chapter demonstrates the need to guard against the automatic imposition of biomedical definitions on the cross-culturally divergent reproductive experiences of women (for more on the questionable anthropological tendency to gloss all ethnomedical understandings as 'beliefs' while reserving the term 'knowledge' for biomedical notions, see Good, 1994).

Setting and Methods

Research for this chapter was carried out in a northeastern coastal village where I lived for a year in 1988 and 1989, as well as in a southwestern fishing village and a central mountain hamlet that I visited in the summer of 1989 (see Sobo, 1993b for a full account of the research).[1] Data were collected through participant observation and interviews that took place in community settings and in private yards. I also solicited drawings of the body's inner workings from participants.

Jamaican villages typically consist of people brought together by ancestry, or by proximity to a small shop or postal agency. In some cases, they are organized around an estate where village members sell their labour. Households are often matrifocal (see Smith, 1988; Sargent and Harris, 1992), and non-legal conjugal unions and visiting relationships (in which partners reside separately) are common. Houses are generally made of wood planks and zinc sheeting; those who can afford to do so use concrete blocks. Often, houses lack plumbing and electricity. People build their homes as far apart as possible but they are usually still within shouting distance of a neighbour.

The majority of the villagers where I lived were impoverished descendants of enslaved West Africans (as are most islanders; accordingly, I refer to participants simply as 'Jamaicans').[2] Many villagers engaged in small-scale gardening, yet few could survive on this alone. People also took in washing, hired themselves out for odd jobs, engaged in part-time petty trade such as selling oranges, and relied on relatives for help. Ideally, there is reciprocity between kin. Although factors such as poverty and migration to the cities and overseas have weakened many family ties, almost all villagers belong to extended kin networks.

Pregnancy and Pregnancy Loss

Personality and situational differences meant that each account collected of pregnancy and pregnancy loss was necessarily unique. The following is a composite account of the basic principles referred to by most participants in most contexts.

Conception begins when male and female sexual fluids meet in the female body, blend, bond, and begin to grow. Slowly, mostly through the process of accretion, the clot of mixed fluids or *bloods* gets bigger; soon, it will *form up* into a fetus.[3] A non-pregnant woman becomes a truly pregnant *bellywoman* not when her period is late, but when the quickening occurs.

A missed period is not a sure sign of pregnancy. A number of other physical conditions can delay the menses and cause symptoms that mimic pregnancy. For instance, a wayward clot of mucus may settle into a woman's vagina or *tube*, blocking the menstrual path, causing a backlog of blood and toxins that swells her belly and makes her nauseous. (Regarding the health-related importance of menstrual flow to Jamaicans, see Sobo, 1992.) The menses lack significance in terms of defining when a pregnancy begins because a clot of blood is not a fetus. Until the quickening, when the clot turns into an active being that moves about in the *baby bag* or womb, a woman cannot truly be described as pregnant. Accordingly, anything that issues forth from the vagina before the quickening (whether due to health-related manipulations or to a spontaneous change within the body) is not seen as human remains. The blood clots that might come down are simply those that have been dangerously blocked from exiting the body. Any accompanying pain is simply part of the process of resolving the particular problem that caused the blockage in the first place. (Regarding menstrual regulation in Jamaica, see Sobo, 1996.)

After the fetus has taken form and grown active, sudden physical movements or heavy labour can knock it out of its nest in the belly. For example, one village girl dislodged a pregnancy when diving off a high rock into the sea; another did so when carrying cement blocks. With the exception of detachment, no other natural causes for lost pregnancies seem to exist.[4]

When an obvious pregnancy turns *funny* – when labour begins very early, when the belly grows too rapidly or in a strange shape, or when a monstrosity emerges in lieu of a humanly-shaped baby – it becomes clear that what a woman carries is not a real pregnancy but a *false belly*: that is, an unnatural pregnancy.[5] Jamaicans combine their cultural model of how the body works with social and moral understandings so that social causes can be found for *false belly*, just as they can for other *funny* or created sicknesses, making *false belly* manageable, meaningful, and useful for discourse concerning social and moral affairs.

Causes for *false belly* are found in the realm of gender relations, and these causes, like *false belly* itself, implicate sociocultural tensions. That is, problematic social relationships are generally identified as having caused the trouble, and the problems entailed in these relationships are traced out in the course of treatment. *False belly* thereby serves as an idiom for the expression of subversive commentary on gender relations and on the burdens of kinship obligations. Therefore, before I describe how *false belly* can be created and alleviated, I shall briefly outline some of the kinds of resentments that *false belly* discourse is used to express.

Obligation and Resentment

Traditionally, Jamaican kinship involves reciprocity and altruism. The desire to care for one another stems from consubstantiality or consanguineality – from having shared blood (see Sobo, 1992, 1993a, 1993b, 1994). Like kin, conjugal partners are obligated to help each other out. Conjugal obligation is not justified ethnophysiologically as being due to shared blood, because then incest would be implied, and conjugal unions can break up while kinship endures. But couples should act as if they are kin, caring and providing for one another according to the relational model that blood kinship provides.

Because relationships entail obligations, even the closest kinship or conjugal ties can involve tensions and ambivalences. Fulfilling obligations in the context of poverty can mean a constant drain on already scarce resources. Kin are often resented for their demands but, because of the ideology of physically engendered altruism, one's kin resentments must remain private. Cultural constructions of gender, on the other hand, lead to openly adversarial male-female relations.

Poor economic conditions can prevent men from supporting their children on a regular basis. Cultural expectations also play a role in men's frequent failure to help their *babymothers* (babies' mothers) financially. Often raised single-handedly by women who view them as irresponsible and so treat them as such, men are not taught how to be responsible parents (Clarke, 1957). Accordingly, women bear many of the monetary and other burdens of child-rearing.

Duppies

The tensions that everyday kinship and gender relations involve are often projected on to the dead. Ancestral ghosts or *duppies* are frequently implicated in bringing on the horrible and perilous condition of *false belly*. Male *duppies* are known to interfere with, *trouble*, or – *to talk it straight* – rape women as they sleep, creating unnatural babies.

New *duppies* do not understand that they are dead and so they often try to do the things they did in life. Every ghost walks about for a bit, but those people known for wickedness in life persist in causing trouble long after the recognized posthumous transition period of forty days and nights. Promiscuous, *girly-girly* men are certain to return to their lovers' yards. So along with women with newly dead mates, those whose men were labelled 'sinners' when they lived must take precautions. But women must always beware of male *duppies*, for, dead or alive, men are said to seek sex constantly.

Wary women, particularly those with dead mates, must not sleep on their backs (a vulnerable position) and must wear red or black panties when they sleep (panties are barriers and these colours scare *duppy* rapists). Surviving lovers must move their beds and can rearrange other furniture and paint their houses or verandah stairs to confuse the dead. *Duppies* are easy to outwit, and the ability to exert at least some control over *duppies* alleviates some of the distress that belief in them brings.

Baby Stealers

Some *duppies* lay in wait under the beds of women in labour, intending to kidnap or to kill their babies as they are delivered. These attacks bespeak the tensions womanhood entails, and the dynamics involved can also be implicated in *false belly*.

Generally, the *duppies* who do this are dead mothers who do not like their daughters' *babyfathers* (the fathers of their daughters' children) or who feel threatened by their daughters' becoming adults and mothers. Children embody the union of male and female, so attacking them is, by extension, attacking that union. Daughters resent controlling or competing mothers, and they can feel guilty for these emotions. The tradition of baby violation by older female relations provides an idiom in which the problems entailed in female rivalries that centre around a daughter's maturation can gain expression.

Female rivalries can include competition for children. People told me that others, women especially, steal unguarded 'pretty' babies. This belief affirms the value of children to women, also reflecting a general distrust of others' intentions, as well as affirming, and confirming, the importance of physical characteristics. Even maternity nurses, people contend, steal pretty children. A pregnant nurse must leave her job, one woman explained, asking rhetorically how I thought nurses got their families. So even one's motherhood, one of the few sources women have for self-esteem, can get stolen away by competitors in the guise of altruistic helpers (which kin too pretend to be). Women compete for social adulthood and some will steal children to gain *ownership* instead of putting in their own labour.

To *Set* a *Duppy*

Because *duppies* lack sense, *Obeah* or sorcery workers can use them to do evil deeds.[6] The less sense one has, the more one gets ordered about and the more likely one is to follow commands. Adult mortals cannot be ordered about, as they have developed the ability to make decisions sensibly. They also have the right to autonomy. Infant *duppies*, doubly lacking sense (being both babies and dead) are easily compelled. Vengeful people seek out *Obeah* workers who, alone or with the aid of demons, command duppies and set them to work *inequity*. Spirit pregnancies often are *cause from* someone setting a *duppy* on a woman to *trick* or *fix* her and *bring her down*.[7]

Obeah workers or sorcerers break moral rules. They do dealings privately, without a church and sometimes even without keeping patrons informed. Patrons themselves fear sorcerers and also fear what others may say if they are seen to be employing them. They consult sorcerers during hours when they are least likely to be seen, or seek out sorcerers who live out of the village. But everyone knows that people rising early or riding on the first bus (which runs before dawn) with no justification have evil in mind.

While *Obeah* workers traffic at night and with spirits of the ground, church-affiliated healers deal with God and sky-dwelling spirits to bring good to the world. They generally work in the daytime. The form for dealing in the supernatural or *created* world is similar for both *Obeah* and healing, as both grew from one African root. But while sorcerers separate themselves from society, healers ally themselves with it.[8]

Each sorcerer has a distinctive method to capture and *set* a *duppy* but most (for large sums of money) use incantations and props such as animal bones and graveyard dirt. Some use imported occult manuals (those from the DeLaurence company in Chicago are especially popular and so Jamaicans often call sorcery 'DeLaurence'); others rely on traditional knowledge. Sometimes sorcerers ask clients to provide property belonging to the intended victim (such as hair or dirty clothing) or to carry out tasks (such as burying a bundle of props and reading prayers) to strengthen the spell.

Obeah usually involves oils or *medicines* purchased in towns at special pharmacies. Coloured, and often fragrant or stinking, oils and perfumes with names such as 'Oil of Deliverance', 'High John the Conqueror', 'Protection', 'Evil', 'Compel', 'Dead Man's Bones', and 'Success' could be bought in 1989 for about US $1.50 for a two-ounce bottle. Sorcerers often mix oils. Sometimes, the intended victim's name is written on paper and wrapped around a bottled concoction which is then buried. This works against the named individual through sympathetic magic, just as using someone's old clothes as floor rags keeps him or her from *uplift*.

Like the oils, clothing is useful. Once *sweat up*, or otherwise imbued with the owner's essence, clothing can be *fixed* or treated and shown to a *duppy*, buried at a grave, or otherwise used to work magic; underclothes are preferred. Sometimes, the article is prayed over and sprinkled with magical powder (for which, as for oils, the *Obeah* worker supplies a *prescription*). It is then secretly returned to its owner in the hopes that s/he will use it and so absorb the magical forces that now inhere in it. Knowledge of this kind of duplicity saved forty-six-year-old Miss Emelda from trouble: she noticed that her favourite frock was missing and announced that the first one to see that dress must burn it. When it turned up behind a barrel she destroyed it, as wearing it would have been very dangerous.

Candles (often black) and incense are lit and incantations made by those intending evil. Sorcerers also rely on modern props. One sorcerer I visited used flash powder, a plastic light bulb which glowed when its base was pressed on the pot-metal finger-ring that he had for sale as a *guard* against misfortune and malice, and a children's fortune-telling toy widely available in the USA. Most *Obeah* workers do not use as many modern props but rely instead on their own charisma. They also rely on *confederates* who bring them customers, inform them of social rifts and squabbles, run ahead and bury things in a potential customer's or victim's yard, and dispense poison unseen.

Spirit Interference with the Belly

Sorcerers can *set duppies* to rape and impregnate women. *Witchcraft baby* refers to those resulting from this sort of premeditated rape; *false belly* is a more generic term that includes *bad bellies* brought on by *duppies* of their own accord. The phrases, however, are interchanged regularly, as with sorcerer labels (see note 6).

Some villagers argue that *witchcraft babies* cannot come from ejaculate, which rape can entail, because, as one man said, 'duppy cock it rotten off, don't it!' But all agree that it can come from the *unclean* or *bad air* that a spirit troubling a woman's body leaves behind. Whether odious air or discharge, *duppy* leavings penetrate a woman through her vagina and move to her belly, sometimes *catching* an egg and moving to the womb, always making the belly swell (quickly or slowly) as if the woman is pregnant.

A spirit pregnancy can mimic a regular one so well that a woman might think it natural until the time of delivery when only clots of *cold* (mucous), *sinews* (any light-coloured bodily fluid, like vaginal secretions or pus), and bad *gas* or air come out. Sometimes, a monster baby develops. People told of frog-like creatures, memberless torsos, and children resembling monkeys. It was said that Miss Lisa, who lived up the hill, gave birth to a cow head. Monster babies can result from being raped by a *duppy* when pregnant as well as from being impregnated by a *duppy* rape; in the former case, *duppy* leavings damage an already-present fetus.

Beside its own essences, a spirit can insert a miniature creature into a woman's body through her vagina. Placement is usually by hand, but a *duppy* could place a tadpole, say, on the tip of his penis and shoot it into the victim. In such a case, a toad or frog will be 'born'. One old woman passed a large lizard which spoke up and told her healer, 'I been there since a tot.' A *duppy* must have inserted that lizard years ago, a cousin explained.

Sometimes, if a woman's food is left unguarded, a *duppy* can trouble or *play with* it, spontaneously infusing it with *duppy* essence. Some of this essence enters the woman's belly as she eats, and impregnates her or affects a previous conception. She can take active precautions, such as always using salt and hot pepper (which *duppies* hate) and never leaving her food unguarded.

A *duppy* might punch a pregnant woman in the belly, which can harm her fetus. This happens rarely, and when it does it is more often a childish reaction to being knocked into or ignored than an act of malice. In any case, women fear vaginal penetration far more than this or troubled food. Sleeping women cannot actively protect themselves from anything. Locked doors do not always deter human rapists; they can never stop *duppies*.

Tension between Women prompts Sorcery

A *witchcraft baby* might be instigated by a neighbour woman who wants the victim's man for herself or her daughter, or a mother-in-law who wants her son back, or anyone believing that the victim has *uplifted* too high. Instigators are normally women, although now and again a man seeks to *punish* another man by hurting his wife, or tries to remove a woman who has gained a promotion at work over him (expressing the ideal that pregnant women should not do paid labour or compete with men for jobs) or to hurt one who rejected him.

People listening to tales of *false belly* generally surmise that the woman attacked was suspected by another woman of carrying on sexually with her man. A teenage girl explained it this way: 'Supposing that I have a boyfriend and you saw him and get acquainted, and I found out. I can hurt you for it. All I have to do is go to an *Obeahman*. So I tell him I want to give you a false belly, and I'll pay him the amount he ask for. And then he'll send the spirit to your house and get you pregnant and you are going to say it belongs to my boyfriend.' This breaks up the affair, probably at once, but certainly later, when he sees what gets born. The *false belly woman* (in this case, me) would deliver a toad or 'something funny,' or would 'just have that stomach for the rest of your life – until you die'.

Misfortune often follows *careless*, anti-social behaviour. An instigator is wicked and *bad mind* for *dirtying* her hands with *unclean business*, but a victim is wicked too if she has *taken up* another woman's man and *mashed up* a union; immoral, she forfeits God's protection.

In addition to highlighting the social tension between two women, *false belly* expresses larger tensions created by role expectations inconsistent with socioeconomic reality. For example, a lack of resources may have forced a victim to seek a second or *outside* lover in order to capitalize on gifts or money that the second man might give her. Male gender expectations for *reputation*, which include having sex with many women, encourage other men's complicity.

Tension between Women and Men is Expressed

Spirit pregnancies allow people to discuss culturally perpetuated intergender tensions. Nutritive substances associated with life (semen, food) are exchanged between men and women through bodily orifices. But gifts that should bring life can cause destruction instead, so one must be cautious about what one takes in. Prestations or gift exchanges involve rights and obligations; as with food-sharing, an exchange of sexual substances demonstrates obligations. Since social relationships in Jamaica generally exist in an unegalitarian fashion (as opposed to idealized, selfless, horizontal parity), occasions for exchange, sex included, can be used to inflict harm just as easily as to establish or renew trust. The substances men give women can turn to poison, both figuratively and literally, just as the food women give men can poison them (regarding women's coercive use of food laced with menstrual blood, see Sobo, 1992). One must, therefore, guard one's vulnerable orifices well.

The vagina or *buddy mouth* takes in semen as it takes in the *buddy* or penis. Sperm is a kind of food, for it *grows* babies, as does female blood, and it ends up in a woman's belly (where the *baby bag* is). In the belly, substances mingle and good food gets converted into bodily components. Foul substances generate sickness and, just as they may reach the belly through the *food mouth*, they may reach it through the *buddy mouth* too. Foul substances include semen from irresponsible or otherwise contemptible men and bad air or discharge left by spirits.

Men *breed and leave* women so frequently that almost any mysterious swelling of the female belly gets attributed to some man – alive or dead – having left a baby of some kind. An *owner* will be named unless the healing process brings sufficient mental relief. The rare spirit pregnancy not attributed to a specific *duppy*, a particular social crime or a certain enemy's instigation still comments on social tensions because the mechanism of spirit impregnation itself implicates them.

Night-time Visitation Experiences

People in many societies have reported that they have been awakened while sleeping on their backs by an anthropomorphic presence that exerts pressure on the chest (Hufford, 1982). Jamaicans know that sleeping on the back leaves the *privates* vulnerable to *duppy* rape. Girls learn to sleep on their bellies, and people always wear nightclothes to bed. Prayers should be said and all shutters or windows should be shut tight and locked at night for fear that *duppies* (as well as cool night-dew and cool draughts) might enter and bring sickness.

When many share one bed, any movement against one's sleeping body can trigger a visitation experience. One woman, Sam-sam, told me that sleeping alone – which she had probably never done in her whole life – is one way to be sure about the reality of intrusions. Sam-sam had been sleeping with her small son when she thought that she felt him pressing her left breast. Sam-sam woke and, realizing that her boy was sleeping at the foot of the bed, grabbed her bible and rebuked whatever *duppy* had come to trouble her that night. 'Some *duppy* they smart', Sam-sam said, explaining that this one tried to outwit her by easing on to her as if he were her son. A *duppy* may even come in the shape of one's regular sex partner. Maya's dead lover did this to her. She conceived a spirit baby made of *cold* (mucous), bad air, and *sinews* (slimy light fluids), which threatened her life, giving her great pain and 'a salt provision and a half' between her legs (a swollen, suppurating vagina or *salt thing*). She survived, but her condition led to her legal husband's discovery that she had cheated on him.

Jumbled Sleep Cycles and Night Visitors

In a review of the literature on night-time visitations, Hufford (1982) reports that the experience of being visited at night by an anthropomorphic presence is universal and remarkably uniform. Fifteen per cent of the general population in North America has experienced a nocturnal visit. Knowledge of a cultural tradition concerning night visitations has no causal link to the experience: visitation and knowledge of its possibility are negatively associated.

Citing the cross-cultural consistency of experiences of night visitation and the lack of any correlations between these and psychopathology or social deviance of the sort that psychoanalysts generally ascribe to sexual repression, Hufford (ibid.) rules out a psychodynamic explanation. This does not cancel the psychodynamic aspects of the content of culturally constructed interpretations of such events; it simply suggests that the causes may not be psychodynamic. Hufford locates these in the biological basis of sleep itself. Night-time visitations are a type of hallucination that can occur when the sleep cycle gets jumbled. This can happen if noise, whether misfiring neurons or bumps in the night, disrupts sleep. Hallucinatory attacks are often accompanied by sleep paralysis, associated with the motor inhibitions of sleep, and so, in their terror, some people cannot move.

Extreme fatigue, which may overtax the sleep cycle, has been associated with sleep-related hallucinations (Hufford, ibid.). The hard labour which rural Jamaicans do and the impediments to undisturbed rest with which they must deal, such as sharing quarters with many people, often leave them unrested. Sleeping on one's back (the position Jamaicans warn about and one linked with snoring) may distort air intake and so trigger hallucinatory attacks, as might pre-sleep eating (Jamaicans notice that late suppers can generate nightmares and *foolish* dreams).

Seeking Healing

Most *false belly* sufferers described to me and those I met were mature women who already had children. The first victim I encountered (we met at a healing or *balm* yard) was about forty-five and had long since had all the children she wanted. Some women approach healers directly after experiencing night visitations; others wait until symptoms show. Not all women with *false belly* recall an intrusion, so not all attribute an unnatural dimension to their conditions. But when labour comes suspiciously early (or when it is delayed, or when the bellies of women who know they cannot be pregnant *rise*), women usually seek a healer's help.

Traditional healers normally make sure that patients have consulted clinicians so that, should anything happen, no accusations of practicing medicine without a license or inquests into the circumstances of death need be made. Often, clinicians provide biomedical assistance which healers augment with herbal medicines and ritual religious practices. In the case of a biomedically defined miscarriage, a woman may seek clinical help immediately (proximity and time is a key determinant of this) or she may go to the clinic to make sure that all is well and nothing has been left unexpurgated after passing the *false-belly* baby. But the ultimate cause of the problem usually cannot be addressed without a healer's aid.

Healers generally consult with a potential patient and feel or *sound* her belly before offering diagnoses or commencing treatment. However, during a public service, Mother Geddes (a church-affiliated healer) excitedly advised a young, apparently pregnant woman, in attendance for the first time, against buying diapers, as her belly held no baby. An observant church member commented that even though Mother had not *sounded* the woman, anyone could tell by looking that the belly held no child; its shape gave that away. The patient, a mother of three named Georgina who probably sensed trouble or she would not have gone to the healing yard, agreed. Her common-law husband, Mac, had run off with her neighbour Yvonne and, although Georgina and Mac had had sex recently, Georgina believed that she had not conceived. Georgina had no money to feed those children she already had and no man to support a new baby. She proposed that Yvonne had set the false belly to make sure that Mac, who held a well-paid job, did not return home. Whether the pregnancy was natural or not, Georgina, diagnosed with false belly, now had a moral right and physical necessity to abort or *dash away* the forming fetus.

Antisocial *Obeah* or the Idealistic Church

The relief that traditional healers offer is psycho-social as well as physiological. With *false belly* as with other unnatural sicknesses, a person seeking vengeance can consult an *Obeah* worker, who sets a *turnback blow* or *hex* on the person who caused the problem. If a victim cannot name her attacker, the *Obeah* worker, through supernatural communications, helpful *confederates*, an informed neighbour or the story told by the patient herself, can find out. *Turnback blows* help victims release anger and assuage feelings of powerlessness.

Church-associated healers keep people from expressing anger directly. The *Obeah* system thrives on revenge (and perpetuates a climate of interpersonal anxiety over others' intentions), but the Church leaves vengeance to God. This is not to say that church-goers never seek revenge or consult sorcerers – they do – but church teachings discourage hate and destructive confrontations. One villager, who helps with the healing work at a Revival church and often gets *taken away in the spirit* and learns who has *set hexes*, told me, 'God is not the author of confusion'. He never reveals their names, as this would cause *hatrage* (hate and rage) and encourage acts of revenge. The Church promotes *one love* and not cycles of vengeance. Patients' psychological or emotional needs are met through the attentive healing process (see Wedenoja, 1989).

Delivering a Spirit Child

False bellies become apparent when labour comes early (as for a miscarriage) or at nine months when no babies show. A wizened midwife or *granny* who had delivered many monsters (e.g. a bodyless head; a set of buttocks without trunk, head, arms, or legs; an alligator; a monkey; a plethora of frogs) explained that she normally inserted her hand into the vagina to check for a head during labour. If no head was found, or if labour was extremely late or surprisingly early, she knew to expect a *witchcraft* or *false-belly baby*. Sometimes, she said, these so-called babies were 'just a bunch of gook'. She buried them, usually in the yard where the birth took place, although anywhere would do.

Upon determining the nature of a case, this *granny* (her methods typical of old-time midwives and of many present-day healers) would promptly light a white candle, which she passed between the legs and over the head of the patient three times, chanting the eighteenth Psalm (generally a well-known psalm and one that she liked). Once she had used candles of any colour, but Granny changed to white after being taken to court in the 1920s for using black ones. Her competitors, she claims (mostly male medical doctors), begrudged her the trade and miscast her use of coloured candles as (illegal) sorcery.

The smoke of the candle would enter the vagina and belly, as had the *duppy*'s essences. It would heat and melt out evil matter, or would drive it away, as smoke drives off mosquitoes and forces snakes from their holes. After the fumigation, Granny would wash the *babymother* in cold water (perhaps to force the warming and *opening* of her body for the so-called birth, maybe to cool evil forces) and anoint her, usually with 'Oil of Virgin Mary' and 'Oil of Conqueror'. Next, Granny would place the candle at the front gate, and she would give the patient a big spoon each of castor oil and white rum, which would bring on the birth.

In the post-partum phase, Granny would mix oils of 'Conqueror', 'Devil', myrrh, cinnamon and thyme in a saucer and carry it to the gate, where she would rebuke the spirit of the *witchcraft baby* and any *duppy* intent on hindering things: 'I beseech you to leave this gate immediately'. Then she would bury the mixture, right at the gate. To ease out what remained in the uterus, the *babymother* would drink tea boiled from *sinkle bible*, senna and one half of a lime cut on the tree. This mixture is identical to a tonic for amenorrhea.

Though this *granny*'s explanation of her methods was fairly specific, rituals retain a plasticity that allows for improvisation and substitution depending on the situation. Bible passages differ between midwives and so do the types of oil named, but the sounding, praying, anointing, fumigating, administering purgatives, and the like, always occur.

Now that midwifery is under government control and most *baby-mothers* give birth in hospitals, most *witchcraft-baby* purging is done by healers instead of *grannies*. Sometimes a healer must *work* a hospitalized case from her yard. One healed a woman so sick with *false belly* that doctors had supposedly given up, leaving her on an intravenous *life drip*. She made the distraught husband fetch his wife's nightdress, which she blessed and manipulated. She told the man to put the nightdress on his wife with no one else's help. The wife was released from hospital yet had little relief. She still carried her *false-belly* load and could hardly make it to the healer's yard, where she 'gave birth' in the pit toilet. The day was gruelling for the healer, who spent it praying over, anointing, fumigating, sounding and feeding purgatives to the patient.

Whether the fetid gas, gelatinous clots and toad-like item (toads being tiny and much slimier than frogs) that came out were the remains of a miscarried fetus or the effluvia of a cyst did not matter. The woman found relief through her purge for an otherwise unintelligible, unmanageable physical condition, and she did not have to grieve for a lost child, as her belly had not actually held a baby. Moreover, the woman released herself from certain of the existential and situational tensions entailed in her conjugal relationship. Her *witchcraft baby* exposed an earlier sin of adultery, allowing her to work through her guilt. Happily, her husband forgave her and felt only glad that her life had been saved.

Sweeping Evil Away

Healers sweep out evil, physically removing and deterring demons, ghosts and other invisible, malevolent things. Besides using purgatives to bring inner cleanliness, banners are sometimes waved, flagging away evil spirits, and some healers spin or *turn the roll*, themselves or with their charges, to *spin off* destruction like a centrifuge. Some shake and then break open soda bottles or pierce their lids with ice picks and use them like sandblasters to *drive off evil*, showering people with carbonated beverage in the process. Some speak in tongues. Spiritual as well as temporal healers (like *bush doctors* or herbalists) know that good health depends on driving miscarried and other debris from the body, and on avoiding social trouble and immoral actions.

The Subversive and Conservative Nature of *False Belly*

In traditional rural Jamaica, local knowledge about *false belly* is used to make sense of the emotionally and often physically painful occurrence of miscarriage or the birth of a monstrously malformed baby. It is also used in discourse to express guilty feelings about adulterous liaisons or about a lust for them, and to support and challenge existing social conditions. That is, people can use talk of *false belly* to work through ambivalences over familial obligations and gender tensions.

In blaming ghosts for pregnancies, men can express resentments about the expectation that they will support their progeny, and women can express resentments over many men's irresponsibility and their coercive and promiscuous sexuality. Blaming other women for setting the *hexes* that lead to *witchcraft babies* can provide a vent for resentments about female competition over men. For both men and women, casting a lost baby as a monster can help express inevitable ambivalences or resentments over children's demands. This can also help women express feelings about certain brutish men or male traits.

While women's *false bellies* often symptomize events that biomedical specialists might label as miscarriage and such, this is not always the case. Sometimes, what is called a *false belly* is actually a healthy pregnancy that a women does not want to continue with. As abortions of natural pregnancies find no social legitimacy, unwanted babies are recast according to cultural traditions as unhealthy, unnatural, socially created *false bellies*, justifying their termination. Covertly *taken*, abortions help women maintain the children that they already have, which actually supports social stability. Like the techniques used for delivering natural or created babies, abortion techniques follow the purgative meta-model evinced in menstruation (Sobo, 1992, 1993b, 1996).

Jamaican beliefs about the body construct, as well as represent, the phenomena they purport to describe. They help people understand their bodily workings, and people manipulate their bodies according to these understandings. Further, as people discuss their bodies they discuss society, often challenging, supporting, subverting and maintaining the status quo, all at the same time. The flexibility of meaning systems allows for this sort of multi-layered action. It allows human beings as social actors, through discourse, to announce their social and moral opinions and standings.

Acknowledgements

This essay draws together portions of various chapters of my book *One Blood: The Jamaican Body*, (Sobo, 1993b). The research, funded by grants from the University of California at San Diego and from Friends of the International Center, was carried out with the guidance of Dr F.G. Bailey, to whom I owe great thanks. I also owe thanks to Dr William Wedenoja for inviting me to his field-sites and for sharing with me his knowledge of Jamaican ways, and to Dr Jill Korbin, who supervised my post-doctoral studies and who first brought Dr Cecil's work to my attention. The greatest thanks of all go to the numerous Jamaican people who participated and otherwise helped with the research. Without them, my work would not be possible.

Notes

1. I visited the latter two sites in 1989 with Dr William Wedenoja, who conducted research there regularly (e.g., Wedenoja, 1988, 1989).

2. I also use the term 'Jamaicans' throughout this chapter for efficiency's sake, and because I have not yet detected any significant content-related regional variations in knowledge related to pregnancy termination or to health in general.
3. I use italics to denote idiomatic Jamaican words or expressions. Actual participant testimony is indicated with quotation marks.
4. Here, I should note that the research from which this chapter was drawn did not focus specifically on *natural* miscarriage or pregnancy loss (here, I use the term 'natural' in the Jamaican sense, as opposed to *created*). This was in part because the topic was not a salient one for participants. I concluded that 'no other natural causes for lost pregnancies seem to exist' because participants provided no data indicating that other natural causes are known and commonly invoked, not because participants explicitly voiced affirmations that there are no other natural causes.
5. Regarding the Jamaican-made distinction between natural and unnatural or created conditions, see Sobo (1993b). Regarding the similar anthropological distinction between naturalistically and personalistically caused sickness, see Foster (1978).
6. There is a typology of *negromancy* workers, which include *professors, Obeahmen*, and *scientists*. Seaga (1969), Barrett (1988), and Wedenoja (1988), trace the historical differences between branches of folk religion like Myalism, Revival, Pocomania, and Obeah. *Scientist*s instruct themselves with mail-order books and favour the written; *Obeah* workers have usually been apprenticed and use mainly performance. *Scientists* draw on demonic forces detailed in their books. *Obeah* workers deal with ancestors. *Professors* stand somewhere in between. Jamaicans actually use all labels interchangeably, lump all types of workers of inequity together, and oppose them and Pocomanians to what they call 'children of God', who deal only with good. The opposition between good and evil is what matters.
7. In some *false belly* cases, *duppies* may not need *setting*; adding special powder to the *babymother's* food will do.
8. Sorcerers are generally men. In Africa, sorcery had legitimacy and commanded respect, and in a system in which men cannot *uplift* or effectively control others, it is not surprising that they seek power as *Obeah* workers. The sorcerer's *unclean deeds* bring good pay, and people fear his power. Wedenoja explains, 'Men monopolize public positions of wealth and power, and leave the less lucrative positions to women' (1989, p. 87). Healing, which is generally women's work, pays much less. Women are responsible for their families' health, and women healers exploit this. Childhood experience leads people

to seek mother-figures for healers, and healing women or *Mothers* serve and guide 'children,' who obey, respect and idealize them as perfect mothers.

References

Barrett L., *The Rastafarians* (2nd edn), Boston, Beacon Press, 1988

Beckwith, M., *Black Roadways: A Study of Jamaican Folk Life*, Chapel Hill, University of North Carolina Press, 1929

Blake, J., *Family Structure in Jamaica*, New York, Free Press, 1961

Brody, E., *Sex, Contraception, and Motherhood in Jamaica*, Cambridge, Harvard University Press, 1981

Buckley, T. and Gottlieb, A., (eds), *Blood Magic: The Anthropology of Menstruation*, Los Angeles, University of California Press, 1988

Clarke, E., *My Mother Who Fathered Me: A Study of the Family in Three Selected Communities in Jamaica*, Boston, George Allen and Unwin, 1957

Foster, G., 'Disease Etiologies in Non-Western Medical Systems', *American Anthropologist*, vol. 78, 1978, pp. 773–82

Ginsburg F., *Contested Lives: The Abortion Debate in an American Community*, Los Angeles, University of California Press, 1989

Good, B., *Medicine, Rationality, and Experience: An Anthropological Perspective*, New York, Cambridge University Press, 1994

Hufford, D., *The Terror That Comes in the Night*, Philadelphia, University of Pennsylvania Press, 1982

Hurston, Z., *Tell My Horse: Voodoo and Life in Haiti and Jamaica*, with a new foreword, San Francisco, Harper and Row, [1938] 1990

Jordan, B., *Birth in Four Cultures: A Crosscultural Investigation of Childbirth in Yucatan, Holland, Sweden, and the United States* (4th edn revised and expanded by R. Davis-Floyd), Prospect Heights IL, Waveland Press, 1993

Kay, M., (ed.) *Anthropology of Human Birth*, Philadelphia, F.A. Davis, 1982

Kerr, M., *Personality and Conflict in Jamaica*, London, Willmer Brothers & Haram Ltd., [1952] 1963

Korbin, J., 'Child Abuse and Neglect: The Cultural Context', in R. Helfer and R. Kempe (eds), *The Battered Child*, (4th edn) Chicago, University of Chicago Press, 1987

Laguerre, M., *Afro-Caribbean Folk Medicine*, South Hadley MA, Bergin and Garvey, 1987

Luker K., *Abortion and the Politics of Motherhood*, Berkeley, University of California Press, 1984

MacCormack, C.P., 'Lay Concepts Affecting Utilization of Family Planning Services in Jamaica', *Journal of Tropical Medicine and Hygiene*, vol. 88, 1985, pp. 281–5

——, and Draper, A., 'Social and Cognitive Aspects of Female Sexuality in Jamaica', in P. Caplan (ed.), *The Cultural Construction of Sexuality*, New York, Tavistock Publications, 1987

Morgan, L., 'When Does Life Begin? A Cross-cultural Perspective on the Personhood of Fetuses and Young Children', in E. Doerr and J. Prescott (eds), *Abortion Rights and Fetal 'Personhood'*, Long Beach CA, Centerline Press, 1989

Newman L., (ed.) *Women's Medicine: A Cross-Cultural Study of Indigenous Fertility Regulation*, New Brunswick, New Jersey, Rutgers University Press, 1985

Nichter, M. and Nichter, M., 'Cultural Notions of Fertility in South Asia and their Impact on Sri Lankan Family Planning Practices', *Human Organization*, vol. 46, no. 1, 1987, pp. 18–27

Powell D., Hewitt, L. and Wooming, P., *Contraceptive Use in Jamaica: The Social, Economic and Cultural Context*, Working Paper no. 19, Mona, Jamaica, Institute of Social and Economic Research, University of the West Indies, 1978

Roberts, G. and Sinclair, S., *Women in Jamaica: Patterns of Reproduction and Family*, Millwood NY, KTO Press, 1978

Rylko-Bauer, B., 'Abortion Traditions Cross-culturally', *Social Science and Medicine*, vol. 42, no. 4, 1996, pp. 479–82

Sargent, C. and Harris, M., 'Gender Ideology, Child-rearing, and Child Health in Jamaica', *American Ethnologist*, vol. 19, 1992, pp. 523–37

Scheper-Hughes, N., *Death Without Weeping: The Violence of Everyday Life in Brazil*, Los Angeles, University of California Press, 1992

Seaga, E., 'Revival Cults in Jamaica', *Jamaica Journal*, vol. 3, no. 2, 1969, pp. 3–15

Smith, R.T., *Kinship and Class in the West Indies: A Genealogical Study of Jamaica and Guyana*, New York, Cambridge University Press, 1988

Sobo, E.J., '"Unclean Deeds": Menstrual Taboos and Binding "Ties" in Rural Jamaica', in M. Nichter (ed.), *Anthropological Approaches to the Study of Ethnomedicine*, New York, Gordon and Breach, 1992

——, 'Bodies, Kin, and Flow: Family Planning in Rural Jamaica', *Medical Anthropology Quarterly*, vol. 7, no. 1, 1993a, pp. 50–73

——, *One Blood: The Jamaican Body*, Albany, State University of New York Press, 1993b

——, 'Menstruation: An Ethnophysiological Defense Against Pathogens', *Perspectives in Biology and Medicine*, vol. 38, no. 1, 1994, pp. 36–40

——, 'Abortion Traditions in Rural Jamaica', *Social Science and Medicine*, vol. 42, no. 4, 1986, pp. 495–508

Wedenoja W., 'The Origins of Revival, a Creole Religion in Jamaica', in G. Saunders (ed.), *Culture and Christianity*, Westport CN, Greenwood, 1988

——, 'Mothering and the Practice of "Balm" in Jamaica', in C. McClain (ed.), *Women as Healers: Cross-Cultural Perspectives*, New Brunswick NJ, Rutgers University Press, 1989

–3–

Water Spirits, Medicine-men and Witches: Avenues to Successful Reproduction among the Abelam, Papua New Guinea

Anna Winkvist

Introduction

In most cultures, women are valued for their productive and reproductive capacities. Often, the latter is more emphasized than the former, and women have strong incentives to reproduce continuously. As a result, women's health in developing countries is closely linked to their reproductive experiences. Both production and reproduction take place within complex cultural contexts and mirror women's role in society in general. Thus, interventions to improve women's health will only be successful if based on extensive knowledge of the role of reproduction in women's lives and the distribution of knowledge and power over reproduction among men and women in the society.

This chapter describes how the Abelam, in the East Sepik Province of Papua New Guinea, attempt to gain control over their reproductive health. A 1983 National Nutrition Survey found the Abelam territory to be one of the worst districts in the country in terms of maternal and child health (Heywood, 1985). The ethnographic study reported here was carried out in conjunction with a nutrition study of pregnancy, childbirth and infant growth in the same area, in collaboration with the Papua New Guinea Institute of Medical Research (IMR) in Madang (Winkvist, 1988). The aim was to identify the traditions surrounding fertility, pregnancy and childbirth that impacted upon the health of mother and child.

Methodology

All data were collected between July and December, 1986, by the author, fluent in Melanesian Pidgin, and a trained female fieldworker provided by IMR. All fifty-two women in the central and southern parts of the Abelam territory who gave birth between July and September 1986 were enrolled for the nutrition study. During repeated visits to these mothers, formal and informal open-ended interviews about child-bearing took place. Three villages were selected for interviews with groups of women: Nale, Twaikum and Gunyingi. These villages were chosen because of the presence of some *lapun* (Melanesian Pidgin word for older people), knowledgeable about the past, who might be able to interpret or explain traditions still prevailing. Between ten and fifteen women, either elderly or of mixed ages, participated in each of these group interviews. In addition, informal discussions took place at the local markets in Kunjingini and Gunyingi. Families not included in the nutrition study were sometimes visited, and often the team would stop for a while during the nutrition study and talk with the villagers. Staff at the Maprik hospital, health centres, patrol posts, Maprik High School, Catholic Missions, Maprik Family Planning Bureau and East Sepik Women's Network also were interviewed. Finally, during the nutrition research, many opportunities for observation and participant observation of women's situation during pregnancy and childbirth occurred. Most conversations took place in Melanesian Pidgin, which most people in the area spoke. However, some older people only spoke the local language, Nanakundi; in such cases younger women were used as interpreters. Words indicated by (n) are in Nanakundi; words indicated by (p) are in Melanesian Pidgin.

Below, the contextual background of Abelam society is presented first, followed by Abelam strategies for ensuring successful reproduction.

The Abelam

The Abelam comprise an ethnolinguistic group occupying the area between the southern foothills of the Torricelli Range and the Sepik River in the East Sepik Province, Papua New Guinea. Their language belongs to the Ndu family of languages, which extends further south to the Sepik River and the Iatmül group, and east to include the Boikin people (Laycock, 1961). North of the Abelam are the Arapesh, who belong to a different language stock. The term 'Abelam' is originally the Arapesh name for this people and was used by Mead (1938) in her report *The Mountain Arapesh*.

The Abelam are linguistically and culturally distinct from their neighbours. However, cultural variation also exists among the Abelam villages, so findings from one area should not be extrapolated to other areas without caution. Most of the fieldwork for this study was carried out in the central and southern parts of Abelam territory, called the

Wosera, and it is with reference to this area that the term 'Abelam' is used here.

The Abelam occupy an area of approximately 290 square miles with a population density of 106 persons per square mile (Lea, 1964). However, the people are unevenly distributed, and in the Wosera the density is as high as 400 per square mile, making it the most densely populated area of mainland Papua New Guinea. Typical of the landscape are floodplains and alluvial terraces; the vegetation is mainly forest, grassland and swamp. Starting in October, when the wet season begins, the gardens are planted with yam. Yams plays a central role in Abelam culture, being connected with male prestige, the authority of older men and kinship obligations. The gardens are therefore of two types: *wabi yawi* (n), planted with greater yam (*Dioscorea alata*), which is used for ceremonial purposes especially in the northern Wosera, and *ka yawi* (n), planted with lesser yam (*Dioscorea esculenta*) for consumption.

Families in the northern parts of Abelam territory usually own a sleeping house, a yam-storage house, a cookhouse, a menstruation hut and a pig shelter, whereas it is common for a southern family to have only one large building, said to belong to the man, which serves all these purposes. The most common house type is a brush-hut built directly on the ground, the roof coming up from the ground at the back towards a high triangular front; the two sides of the house are also triangular. There are no windows, and food is cooked over an open fire just outside the door or inside the house, leaving heavy smoke inside the poorly ventilated structure.

Abelam clans are patrilineal kin groups, and within the village several clans are represented. The clans are named and each have a bird totem, *djambu* (n), associated with them. Each clan is also affiliated with *ngwalndu* (n). *Ngwalndu* do not correspond to ancestors or *djambu*, but are ritual objects belonging to the clan (Kaberry, 1941). A man belongs to the clan of his father and inherits his *djambu* and his *ngwalndu*. However, matrilineal principles complement the patrilineal kin groups and play an important role in the society too. Thus, the *djambu* and the *ngwalndu* of the mother's father are also inherited; there are economic and ceremonial obligations to the mother's kindred, and a man has rights to harvest from his mother's brother's land and his mother's brother's son's land. If a man has no children of his own, he may adopt a sister's child. In spite of these matrilineal principles, there is no doubt that Abelam men have a superior position over the women.

Each village has several Big Men, or *nema ndu* (n), who represent the village, maintain its prestige with their skills and direct the initiation ceremonies.

Abelam women earn recognition through hard work and a

productive garden (Heywood Allen, Fandim, Garner, Hide, Joughin, Junembarry, Mathie, Numbuk, Ross and Yaman, 1986). Traditionally, women alone are responsible for the planting, weeding and harvesting of all crops except yams, the collection of firewood and water, the washing of sago, the care of children and of pigs, and the making of *bilum* (p; netbags). The men do everything related to the yam, hunt, build houses, carve masks, spears and figures, and decorate the *haus tambaran* (men's ceremonial house; see Hauser-Schäublin, 1989). Men and women together clear new bush. As Ross (1984, p. 22) says, 'men's work is either seasonal or elective while women perform all the routine day-to-day essential chores and all the more tedious subsistence work'.

Before 1937, the Abelam had had little contact with Europeans. That year, the Australian administration established a patrol post in Maprik, and a year later a Roman Catholic Mission was established in Kunjingini. Today, there is a hospital in Maprik which is the referral centre for the Maprik District's population of 150,000. In the Wosera Sub-district there are four sub-health Centres, each serving around 20,000 villagers. The centres in Kaugia and Kunjingini are both run by the Catholic Mission. The Sub-district also operates six aid-posts, staffed by aid-post orderlies (with two years training), each of whom serves 2,000–4,000 villagers. The role of the latter is especially important in remote areas. Most of them are men, even though in Papua New Guinea culture it is not appropriate for women to approach men with issues concerning pregnancy, childbirth or family planning. As a result, in some districts antenatal coverage is less than 10 per cent (Tremlett, 1986). Maternal mortality is on average about 800–900 per 100,000, but for some areas it is as high as 2,000 per 100,000 (Mola and Aitken, 1984; UNICEF, 1991).

Child-bearing among the Abelam

Among Abelam women, the road towards successful reproduction starts early in life. In Wosera tradition, one clan is said to have special power to be *nianmi* (n), a kind of traditional healer, a tradition that originated around Miko, Twaikum and Apusit but has spread throughout the area to other villages. The *nianmi* deals with all issues relating to fertility. When a girl is about ten years old, the *nianmi* provides her with a special mixture, also called *nianmi*, to ensure her fertility. The mixture consists of a piece of umbilical cord, *liklik hap long snek bilong bilum bilong pikinini* (p), which is cooked, dried, and combined with coconut and breadfruit. Later, when the girl conceives, she must donate a shell-ring to the *nianmi* (traditionally all payments were made with rings from the shell *Tridacna gigas*, obtained from the Arapesh).

At the time of their first menstruation the young girls used to be kept inside the family's house in a corner specially screened off for them. The first daughter would stay inside for one year, but the second or later daughters would only stay for about half a year. However, now most girls stay inside for only one to two months, and it is the girl's father or mother's brother who decides the length of the stay. The girl is not allowed to see anybody but will spend much of her time making *bilum* (p; net bag), one of the most important possessions of the family for their daily life. When the confinement is ended, there will be a big *singsing* (ceremonial event, usually with dancing and singing). In some areas, the girls used to receive scar tattoos on their upper arms, breasts and stomach to indicate that they were ready for marriage and child-bearing, but this is no longer done (Hauser-Schäublin, 1989).

The Abelam theory of conception is a combination of physiological facts and spiritual beliefs. For the Abelam, the world is inhabited by two kinds of spirits: ancestral spirits (sometimes referred to as *ngwalndu*), who can be called upon for help in everyday life; and natural spirits, known as *wala* (n), *masalai* (p). *Wala*, who dwell in rivers and streams, are needed for conception and enter the woman's vagina and insert the child when the woman is in or near the river. Afterwards, repeated intercourse between husband and wife is needed before the woman bears the child. Both husband and wife contribute to the bones and flesh of the fetus; if it is a son it is the father who has given the blood, if it is a daughter it is the mother (Kaberry, 1941; Schofield and Parkinson, 1963; Allen, 1989).

Once pregnant, the Abelam woman has access to yet another specialized traditional healer. In addition to the *nianmi* clan in the villages, another clan has the power to be medicine-men, *poisonman* (p), i.e., those who deal with the curing of all kinds of sickness. In Wosera tradition, there are two kinds of *poisonman*, *kusndu* (n) and *mindu* (n). The *kusndu* may be consulted by anybody in the village, whereas the *mindu* only deals with pregnant and lactating women and children who are still being breast-fed. The *mindu* monitors pregnant women, and he identifies pregnancies by observing when the woman's abdomen enlarges, when her nipples turn black instead of red, when she has white spots in her eyes, or when her legs become swollen. Today, these signs are also referred to by the women themselves as indicators of pregnancy, and they consider themselves two-months pregnant at that time. In addition, women with exposure to Western education recognize that if they miss a menstrual period they are pregnant, and they say that they are one month pregnant at that time. Some women may start to count months of pregnancy, but this is not something emphasized in the society.

Children are seen as a resource, and a large family is often desired. The men especially want sons who can inherit their land. To ensure that a new-born child will be a boy, a man may take a certain black spider, break a coconut or take a yam with the top cut off, roast them and ask his wife to consume them. Girls, however, are also appreciated, as they are needed to help their mother.

A woman knows that if she experiences some pain and the waters break she is close to delivery, and she will then squat in the house. Often she has to deliver in the garden; it can be far away from the house and the women work their gardens throughout the entire pregnancy. It is up to her if she wants to deliver on her own or ask some of her female relatives to help her. In reality, very few women are assisted in childbirth by a skilled and experienced birth attendant. Sometimes family members might be present, but most women choose to deliver on their own (Tremlett, 1986). One reason for this is that women are generally believed to be polluting, particularly during menstruation and childbirth. Contact with such pollution is believed to cause illness, and it will severely affect the growth of the ceremonial yams so important to male honour. Thus if women assist with a delivery, they may not be allowed to touch or cook for husbands or children for up to one week afterwards to protect the family from such pollution. If a woman assists with a delivery outside her family, she is usually paid compensation for the contamination. This can be expensive, so women try to avoid the expense by delivering on their own. If a woman or child dies during labour or delivery, the birth attendant may be accused of murder or sorcery, and compensation will be sought by the dead person's relatives. Even trained village health-workers have been treated in this way. Furthermore, some women deliver alone to protect themselves from sorcery. Finally, many women deliver alone because they do not anticipate problems. There is resistance against delivering at the hospital, because the women are afraid of having to expose themselves to the male staff there, or they may not have money for transport or the cost of a stay (the latter is a misconception, as health care is free). Also, they believe that if they die in the hospital their spirit will not find its way back to their village. Thus, over 90 per cent of all births take place at home.

The following is a description of a childbirth observed in Jambitanget during the course of this research.

> The woman was staying in the hut, with a little fire next to her. There were no traditional midwives and her relatives were not supposed to help her. She squatted close to the wall on one side of the hut, holding both hands on cut branches in the ceiling above her head. Some large green banana-leaf leaves

were put under her. When we arrived, she had been in pain for a long time, and the infant was close to being delivered. Except for the researcher and the fieldworker, only her mother was present inside the hut. The only light was the small fire. The woman pushed, sitting in this squatted position, and the infant was delivered within a few minutes. The placenta came some minutes later without her pulling the umbilical cord. The infant was left on the leaves for some minutes, even though it did not seem to breath. After about five minutes the woman was given a razor blade by her mother, and she cut the umbilical cord close to the infant. The infant had now started to scream and was declared to be alive. Blood was pouring from its umbilicus, and the child was held upside down for a short while to let some drip away. The stump of the cord was not tied on the infant. The placenta, together with the rest of the cord, was put in a ceramic pot to be buried later in the ground at exactly the place where the baby was born.

The leaves were taken away and the mother poured some cold water over the infant to clean it. Nothing was put on the umbilicus.

The whole village stood outside the hut, waiting to hear the results. Only the father was allowed to see the infant immediately. Mother and infant both stayed inside the hut.

Abelam Responses to Unsuccessful Reproduction

Infertility

In cases where menarche is delayed, the girl's parents will collect the vine *ramunjinga* (p) and put some leaves of it on the girl's plate under her food, so that its juice will mix with the food. The leaves themselves are not consumed but are later thrown away. Another remedy is for the girl to go out in the forest herself and find a cardamum-like plant, *gorngor* (p). She turns her back to the plant, pinches off its bud and paints the remaining plant red. Later a new bud will come and the girl will start to menstruate.

After marriage, if the girl does not conceive her father will bring her back to the *nianmi*, donate additional shell-rings, and request that the *nianmi* breathes on her abdomen. His breath is regarded as powerful, and the girl should afterwards be able to conceive. The mother's brother is an important person in a girl's life. He is even referred to as her 'little father'; infertility is sometimes seen as an indication that the girl's uncle is upset over something, and this 'dispute' has to be resolved before the girl will conceive.

There are cases of infertile women but this is not very common, and such women are pitied. A man who does not have any children can request members of his own clan to give him a new-born child, but he may not ask others. If the father of the new-born child agrees, it is given, regardless of the opinion of the mother. Usually the biological mother will keep the new-born child as long as it is breast-fed, which is about two years.

Pregnancy Loss

When miscarriages and stillbirths occur, Abelam explanations are related to social and spiritual rather than physical causes, for example, conflicts within the family, or spirits who have been offended. First, if a girl's payment to the *nianmi* has been ignored, the *nianmi* may retaliate and cause the fetus to become sick and die. Secondly, as described above, *wala* are needed for conception but can actually be harmful to fetuses and infants younger than one month old. If *wala* are offended by a woman passing by the stream and singing loudly or stepping on stones sacred to them, they will enter her body and harm her fetus or enter the body of her child and cause sickness or even death. The pregnant woman and her husband should also avoid using sharp knives, or the child will be born blind or with sores on the body because this offends *wala* (Schofield and Parkinson, 1963). Thus, although *wala* are responsible for causing the miscarriage or the child's illness and death, the ultimate reason is that the parents broke a taboo.

If a woman experiences pain during pregnancy, she will first consult the *mindu*. In exchange for a shell ring he will blow air on her abdomen, place his hand on her back or tell her to consume sago, yams and greens. If this treatment does not help, she may instead consult the *kusndu*.

Some women claim that it is possible for a woman who suffers pain in late pregnancy to stay at home and rest. However, most men want their women to work all the time because, as one woman asked, 'Who would otherwise get water, firewood and work in the garden?' Also, it is said that if the woman keeps working through the entire pregnancy, the new-born will be strong and healthy, 'pikinini bai kamap gutpela' (p). If she stays at home, the new-born will be weak and skinny, 'pikinini bai kamap bonating' (p), and this is often given as the explanation for small new-born children. Small infants are not treated in any special way, but are breast-fed like other infants. 'If it survives, it survives. If it dies, it dies', as one mother put it.

After the child is born, the mother watches to see if it starts to cry. If it does not breathe, it is not helped in any way. It is commonly held that when the infant starts to cry one knows that it is alive, and it will then be washed. This was also noted by Schofield and Parkinson (1963), who wrote: 'If the child does not cry after birth it is not picked up and is left for dead even if it is still moving'. Sickly and malformed infants were traditionally left to die, as they faced a short and miserable life anyway (Allen 1989).

Difficult Labour

If the delivery is delayed, the woman may ask a certain group of women called *gundiui* for help. These women have special knowledge and skills relating to childbirth, and they will provide massage, blow air on the woman's abdomen and hold a *singsing* over water that she must later drink. All these procedures are believed to trigger the delivery. *Gundiui* is actually the name of a bird that inhabits the river's edge. When the bird plays, it keeps turning around in the water. The water used in the *singsing* is fetched in a shell or cup from the river, and the *gundiui* women then meditate and sing over it. When the mother later drinks this water, the baby will turn around within her like the *gundiui* bird in the water, put its head down and be delivered. Further, the mother can herself encourage labour by repeatedly climbing coconut or betel-nut trees, which will make the eyes of the infant open up. Several mothers acknowledged that they had used this method and delivered in the seventh or eighth month of pregnancy. This climbing of trees is often done in combination with drinking the *gundiui* water. If a mother does not want to climb trees, she may walk long distances instead. The reason given for wanting an early delivery is that the mother is tired of carrying her heavy burden, 'mi less long karim dispela bikpela bel, em hevi tumas' (p). Cases where infants had been delivered earlier than nine months were referred to by many women, but this was not regarded as a problem. There are no known means of delaying a delivery.

Within the traditional health system, a woman with a retained placenta would go and see the *kusndu* and the *mindu*, who would both breathe on the abdomen to encourage the placenta to be expelled. However, most people today agree that a woman with a retained placenta or a breech presentation at birth has to be taken to the hospital, because otherwise she will die, although female relatives might try for a while to help the woman by pulling the cord. Sometimes the mother even tries to do this herself by tying the cord to her big toe and pulling it (Tremlett 1986). Several times during this research, mothers with placenta-retention and the umbilical cord still connecting her and her new-born were encountered up to a day after the infant had been delivered. One of these occurred in a remote village where it was impossible to drive closer than half an hour's walk in difficult terrain from the village. The woman was in extreme pain by this time and could not walk by herself. A discussion about how to get her to the car took place. The men did not participate but kept themselves in the background, while the women brought a *bilum* in which the woman was placed. Two other women, both smaller in body size than the woman in the *bilum*, carried it one at a time in the traditional way, with the string around the forehead, all the way to the car. The placenta was removed at the hospital, and the mother recovered within a few days. However, this is a not uncommon cause of death among women if they are not taken to the hospital.

Food Taboos During Child-bearing

According to tradition, all women, but especially pregnant ones, should eat fruit like fig and wild palm fruit. Most women agree that a mother who is pregnant for the first time should not eat lizard, bandicoot, cuscus, snake or a pig that has chased a dog. If she consumes these foods, her delivery will be difficult. For example, her infant will be afraid to come out (if she consumed a pig that had chased a dog), or it will cling to her uterus like the cuscus clings to the trees, or it will stay inside like a lizard that has been chased up a tree will stay there, or the umbilical cord will wrap around the child's neck (snake and cuscus). During later pregnancies she is allowed to eat these foods. Dietary restrictions start when the woman is about four months pregnant.

Following the birth, the mother may not eat coconut, greens or meat for about one month, or the infant will not sleep in the *bilum* but will cry all the time. Some say that if the mother chews betel-nut, the infant will get sores around the anus and mouth. These restrictions end at the first full moon after the delivery.

Some women do not feed the infant the first milk, colostrum, while others do. One mother said, 'sapos yu larim istap, em bai indai pinis' (p), 'If you don't feed it, it will die.'

If the milk does not come, the remedy is that the husband or a *gundiui* woman take a banana, heat it and spread the mashed meat, *wara bilongen* (p), over the breasts. The breasts are then massaged with the banana paste, and this helps initiate lactation. This method is widely mentioned and used. If a mother cannot breast-feed at all, a relative will nurse her infant, and only rarely are the clinics asked about powdered milk. Bottles and powdered milk are only sold by prescription, and breast-feeding is almost universal. A mother who is not able to lactate should go to the *mindu*, who will instruct her to eat a soup of coconut milk and yams. If the breast-fed child is malnourished, the *mindu* will tell the lactating mother to eat this soup together with wild palm fruit and figs.

Contraceptives

The coconut shells in which the women received their *nianmi* mixture when they were young are kept by the *mindu*. Thus, when a woman does not want to have any more children, she asks the *mindu* to dispose of the shell and she will supposedly not conceive. If she does not want to make such a definite decision, she may chew raw ginger as a traditional contraceptive, either on its own or mixed with yams. In some places women also use *singsing* (p), i.e. a collective singing session.

As mentioned above, women are not allowed to have sexual intercourse while pregnant (the mother will become defiled) or while still breast-feeding (the breast-fed child will become weak and will not be able to walk), which often occurs for up to three years. This proscription is strong, so if a woman becomes pregnant while breast-feeding, she will first deny being pregnant, and later, when her condition becomes visible, she will explain that the first child has already been weaned, even if that is not the case.

During the time when the men are growing the large ceremonial yams they are not allowed to have intercourse, and this restriction, together with that of lactation, has traditionally been effective enough to give a spacing of births of about three years without the use of contraceptives. Today, however, these restrictions are often ignored by younger people, and there is a perceived need for information about family planning. The only modern method of birth control encouraged by the two Catholic sub-health centres in Kaugia and Kunjingini is the ovulation method. In 1985 the UNFPA started an East Sepik Family-planning project, with a nurse stationed in Maprik. Initially, the information and contraceptives provided were appreciated. A written agreement from the husband was needed, but this was rarely a problem. However, open criticism by the Catholic Missions, including the health centres which are against artificial birth control and do not perceive large family size as a problem in the area, made people afraid of using this facility.

There is an awareness that some women do not resume menstruation quickly after delivery, while others do. The explanation given is 'taim pikinini ilusim susu, sik mun isave kam' (p); that is, when the child is breast-fed, the period will not occur. When the child stops being breast-fed, the menstrual period will resume. If the woman now has intercourse, she will get pregnant, whereas if the child is still being breast-fed, she will not become pregnant even with intercourse, 'Sapos man istap klostu, meri ikamap bel gen, tasol sapos pikinini isusu, nogat.' (p).

Discussion

Adherence to the Traditional Health System

Several villages still have a *nianmi* and *poisonman*. In addition, many women mentioned using the service of *gundiui* women during labour. Ideas about taboos concerning food during pregnancy and lactation varied. Some women claimed that there are none at all and never have been, while others, especially older women, emphasized that there are some. Most women agreed that they would go to the health centre if their children became sick, but if the treatment was not effective, they would use traditional medicine.

Thus, Abelam traditional medicine is still used in parallel with Western medicine. This combination of traditional and Western medicine is the rule rather than the exception in most parts of the Third World today, and its features in different societies in Papua New Guinea have recently been reviewed (Frankel and Lewis, 1989).

The Power to Act: The Abelam Health System Through a Gender Perspective

As in most societies, fertility plays an important role in Abelam culture. Among the Abelam this is reflected in the multitude of people and spirits with power over reproduction and reproductive health. The *nianmi* ensures that adolescent girls become fertile by providing a special mixture and can later be consulted for infertility, while water spirits called *wala* are needed for conception to take place. However, both the *nianmi* and *wala* also have power to harm the fetus or young child if offended, causing miscarriages, deformities, neonatal death or neonatal illness. Further, the *mindu* monitors pregnant women and treats pain during pregnancy, placenta retention, insufficient milk production and malnutrition among breast-fed children. The *mindu* is also consulted by women who want to stop reproducing. Finally, *gundiui* women are consulted during labour.

However, women have relatively little control over reproduction. As described above, the responsibility for ensuring successful reproduction is mainly that of the *nianmi* and the *mindu*. *Gundiui* women only have knowledge about how to induce labour and will not assist at the birth. One of the few instances of female control is at the time of delivery: women themselves know and use several methods for inducing labour, including the climbing of coconut or betel-nut trees and drinking *gundiui* water. Still, rather than being recognized as the owners of knowledge which controls reproduction, women are seen as potential sources of misfortune. In cases of miscarriages or deformities the woman may be blamed for having offended the *nianmi* or *wala*. The husband's role is here limited to causing minor infant morbidity by offending the *wala*. If the baby is born too small, the mother may be blamed for not having worked hard enough during the pregnancy. Also, as mentioned earlier, women are seen as polluting particularly during menstruation and childbirth, and if a polluted woman touches the food of others she may cause illness and poor yam harvest.

The weak position of women relative to men is also reflected in the general Abelam health system. In Abelam tradition, death and illness are ascribed to four main causes. First, the *wala* may cause miscarriages and harm new-borns. Secondly, witches called *sanguma meri* (p) may sometimes help sick children but they may also cause malnutrition by eating the flesh of the child. *Sanguma meri* are mostly known for their habit of uncovering corpses and consuming their flesh, which is why the bodies of children and young adults are buried close to the village so that their graves can be watched. *Sanguma meri* are actually only the spirits of village women, who leave the women's bodies during the night while the women are asleep. If a spirit is prevented from returning to the body the woman will die during her sleep, and if the spirit cannot completely re-enter the body she will become insane. *Sanguma meri* pass on their tradition to their daughters but never to girls of other families. As a consequence, the tradition is only inherited within certain families.

Thirdly, serious accidents, sickness or death among people older than two years are said to be caused by a sorcerer in another village who has been paid by some enemy. Samples of a victim's hair, blood, faeces or uneaten food scraps are required to carry out the necessary malevolent rituals, and these are later mixed with powerful paints by the sorcerer. Sorcerers are actually referred to as *kwis ndu* (n), meaning paint man (Forge, 1970). Here, the only recourse is to identify the sorcerer and pay them to discontinue the sorcery, or to identify the enemy and use counter-sorcery against him. Often the village Big Men are asked for help with identifying the sorcerer and delivering the payment, as Big Men are assumed to have contacts with sorcerers. The sorcerers learn from similar practitioners how to make drugs and poisons, which are tried out first on animals like frogs and dogs, and later on humans. The belief in *sanguma meri* and sorcerers is still strong; many villagers spoke of knowing who these people were in their villages.

Fourthly, old men or women are said to die because of old age and no spirits are held accountable. Nor is sorcery implied in cases of murder or war (Schofield and Parkinson, 1963).

Thus, men represent central and controlled knowledge and power in the traditional health system. A sorcerer, who is always male, is a regular human being who has learned his skill and who deliberately causes illness and death on behalf of his client. He actively uses destructive power and is held accountable for his actions (Stephen, 1987). In contrast, women's knowledge and power is peripheral and uncontrolled. In Abelam tradition, witchcraft is innate and may take place without the conscious intention of the witch (Forge, 1970). The witch, who is always female, is simply the passive vehicle of destructive power, and the destruction is unpredictable and illogical.

In summary, Abelam men possess knowledge and control over the initiation, maintenance and termination of women's reproduction. Women control the moment of delivery, but consult male traditional healers for all other purposes. In the general Abelam theory of illness and misfortune, men represent deliberate evil actions, whereas women represent mishaps due to carelessness or being the passive agent of evil forces. The explanations for miscarriages, fetal deformities, low infant birth-weight and neonatal deaths, are all related to women's carelessness.

Acknowledgements

I am most grateful for the support and cooperation of Dr Peter Heywood at the Institute of Medical Research in Madang, Papua New Guinea; Dr Milton Barnett and Dr Kathleen M. Rasmussen at Cornell University, Ithaca, N.Y., USA; and Diana Lai and all mothers in the Wosera area. The research was supported by the Swedish Institute; SAREC; the Fulbright Commission; the Sweden-America Foundation; the Institute of Medical Research, Papua New Guinea; and DNS Small Grants, Cornell University.

References

Allen, B.J., 'Infection, Innovation and Residence: Illness and Misfortune in the Torricelli Foothills from 1800', in S. Frankel and G. Lewis (eds),

A Continuing Trial of Treatment. Medical Pluralism in Papua New Guinea, Boston, Kluwer Academic Publishers, 1989

Forge, J.A.W., 'Prestige, Influence and Sorcery: A New Guinea Example', in M. Douglas (ed.), *Witchcraft, Confessions and Accusation*, London, Tavistock Publications, 1970

Frankel, S. and Lewis, G., *A Continuing Trial of Treatment. Medical Pluralism in Papua New Guinea*, Boston, Kluwer Academic Publishers, 1989

Hauser-Schäublin, B., *Kulthäuser in Nordneuguinea*, Berlin, Akademie-Verlag, 1989 (summary in English)

Heywood, P., *1983 National Nutrition Survey: 1. Preliminary District-level Analysis of Length and Weight Data*, Madang, Papua New Guinea Institute of Medical Research, 1985

——, Allen, B., Fandim, T., Garner, P., Hide, R., Joughin, J., Junembarry, J., Mathie, A., Numbuk, S., Ross, J. and Yaman, C., *A Rapid Appraisal of Agriculture, Nutrition and Health in Wosera Sub-district, East Sepik Province*, Madang, Papua New Guinea Institute of Medical Research, 1986

Kaberry, P.M., 'The Abelam Tribe, Sepik District, New Guinea. A Preliminary Report', *Oceania*, vol. 11, 1941, pp. 233–58, 345–67

Laycock, D.C., 'The Sepik and its Languages', *Australian Territories*, vol. 1, 1961, pp. 35–41

Lea, D.A.M., 'Abelam Land and Sustenance: Swidden Horticulture in an Area of High Population Density, Maprik, New Guinea', Ph.D. thesis, Canberra, Australian National University, 1964

Mead, M., *The Mountain Arapesh*, Anthropological Papers of the American Museum of Natural History, New York, Natural History Museum Press, 1938

Mola, G.D.L. and Aitken, I.W., 'Maternal Mortality in Papua New Guinea, 1976–1983', *Papua New Guinea Medical Journal*, vol. 27, no. 2, 1984, pp. 65–71

Ross, J., 'Subsistence Under Stress: Nutritional Implications in the Wosera, Papua New Guinea', MS Thesis, University of Guelph, Canada, 1984

Schofield, F.D. and Parkinson, A.D., 'Social Medicine in New Guinea: Beliefs and Practices Affecting Health Among the Abelam and Wam Peoples of the Sepik District, Part I', *Medical Journal of Australia*, vol. I, no. 1, 1963, pp. 1–8

Stephen, M., *Sorcerer and Witch in Melanesia*, New Brunswick NJ, Rutgers University Press, 1987

Tremlett, G., *Strengthening Service Delivery and Information, Education and Communication Activities of Maternal and Child Health/ Family Planning Programmes*, World Health Organization Report,

PNG/84/P01, 1986

UNICEF, *The State of the World's Children*, Oxford, Oxford University Press, 1991

Winkvist, A., 'Infants Among the Abelam: A Nutritional and Ethnographic Study of Pregnancy, Childbirth and Infant Growth in Papua New Guinea', MS thesis, Ithaca NY, Cornell University, 1988

–4–

Explaining Pregnancy Loss in Matrilineal Southeast Tanzania

J.A.R. Wembah-Rashid

Introduction

This chapter explains beliefs concerning miscarriages, stillbirths, the gestational stage at which pregnancy is recognized and when the fetus/ baby is considered human among the peoples of southeast Tanzania. Southeast Tanzania is inhabited by Wamakonde, Wamakua, Wamwera and Wayao, who are part of the Yao cluster. Others in this cluster include the Mozambican Wamakonde, Alomwe, Wamatambwe and Wangindo (Murdock, 1959). The peoples of the Yao cluster occupy the area between Lake Malawi, the Indian Ocean and the Lukuledi and Zambezi rivers (Tew, 1950), thus inhabiting the northern part of Mozambique and adjacent areas of southeast Tanzania and southeast Malawi. However, this study is restricted to sections of these groups that live in southeast Tanzania, i.e. the current administrative regions of Lindi and Mtwara, and Tunduru district in Ruvuma region.

This is an area of forested highlands and plateaus, undulating wooded grassland plains and swamps, where soils and rainfall are highly variable. Most of the soils can be cultivated, especially on the plateaus and in the alluvial river basins, and allow villages to remain on the same site for thirty years (Gough, 1961; Wembah-Rashid, 1983).

The peoples examined here have much in common. They have, as a matrilineal group, settled the same corner of Tanzania and been cut off from the rest of the country by natural barriers for over two centuries. Their various histories of their origins and movement into the area are closely related. Their ancestors were part and parcel of the Bantu peoples who arrived from the hinterland during the first millenia AD. Their grandparents took part in the East African slave trade as victims or as slave-buying agents. About a century ago they fought against the Ngoni, and resisted and finally succumbed first to German and then to British colonialism.

Although the above groups speak and identify themselves with the various languages noted above, most of them have been speaking Kiswahili and the languages of their neighbours for the past century. This has been possible because of language-group integration through intermarriage, settlement and the high mobility of individuals and groups within the area. It is not uncommon for a single village to be settled by different language groups, who also share cultural, economic and political systems. Until the arrival and penetration of Europeans into this area, the major economic activities comprised, among others, agriculture, hunting, fishing, foraging and regional trading activities. The main crops grown were millet, eleusine, pulses, legumes, yams, potatoes, oil seeds, nuts, vegetables and fruit trees. They also domesticated some animals, for example, cattle, goats and sheep, as well as different kinds of birds, for example, chicken, ducks and pigeons. While domestic food production and foraging were jointly carried out by both females and males, hunting and fishing was a male domain.

The matrilineal peoples of southeast Tanzania have lived as acephalous groups for many centuries, during which clans were common means of linking lineage segments to one another in sets of ever widening relations. But as these groups split off from parent groups for various reasons, such as finding new land for settlement, there was more and more contact with peoples of other language groups within the area. In due course colonialism forced the various groups to assume more permanent and autonomous settlements as their habitat became politically and physically demarcated into administrative sections. This process to some degree constrained the natural movement and intercourse between clanspeople and enhanced inter-clan and multilingual networking. In this area, nationalist politics cemented inter-ethnic integration, and the nation-wide resettlement scheme of the mid–1970s brought many ethnic groups together.

Most important is the fact that these groups share elaborate rites of passage. Both Roman Catholic and Anglican missionaries encouraged the continuation of the rites by incorporating them into their church ceremonies. From the mid–1930s the two churches modified the rites by removing what they considered to be heathen elements and introducing other elements deemed appropriate in Christianity (cf. Hokororo, 1960).

In this chapter I draw on material from personal observation as well as participation in some of the rites as a native of the area. I also use oral traditions, collected during systematic anthropological research conducted on and off between 1965 and 1990. Additional information was collected in 1992 from a focus group discussion conducted among traditional midwives from the area now living in Dar-es-Salaam.

Before conversion to Christianity, the people under study did not recognize the fetus or a stillbirth or a baby with congenital defects as human. Offspring became human when midwives pronounced them to be so after expert scrutiny. Miscarriages, stillbirths and the deaths of abnormal babies were not causes for elaborate mourning ritual or mourning behaviour, as would have been the case for the deaths of adults or babies recognized as human. However, every effort was made to prevent miscarriages, stillbirths and abnormal births from occurring. When they occurred curative measures were taken to restore the mother's health.

Loss of pregnancy caused, and still causes, considerable distress and anxiety. As pregnancy is expected to result in a new human being to extend the family, clan and lineage, its loss is perceived as threatening the parent's line with extinction. It causes distress and anxiety because it calls for a socially and medically justifiable explanation for a couple's failure to extend their kinship line.

Students of medical anthropology recognize that menstruation, pregnancy and childbirth can be described and explained both in clinical or biological terms and in social terms. Individuals pass through a number of social statuses in their lifetime, the contents of which are often defined by specific biological as well as social experiences. It is argued, for example, that, for the woman concerned, pregnancy and childbirth are important social experiences as much as they are biological (Standing, 1980). While I agree with this view, I would observe that in the matrilineal societies of southeast Tanzania, where rites of passage are elaborate, these experiences are shared by the women's spouse. Three rites relevant to pregnancy and childbirth are performed: (1) to mark the attainment of puberty; (2) to confirm the existence of a pregnancy; and (3) to prepare the parents-to-be for childbirth. Although menstruation, which biologically indicates the attainment of puberty, is treated as dangerous and polluting, its onset is anticipated and welcomed with a sense of gratification and pride by the young woman concerned and her relatives. It marks a girl's attainment of the potential to create new life and symbolizes fertility, a state that is highly cherished. The same is true of a boy reaching puberty.

These status are emphasized in the series of rites of passage that individuals have to undergo during their lives. During these rituals and ceremonies, initiates are subjected to various kinds of special prescriptions and proscriptions regarding food, clothing and behaviour generally (Leach, 1976). Along with the foregoing, they are provided with medicines for curative and protective purposes for both the parents-to-be and their anticipated offspring. The rites also serve to explain to the initiates in advance the unknown mysteries of the various stages of their bio-social metamorphosis. To the older participants (which include the elders who give instruction, the female relatives of the initiates and all other females present), they are a reminder of their responsibilities and obligations in society.

The Puberty Rite

The puberty rite, known in the area as *mateengusi*, provides the opportunity for older women to instruct a girl (and in some cases her boy partner) about her newly attained status. In the traditional setting when a girl attained puberty stage, the holding of *mateengusi* rite was obligatory. The girl's grandmother, mother and aunt would invite a couple of trainers, i.e. old women who give instruction, from the community or nearby villages and other females who have already gone through the rite. The rite started at sunrise and took about five or six hours. It was characterized by singing, hand-clapping, dancing and limited feasting. During these activities, it was explained to the initiates what menstruation was all about and what the expected behaviour of the couple was when and after it occurred.

The concept of being grown up had two implications, biological and social. A young woman who has attained puberty was expected to marry immediately any agreeable man who approached her, irrespective of stature or age; it was not uncommon for older men to marry younger women. However, there was a perception that older men, or big men in stature, scared young women. This rite instilled a sense of confidence in young women by emphasizing the fact that puberty, or the experience of menstruation, manifested female physical maturation that empowered them to have sex and procreate with any man. Socially, menstruation elevated young girls to the status of young women. They were not expected to associate intimately with young girls who had not reached puberty lest they divulge the secrets of puberty.

There were cases when young people married immediately they came out of their first initiation rites, which included circumcision for boys and labia minora or clitoris elongation for girls. When this was the case, the puberty rite was performed for the couple one day after consummation of the marriage. Consummation was considered successful when the girl's virginity was taken away and the boy effected an ejaculation. However, it seems that in traditional times, blood observed during defloration was taken to be synonymous with menstruation. And, because menstruation signalled fertility and the potential for procreation, its attainment had a higher social value than virginity itself. Menstruation and defloration are referred to by terms from the same word-root in many languages of the region. The term for menstruation seems to imply that the process comes naturally of its own accord, while the term for defloration suggests it is forced or caused by the male. The terms, in Kimakua, are *utenguwa* and *utenguwiha* respectively.

As a result, a young man who deflowered a girl, even outside marriage, was quietly respected by the girl's relatives, especially the women, and he bestowed a sense of pride to his own folk. In some cases he was expected and invited to sit with the girl during the rite to receive instruction and gifts with her. Under normal conditions sex outside marriage would be considered deviant and a punishable crime, but in these circumstances it is approved.

My interpretation of this behaviour is that the girl and boy enjoyed some prestige because they were, through the attainment of puberty, bestowed with biosocial power and the potential to produce children. They were now one rung higher on the ladder of status achievement; they were not just initiated boys and girls, but were among those who had attained puberty. Socially, this higher status is recognized by the community in the initiation rite, *mateengusi*.

For the girl the major biological experiences, are menstruation and being deflowered, and for the boy, ejaculation and deflowering the girl. These experiences are emphasized by punctuated outbursts during the rite made by parents and relatives to the effect that the initiands are now adults. The reference to adulthood is a two-pronged message, telling not only the young people but also their parents and relatives that they are now adults. Since the identity and status of the children has changed, those of their parents and relatives will also change.

At this point, I agree with Standing (1980), that in respect of the changes associated with rites of passage, Western culture places more emphasis on the biological events, in this case puberty and particularly menstruation, than on the social aspects. As earlier indicated, in the societies under study, attaining puberty marked one of the most important rites in an individual's biosocial development. The holding of the ritual and its accompanying ceremony should be seen as a public announcement of this development. It also provided an occasion for the elders to spell out the sorts of behaviour which henceforth would distinguish the initiates from young boys and girls who had not reached the stage of puberty. The girl was thereafter placed in the category of females who have the ability to become pregnant, the boy in the category of males who have the ability to impregnate women.

The Meaning of Pregnancy

Before I describe the reasons for loss of pregnancy as perceived and explained by the peoples under study, it will be desirable to explain the circumstances in which pregnancy should take place. Under normal conditions pregnancy should only occur in a situation of good health. By good health is meant that there must be a state of balance in the moral order where the physical state of the mother-to-be, the universe within which she is a member (i.e., the natural environment), the gods, the ancestors and other supernatural powers are all working harmoniously and in coordination.

All adult individuals in the area understand how pregnancy occurs. During both female and male initiation rites, elders explain to initiates that pregnancy occurs when a male and female who have attained puberty copulate and the former effects an ejaculation inside the latter's reproductive organ. However, not every individual can explain with accuracy the biological parameters within which pregnancy takes place inside the female body.

Elderly women, particularly midwives and experts in female initiation rites, possess knowledge that can be considered biological. They know that every female possesses a womb, which is an extension of her genital organ. This womb, variously referred to as *irukulu* or *nthunkwa* in Kimakua and *chituumbo* in Kimakonde, Kimwera and Kiyao, is conceived of as a bag. The male's seed is contained or 'planted' in this bag to develop into a fetus or baby. These female experts (nor even their male counterparts) do not differentiate between semen and sperm, the term *ikanja* in Kimakua, and *ubiila* in the other three languages, being used for both. It is known that the testicles are associated with the manufacture of sperm and semen, because it is explained that castrated males fail to impregnate women because they cannot produce semen and sperm. There seems to be no knowledge about the presence of ovaries in the female.

Detecting and Explaining Pregnancy

There are many signs for knowing when a woman has conceived, especially in the case of her first pregnancy. In marriage the first of these signs may be recognized by the couple. During the puberty rite, the young woman would have been instructed that the menstruation she had just experienced would be a monthly occurrence. She would also be told to abstain from sexual relations during the whole period she is in that state. During menstruation she would be unclean and must observe certain taboos. She should not, for instance, add salt to her cooking; instead she would have to ask someone else to do it for her. She should not share the same bed with her husband, but if she has to she should not sleep face to face with him.

Sleeping face to face with one's sexual partner is a proxemic expression of the readiness to participate in coitus. This rule goes for the male too and is part of the instructions given to him during initiation. In principle, therefore, one can abstain from sex and assume this sleeping posture only when sick, although merely sleeping face to face does not indicate that coitus must take place.

By implication, therefore, when a husband observes that his wife has shown a desire to have sex continuously for more than one month, he begins to suspect something. Through a process of elimination, for example, that she has not complained of being sick or they have not quarrelled, the only possible explanation is that she has conceived.

Instructions at puberty also warn a young woman that immediately she notices that she has missed her monthly period, she should inform her mother or grandmother or some other elderly woman confidant about it. Whoever obtains this information first passes it on to others on both sides, the wife's and the husband's. Some elderly women experts, that is midwives and female ritual specialists, set in motion a secret process of examining the young woman closely for other more telling signs. These signs are changes in the young woman's morphology. Her breasts, for example, begin to grow large and firm and become more pronounced. In the traditional setting this was easy to notice since breasts were not covered. It is also known that a pregnant woman's heart beats faster than normal at this time, which can be observed at her throat and chest. Another sign is that her face and hands become brighter in complexion and her skin generally turns tender. In some cases, after two or three months her belly begins to protrude and her buttocks become more pronounced.

Some women develop, at this stage, certain characteristics such as liking or disliking certain types of food and drink and even certain people. There are many reported cases where women in this state develop an insatiable desire for eating termite mound clay or some other form of soil, and sour foods such as raw mangoes, tamarind fruit, lemons and limes. Other women desire sweet foods, for example, sugar, ripe fruits and honey. Others develop a strong hatred for certain individuals, including their husbands, and they may pick quarrels with them for no apparent reason. They may also vomit frequently and experience fatigue and weariness most of the time.

Loss of menstruation, and therefore the possibility of conception, may be detected in the second or third month by the woman and her husband. However, in cases of first pregnancies and marriages, the elders must confirm this fact by looking for the physical signs described above. It is often only after these observations that the couple, or the pregnant woman and the general public, are officially told that she is pregnant. In the past, this exercise was done through a rite called *uvahiya ikahi* among the Wamakua and *kwaapa lukaata* among the Wamwera and Wayao.

Announcing Pregnancy: *Uvahiya Ikahi*

From the time elderly women experts establish that a woman has conceived, especially in the case of a first pregnancy, they prepare the rite for her and her partner to be performed during the third or fourth month of pregnancy.

Ikahi or *lukaata* is a vessel out of which people drink water and other beverages, made by cutting a gourd into two halves from its top to its base. Its contents are scooped out and its inside cleaned. There is, or rather was in the past, a common vessel in each household. For the rite a new vessel is made specifically for the exclusive use of the young pregnant woman, since she is not allowed to share a drinking vessel with any other person during the time she remains pregnant, not even her own husband or relatives. It is feared that sharing a drinking vessel with other individuals may directly or indirectly endanger her pregnancy. It is said that jealous or wicked people can 'spit' their evil wishes into the vessel as they drink out of it which would be transmitted to the pregnant woman if she drank from it afterwards. Moreover, if an unclean individual used a drinking vessel which was then used by a pregnant woman, the pregnancy would receive a shock which could result in a miscarriage or stillbirth if not treated, particularly first pregnancies. To guard against these dangers the young pregnant woman has to carry this vessel about with her all the time she is pregnant and ensure that it does not get into wrong hands. The fact that she carries the *ikahi (lukaata)* around also alerts any person of good will who knows that he or she is unclean to avoid meeting her face to face, for it is the eyes meeting that transmits the shock waves to the pregnancy if the other party is unclean.

Another important aspect of the rite is that the young woman and her husband who are at the centre of the rite are officially told about the pregnancy for the first time. It is explained to them that this is the reason she has been missing her monthly periods. The rite also provides the opportunity to inform the couple of the taboos they should observe during pregnancy. For example, they are instructed not to abstain from coitus. It is believed that continued sexual activity is good for both the fetus and the mother, ensuring the healthy development of the fetus, because it is believed that the fetus feeds on sperm in the early stages of pregnancy. Continued sexual activity also ensures safe delivery, which can only be achieved through the preparation or enlargement of the baby's passage. The young woman must enlarge her vagina or baby passage to equal that of the mouth of the vessel given to her. She is told that to achieve this she must do two things, continue having coitus, and consistently massage her passage to widen it.

Continued coitus in itself is seen as an activity that discourages contraction of the passage. Through coitus the passage muscles become loosened, and the semen and sperm act as a lubricant which the woman uses after coitus to work on or massage her baby passage with her own hands and fingers. It was suggested by some informants that this is one of the reasons why she was given her own drinking vessel. It is thought to be improper or 'unhygienic' for her to share the usual household drinking vessel with other people when she is constantly handling her own genitals, and semen and sperm; this renders her unclean.

She was also forbidden to talk to strangers; if she could not avoid meeting strangers then she had to 'spit them'. The action of 'spitting' expelled any alien spirit that might have entered her and would protect the fetus from shock. Other protective measures included concoctions of the pounded leaves and barks of certain trees, which were mixed with her bath water until she gave birth. During the evening of the day of the puberty rite, a midwife or elderly woman in the family made a twisted waist band of fibre from the bark of a tree believed to have protective powers. The husband then tied it round his wife's waist while both of them stood naked in the doorway. This medicated waist band was, and in some cases still is, believed to protect the first stages of pregnancy and nurture it through to a safe delivery.

Other protective medicines were administered to her relatives, particularly young male in-laws and siblings who might indulge in sexual activities outside marriage. Some herbs were prepared, usually by elderly women or men, and mixed with water. The water would first be used by the relevant young male to wash his private parts and hands before being mixed with the medicine. Then the mixture would be given to the pregnant young woman, who would pour it on to the front part of her body from her breasts down to the abdomen. From then on, she would not be affected by the activities of such people, even if they came face to face to her after committing adultery.

In view of the foregoing a husband whose wife is pregnant was, in the past, not allowed or expected to have extra-marital sexual relations. However, if he had other wives or concubines, he could continue having sex with them after going through the self-cleansing process described above.

Child-birth Procedures

During the seventh or eighth month of pregnancy, a second rite was, and still is, performed, called *ntaara* among the Wamakua and *litiwo* among the Wayao and Wamwera (Hokororo, 1960; Wembah-Rashid, 1975). It is a day-long rite beginning at sunrise and ending at sunset. Except for the husband, all the participants are women who have given birth before and therefore have themselves been initiated into this rite. At the centre of the rite are the pregnant woman and her husband.

The main purpose of this rite is to tell the young couple officially how the baby is going to come. The emphasis is on the physical and mental strains that the woman has gone through and will go through. It tells of the strains of initial sexual experiences, the dangers of pregnancy and delivery, the pleasures of coitus and of bringing forth a new life. It is thus a psychological reminder of the past and a preparation of things to come. It also marks the time when the couple should cease coitus until further instructed. These messages are transmitted by means of practical demonstrations, songs and dramatizations.

Reasons for Pregnancy Loss

According to traditions that prevailed in the area in the past, and still believed by some people today, there are four main reasons for pregnancy loss: meeting with an unclean person; a dispute involving the victim; the displeasure of ancestor spirits; and illness or general physical weakness of the mother-to-be.

Meeting with an Unclean Person

When a pregnant woman, especially in the case of a first pregnancy, meets an unclean person face to face, it is believed that the fetus receives a shock, irrespective of whether the pregnant woman is aware or not of the state of uncleanliness of the person she meets. The shock destabilizes it and, if not treated, causes its death through miscarriage or stillbirth. A person is considered to be unclean if he or she has indulged in coitus with a partner other than his or her spouse. This shock is known as *itundumara* in Kimakua and *nduundumala* in Kiyao and Kimwera.

Dispute Involving the Victim

Loss of pregnancy can also occur if there is, or was, a dispute between the pregnant woman or her husband or any of their relatives on the one hand, with an individual or group of people on the other. A dispute may have existed before the pregnancy or develop during it. The party that thinks it has been wronged may decide to curse the other, in this case the pregnant woman or her husband or relatives, by calling upon whatever powers she or he appeals to, in order to cause the loss of a pregnancy, whether existing or anticipated. The curse may be directed to a specific individual or to any females of the enemy camp capable of conceiving (including domestic animals, though the focus in this discussion is on humans). The effects of the curse will be realized when there is a pregnancy loss from among the party that was cursed. Curses meted out in this manner are considered to be witchcraft and are rarely made publicly. However, they can be detected through divination.

In traditional, pre-Christian times, there was a strong belief that death (including stillbirths and miscarriages) was often caused by human machinations. Abdallah (1973, p. 20), himself a Yao writing of his own people after conversion to Christianity, observes:

> Because we Yaos think like this – if a man falls sick or dies, we say that somebody has bewitched him; it is not mere chance. Of course we know that God has taken him, but God merely receives him, somebody has caused his death by witchcraft. That is what we believe.

Strained relations between family members, relatives or neighbours on the one hand and the pregnant woman or her spouse on the other may cause frustrations which often lead to the destabilization of a pregnancy. For instance, accusations of witchcraft, theft, adultery and other social misconduct are commonly cited.

The Displeasure of Ancestor Spirits

This explanation for pregnancy loss is in principle similar to the foregoing one. The displeasure of ancestor spirits can be seen as a dispute or conflict between spirits who are the living dead of a community and their living descendants. This conflict can be caused by misdeeds of the victim, her husband, family or lineage members which affect one of the spirits or the community of both the living and the living dead generally. The ancestor spirits choose one form of punishment, for example, to withhold an individual's fertility or cause pregnancy loss for a specific pregnant woman. Such a punishment is meted out to the woman because of her own misdeeds or to pay for the wrongdoing of those related to her.

Sometimes the spirits may sound a warning by destabilizing the pregnancy. Under such circumstances the woman will begin feeling unwell. If diviners are consulted in time and appropriate diagnosis obtained, remedial measures can be taken to save the pregnancy. Common remedial measures include appeasing the spirits through sacrifice and prayer.

Loss of Pregnancy Through Illness

Generally, when pregnancy is lost through illness or poor health (that is because of the physical weakness of the mother-to-be), it is considered a natural loss. It is understood that a sick woman cannot endure the hardships that go with carrying a pregnancy for nine months. So when a woman known to have been sick loses her pregnancy, members of the community are not surprised, nor do they consider that any party is to blame for it; rather, they pity the woman.

However, the nature and duration of the sickness or the reasons for the woman's poor health or general physical weakness may be questioned. Some of these conditions may be known to have resulted from the woman's carelessness, for example, from not eating well, from not observing simple rules of hygiene, or from disease inherited from members of her family. In such cases, the pregnancy loss is seen as natural and not in any way due to foul play. However, if her poor health is the result of starvation or improper feeding through lack of food, her husband will incur blame.

The first three explanations for pregnancy loss are based on the belief of the effect of external forces upon the pregnant woman. The fourth explanation sees the forces originating from the woman herself or from nature. In other words, both naturalistic and personalistic reasons are advanced to account for pregnancy loss (Foster and Anderson, 1978). Overall, the explanations illustrate these societies' beliefs in the meaning of pregnancy loss, namely that it is categorized as a disease. The explanations are indicative of beliefs in the influence that individuals, from both the living dead and the still living communities, have over pregnancies and babies.

There is a strong belief that producing babies is a very delicate and important undertaking, needing the cooperation of all community members and the prevalence of a state of equilibrium or a peaceful environment within which the pregnancy can develop into a human being. These two elements are paramount for the successful creation, development and healthy birth of babies. In other words, for women to conceive and nurture their pregnancies up to giving birth, the family, lineage and clan members, both those still living and the living dead, and neighbours must in a way 'consent' or 'give their blessings' to the process.

Despite these beliefs, recurrent pregnancy loss was often blamed on the male partner. It was believed that unfaithfulness by the husband was responsible for his wife's and the fetus's shock and destabilization. An unfaithful married woman who conceived through a lover would also cause her own miscarriages and stillbirths if she refused to disclose her lover(s) to the midwife or elderly women relatives before or during labour to allow a cleansing process to be performed.

In certain circumstances, it was believed that both husband and wife could indirectly cause a miscarriage or stillbirth. It has been explained earlier in this chapter that during the initial months of pregnancy, couples were encouraged to engage in sex. However, during the seventh or eighth month of pregnancy coitus was disallowed. It was believed that the baby's head was close to the passage and therefore deep penetration by the father could damage it. If it were necessary for coitus to continue (allowed only with women who had given birth before), the couple were prohibited from using the missionary position. Instead the father approached from behind while the couple lay on their sides. In this context, therefore, it would appear that use of inappropriate positions during coitus in the advanced stage of pregnancy could cause miscarriage or stillbirth.

Disposal of the Products of Miscarriage or Stillbirth

Whenever a miscarriage occurred, the fetus and contents of the uterus were disposed of by midwives or elderly women who had achieved menopause. The form of disposal is explained as 'throwing away' and was done at the jar where all the refuse from the house and compound is thrown. The midwives or elderly women dug a pit, put the remains in it wrapped in some rags, and covered it. This was done for all miscarriages and stillbirths and was undertaken only by women. The husband and close relatives were informed later of what happened.

In all the languages of the area under discussion the words used to break the sad news about a miscarriage can be translated as either 'the pregnancy fell down' or 'it ended up in the labour room'. When a stillbirth occurs or an incomplete baby is terminated by midwives, the situation is described as 'the baby returned to where it came from' or 'it was unable to go out of the labour room'.

Miscarriages and stillbirths which occur in urban clinics and maternity hospitals are handled differently. During the colonial period and immediately after independence, the remains were dumped in the usual dustbins used for refuse and collected by municipal garbage collectors. However, because garbage disposal was not properly carried out by some municipalities, some remains were seen being eaten by stray dogs. Government regulations now state that any remains of miscarriages or stillbirths must be handed back to their owners to dispose of them. When this happens, the fetus and other remains are either disposed of in the traditional way or treated as full humans and buried accordingly, though no funeral rites or mourning take place. Nevertheless, the affected couple appear bereaved for some days.

Protective Measures After Pregnancy Loss or Normal Birth

Following a miscarriage, stillbirth or normal birth, a woman was subjected to rigorous massaging and hot-water baths and provided with plenty of food, all of which were believed to be important in the restoration of her health. She was also treated with medicines. Some were for oral use, to help her in cleaning her womb, while others were to be used when bathing in order to protect her from developing a disease known as *itaya* or *uloongo* among the Wamakua and Wayao respectively. This disease is described as causing the body to swell. In some cases the victim was given protective medicines in the form of talismans or waist bands. This was done when it was suspected that previous miscarriages or stillbirths were caused by human or spirit machinations. These medicines were concoctions of organic and non-organic materials prepared and administered either by midwives or by specialist medical practitioners, who could be male or female.

After Miscarriage, Stillbirth or Ordinary Birth

Following a miscarriage, stillbirth or ordinary birth, the couple resumed sexual activity after observing certain measures and going through a special rite. As already indicated, the woman was first given curative and protective medicines to clean her womb and give her back her health and energy. Usually, after one month or forty days, if she had ceased bleeding, she would be ready to start sleeping with her husband again.

In the case of a first pregnancy, a midwife or elderly woman prepared a medicine in a small clay cooking-pot during the evening of the night the couple intended to resume sleeping together, and placed it in their bedroom. They both washed their genitals with the medicine, thereafter resuming normal sexual intercourse throughout that night as they desired. Very early the following morning, between three and five, they took the pot and its contents together with a ladle to crosspaths in the neighbourhood, where the pot was turned upside down, thus spilling its contents on the ground. Using the ladle, they made a hole in the centre of the bottom of the pot. Both pot and ladle were left at the spot, and the couple walked back to their house without turning or looking back. Usually passers-by would tread on the remains of the pot and medicine without paying any particular attention to them, and in that way they disappeared.

Fetus, Baby and Human Being: What are They?

Discussions were initiated with expert midwife informants who were also indigenous medical practitioners and with respected knowledgeable elders to establish definitions for the three terms above. Many informants considered that when conception takes place, a ball of jelly-like blood is first formed, known as *ikukuruso* in Kimakua. When it develops into a form in which organs are recognizable it becomes *nrolo* in *kimakua*. The *nrolo* then becomes a more human-like individual or *mwaana*, which, in all languages, means 'baby'.

However, this recognition cannot be confirmed until the baby is born, given the possibility of a stillbirth or the birth of an unformed baby. In other words, some informants advanced the notion that a baby may or may not develop into a full human being. When a baby is born, before it is pronounced human, midwives must examine it thoroughly to establish whether it has the minimum characteristics acceptable for defining a human being in these societies. If it was born with defects which would not allow it to function normally as an individual, performing the duties and carrying out responsibilities expected of it when it becomes an adult, it was declared non-human and was eliminated. For instance, babies born without an opening for the anus or without genitals or without fingers or toes were killed instantly and buried by midwives without the knowledge even of their mothers, who, with their husbands, were told that the babies had returned to where they came from, that is they were never able to go out of the labour room. However, these practices are now discontinued, following the conversion of more and more people to Christianity after the 1920s and the growth of the allopathic health service after World War II.

However, some babies were born with minor defects which could be rectified by the midwives. Such babies were allowed to live because this rectification rendered them normal and therefore acceptable as humans. Common defects which could be rectified by the midwives included an extended membrane attaching the tongue to the lower mouth, having extra toes or fingers, or having some outgrowths on any part of the body. These abnormalities were attended to by midwives who performed surgery either immediately the baby was born or some time later.

It is clear from the foregoing discussion that there exists an ambiguity in what is considered biologically or socially human. Among the pastoralist Barabaig of central Tanzania, for instance, handicapped children have no right, or rather cannot be allowed, to live. As recently as 1992, while I was conducting research in Manyoni, in the Singida region, a case arose in which the parents refused to take back their two-year-old child after it had had its foot amputated during treatment at the Catholic Mission hospital in Manyoni town. The parents stated categorically that they would kill the child if they were forced to take it back because their society has no place for amputees. The hospital management and local government officials intervened by having the child placed in an orphanage.

The Effect of Miscarriages on Spouses

Miscarriages and stillbirths caused health concerns to the woman, and social and psychological anxiety to spouses and relatives, especially if such losses occurred repeatedly. However, even recurrent pregnancy loss was not an automatic cause for divorce: several other factors had to come into play first. Among the peoples under discussion it was unknown for women or their husbands to deliberately cause miscarriages or stillbirths. Such an act would be described as witchcraft and murder, and could lead to a demand for divorce by the spouse who believed that the other was in the wrong.

Most of the beliefs and practices described prevail among believers in indigenous religion, Muslims and Christians. Along with Sunni Muslims there are two major Christian denominations in this area, Roman Catholicism and (Higher) Anglicanism. Whatever their religious affiliations, however, most people in the area practise dual religionism: traditionalism and Christianity or Islam. It seems that it is the general belief of Christians and Muslims alike in this region that before the fetus manifests human features, it is non-human. Where miscarriages occur, no special Christian or Muslim religious rituals are called for. However, a stillborn child may be placed in the category of angels and buried with special prayers. I have personally observed in my own village church, and other informants have confirmed, that such children are buried in the church cemetery and that no requiem mass is said after burial because they are believed to be free from sin.

Pregnancies are considered to be one of the blessings that human beings receive from God and from their ancestors. Pregnancy is not considered a disease because only healthy and clean women can conceive and carry the fetus through to the birth of a new human being. They are blessings because babies extend the line of their parents. However, pregnancies are dangerous and delicate, demanding a peaceful atmosphere and a clean environment in order for them to develop properly. Southeast Tanzanians believe that pregnant women should therefore be given all possible assistance and the attention they need in order that they may carry the fetus to term. It is considered wrong for anybody to pick a quarrel with a pregnant woman, because anxiety, a disturbed mind or frustration may destabilize the fetus and cause a miscarriage or stillbirth. Stillbirths can be detected before the time of labour because the fetus ceases its movements. The mother or midwives and elderly women who visit her constantly and talk to her are the people who make the first detection. Midwives know appropriate medicines to induce labour even in cases of stillbirth. For this reason, and because pregnancy is not considered to be a disease, pregnant women are encouraged to go about their household and outside chores as usual up to the eighth or ninth month. Outside chores are, of course, limited to the area in which the women can go; this is particularly so in the cases of first pregnancy. This is to avoid the risk of young and inexperienced women going into labour away from midwives or any form of assistance.

Conclusion

Miscarriages and stillbirths are considered types of disease among the matrilineal peoples of southeast Tanzania. Their causes may be personalistic or naturalistic. In the former case, ways of averting them include the use of protective medicines or charms and the establishment of cordial relations between both the living and the dead individuals within families, lineages, clans and neighbours. Protective measures for naturalistic induced disease are assumed to be embedded in the good conduct of the whole community, that is as long as individuals and family, lineage and clan members conduct themselves in a manner that is pleasing to God, nothing wrong will happen.

Naturalistic reasons operate at two levels: first, they are considered to be the will of God, and secondly, they are accounted for through the indirect harmful activities of the woman herself, or together with her spouse, or of the community within which she lives. The will of God is considered to be at work when the results of divination identify neither a person nor spirits as responsible for what happened, nor is it established that there was neglect on the part of the woman and her husband or relatives. Alternatively, the general ill health of the mother may be due to natural causes, for example, inherited disease, or ignorance and neglect, such as not eating the right kind of food. The woman or her spouse may also cause a miscarriage or stillbirth through careless and/or excessive sexual activity.

Following miscarriages and stillbirths, curative measures are needed.

Where the reasons are pronounced as personalistic and arising directly from living humans, a reinforcement of previously used medicines and charms may be administered. If the cause was established as that of spirit displeasure, their appeasement through sacrifice and prayers will be essential. In addition to the foregoing, general curative medicines are administered to restore the woman's health. Pregnancy loss through naturalistic reasons is treated through prayers and sacrifice to God, curative medicines, and a general call to the community for good conduct.

Miscarriages and stillbirths are causes for bereavement to the couple concerned, their family and lineage members. Although there is no elaborate mourning, the couple receive great assistance, consolation and counselling from their relatives, friends and peers. They are encouraged to forget the loss and look ahead with courage and enthusiasm because they possess the potential for having babies. This last point is particularly true for young couples. Elders cite examples of couples in the community who lost several 'children' and are now enjoying large families.

References

Abdallah, Y., *The Yaos: Chiikala cha Wayoa*, London, Frank Cass, 1973.

Foster, G. and Anderson, B.G., *Medical Anthropology*, Chichester, Wiley and Sons, 1978

Gough, K., 'Descent-group Variation Among Mobile Cultivators', in D.M. Schneider and K. Gough (eds), *Matrilineal Kinship*, Berkeley, University of California Press, 1961

Hokororo, N., 'The Influence of Church on Traditional Customs at Lukuledi', *Tanzania Notes and Records*, vol. 54, 1960, pp. 1–13

Leach, E., *Culture and Communication*, Cambridge, Cambridge University Press, 1976

Murdock, G.P., *Africa: Its Peoples and Their Culture History*, New York, McGraw Hill, 1959

Standing, H., 'Beliefs About Menstruation and Pregnancy', *Mims*, vol. 15, 1980, pp. 21–7

Tew, M., *The Peoples of the Lake Nyasa Region*, London, International African Institute, 1950

Wembah-Rashid, J.A.R., *The Ethno-History of the Matrilineal Peoples of Southeast Tanzania*, Vienna, E. Stiglmyr, 1975

——, 'Socio-political Development and Economic Viability in a Rural Community: The Case of Nakarara Village, Mtwara Region, Tanzania', unpublished Ph.D. Dissertation, Department of Anthropology, University of Illinois at Urbana-Champaign, 1983

–5–

'Children of the Rope' and Other Aspects of Pregnancy Loss in Cameroon

Olayinka M. Njikam Savage

Introduction

Life-death, The Two-headed Janus

In Cameroon and indeed in much of Africa, traditional religious beliefs and cosmic views are closely intertwined with health beliefs. Thus, health and ill-health are as likely to be caused by deities, ancestral spirits, malevolent spirits, witches, sorcerers, curses and the breaking of oaths as are good fortune and misfortune. Deities and ancestors may cause illness, usually in order to demonstrate displeasure or chastise descendants for inappropriate behaviour. Witches, on the other hand, operate out of malice and are out to do harm. As such, death is perceived not as an ultimate end in itself but as a sign of departure into new beginnings. The dead, over time, become exalted to ancestral spirits. They thus continue to live, communicate, mediate and intervene in relationships with the living (Fortes, 1949; Mbiti, 1989). Among the Yoruba, the dead are commemorated individually as ancestral spirits through the *egungun* rites performed by masquerades of the male *egungun* cult (Morton-Williams, 1960).

Death is a natural and expected phenomenon, especially in the case of the very old. If the dead person has also been wealthy and has had several children and grandchildren, then he is perceived as having had a successful and well spent life. In these circumstances, death marks the end of a fulfilled existence. The passage is marked with little mourning but with feasting. On the other hand, the death of the young is an unnatural and horrifying event, especially as children are supposed to bury their elders and not *vice versa*. Mothers are often forbidden by custom from attending the burial rites for their children, which are performed quietly and quickly.

Descendants are therefore essential not only for the continuation and survival of the lineage but also to ensure appropriate and befitting burial ceremonies for the dead and subsequent funeral rites. Also, ancestors must be remembered and venerated through regular offerings of oil, salt, food, etc. Fertility is thus an essential factor in the process of ensuring a continuous link between the living and the dead through deities and ancestors. The safeguarding of fertility is therefore an important feature of traditional religion. Consequently, diseases or illnesses that threaten the reproductive system or specific organs not only receive considerable attention but are classed in a special category. Witches or malevolent spirits are usually held responsible for reproductive morbidity.

Ancestors demonstrate their happiness or pleasure with the living by ensuring fertility through births and rebirths. The dead are often reborn. Such births are identified through the predestined names given to such babies. In Zambia as in Cameroon, divination is used to identify reincarnated ancestors to ensure that an appropriate name is given (Stefaniszyn, 1954). Reproductive morbidity or the inability of a woman to bring forth an offspring, whether through failure to conceive, miscarriage, stillbirth or infant or child mortality, is therefore an indication of disharmony with the living and/or between the living and the dead. Within the context of traditional society, health is therefore perceived as a harmonious state where the social, religious or supernatural realm clearly impinges on physical and psychosocial well-being. Pregnancy, par excellence, is one of these states.

Methodology

Group discussions were conducted among groups of women representing the Bamileke (West Province), Beti (Centre Province) and Bakweri (South-West Province) between December 1991 and July 1993. Unlike the traditional focus discussion group which usually comprises about ten women, there were about twenty women in each discussion group. In all, eleven group discussions were undertaken, three from West and South-West Province and five from Centre Province. In addition, five case histories were recorded among each provincial group from women who had experienced between two and five episodes of pregnancy loss. The data presented here are drawn from these group discussions and case histories. The five groups from Centre Province were compressed into three because of the similarities of their results. The women were aged between twenty-five and forty-five. None of them worked in the formal sector, although they all had food farms from which they fed their families. They were all Christians from different denominations. About 10 per cent did not have children and 30 per cent had experienced reproductive morbidity; parity ranged between two and seven births.

Participants were selected from women who had turned up for the discussion on the appointed day. In most of the villages, a lot more women than expected turned up, with the result that it was difficult to restrict the size of the groups to fifteen or less as had been intended. The venues of the group discussions were meeting halls, houses of the female opinion leader, the village green and the health centre. In this study, pregnancy loss, or fetal death, was broadly defined as spontaneous miscarriage and stillbirth, with the exclusion of induced abortion. No attempts were made to distinguish early from late fetal deaths.

A focus-group guide was developed and administered to all groups. Warm-up questions focused on menarche and fertility. The guide contained the following issues: perceptions of pregnancy and appropriate behaviour, vulnerable periods and pregnancy loss. Successful pregnancies were discussed within the context of self-care and conjugal, kin, social and community responsibilities as well as use of health-care facilities (modern and/or traditional).

The discussions, which were all taped, started out in French but often lapsed into pidgin and local dialects. The main points of each discussion were summarized at the end of the session. The tapes were subsequently translated into French and English and then transcribed. The results were analysed using content analysis and the cut-and-paste method.

Socio-cultural Perspectives of Fertility

Traditionally, the sole role of the female child was, and still is, that of wife, the potential bearer and rearer of children. This is amply demonstrated by a custom of the Grassfield Belt of Cameroon (this phrase is roughly used to refer to West and North-West Provinces): just before the delivery of a woman, a potential suitor makes a presentation of a bundle of firewood to the expectant mother, thus declaring his intention to be a prospective son-in-law should a female child be born. Thus even before birth the status and cultural expectations of the female child are clearly outlined. There are numerous sociocultural practices which reiterate and reinforce this image at various stages of a female child's developmental cycle. For example, female children are discriminated against as regards education, especially beyond primary school level (Demo, 1987).

Menarche is therefore perceived as a significant phase in a girl's physical and social development. It is an indication of her potential reproductive ability and status as a wife and subsequently mother. Among the Beti of Centre Province, it is also the marker for the commencement of sexual relations. Sexual relations before menarche are perceived not only as polluting the girl but also as the cause of infertility in later years. The commencement of sexual relations and subsequent acquisitions of boy friends and suitors is perceived by young girls as enhancing their social status. Overnight, as it were, they undergo a social transfiguration and are suddenly sought after as potential girl friends, wives and mothers. Young girls therefore not only await menarche eagerly but attempt to provoke it by douching with petro-chemical substances.[1] With menarche one can 'safely' indulge in sexual activity without the fear of social and supernatural sanctions, especially infertility (Njikam Savage and Tchombe, 1995). Consequently, menstrual patterns are keenly observed and deviations quickly noted, as they may be indications of illness and especially reproductive morbidity.

Ancestral Approval of Marriage and Pregnancy

Marriage is a union between families during which the approval of kinsmen, God, deities and ancestors is sought to ensure a successful union which will culminate in the bearing of children. Ancestral spirits are invoked to approve, witness and take part in the ceremony as well as to protect the new couple from misfortune. Pregnancy is thus the fulfilment of a social and moral obligation first to one's family and secondly to the community. It is the ultimate rite of passage in the transition from girlhood to womanhood. Childbirth is considered to cement a marriage. In many societies in Cameroon, this transition is marked by a corresponding change in nomenclature. Suddenly, it becomes impolite for the new mother to be called by her name, as had been done before. A prefix is now attached to her name in cognizance of her new status. In the Grassfield Belt especially, women who have had multiple births, particularly twins, are held in even higher esteem. Twin mothers are called *manyi* and their fathers, *tanyi*. Special positions of honour are reserved for them during public ceremonies and they are given privileges which shield them from undergoing unsavoury funeral rites. Twins are regarded as special beings who have supernatural powers and are predisposed to being capricious and/or benevolent. Parents and family members are therefore careful not to incur their displeasure. Twins of different sexes are believed to be the most capricious.

Perceptions of Risk in Pregnancy

Among the Bamileke of West province, successful childbirth is the ultimate proof of the consummation of a marriage and of ancestral approval of a physical relationship contracted here on earth. Pregnancy represents a period of conversation, throughout which the fetus is in constant communication with the ancestral spirits. Childbirth is the logical culmination of a fruitful period of conversation. The resulting offspring is therefore perceived not just as proof of the existence of the ancestors and of their desire to perpetuate the family line, but as a supernatural gift, the physical embodiment of an ancestor pleased to be reborn into the family. Delayed conception after marriage, miscarriages, stillbirths and infertility are all indications of female ancestral displeasure particularly.

Nonetheless, in all ethnic groups, pregnancy and childbirth are perceived as particularly vulnerable times, during which the expectant mother is perceived as walking the fine line between the living and the dead. It is therefore necessary to shield both mother and fetus from malevolent forces, both those who aimlessly roam about in search of vulnerable prey and those out for particular targets.

Among the Beti, so important is the demonstration of fertility that by tradition a woman is expected to have a child out of wedlock whom she leaves in her natal family on marriage. This enhances her chances of marriage and also ensures the continuity of the household. Nonetheless, pregnancy is still fraught with risks. Particularly vulnerable are the first three months, when the risk of pregnancy loss is high.

Perceptions of Pregnancy Loss

Natural Causes

Pregnancy loss may be caused by natural and/or supernatural factors. An excessive physical work load during pregnancy, like carrying heavy farm produce over long distances under the hot burning sun, and physical abuse from one's spouse may cause miscarriage. On the other hand, lethargy and undue laziness result in a prolonged and difficult delivery. It is therefore important for the expectant mother to achieve a delicate balance between work and rest.

Female sexual misconduct during pregnancy has dire consequences for fetal survival. Sexual intercourse with a person other than the father of the expectant child results in the intermingling of semen and blood of various origins, causing incompatibility and subsequent fetal wastage. Dietary restrictions are also important during pregnancy to prevent fetal deformations and pregnancy loss. Food restrictions usually include the avoidance of game and uncommon sea creatures.

Spousal Role in Pregnancy Loss

Capricious males endanger the lives of their wives and babies by hindering delivery. Such men are found to have erections while their spouses are in labour. Consequently, women are advised not to publicize the fact that they are in labour. During pregnancy, regular sexual intercourse is essential for adequate fetal development as well as to facilitate delivery in the last trimester. This belief is also shared in West and North-West provinces of Cameroon and elsewhere in the Central African region (Taylor, 1990), contrary to the practice in much of West Africa (Caldwell, Caldwell, Ankrah, Anarfi, Agyeman, Awusabo-Asare, Orubuloye and Orubuloye, 1993), where sexual intercourse is forbidden during pregnancy. To a lesser extent, male sexual transgression constitutes a contributory factor in that multiple sexual partners increase the risk of sexually transmitted diseases, which may also cause fetal wastage. Women may refuse to have sexual relations with their partners if they suspect they have a sexually transmitted disease, in order to safeguard the lives of their unborn children.

Supernatural Causes

The supernatural causes of pregnancy loss are more complex in origin, difficult to decipher and treat. They involve interventions by ancestors disapproving of social and religious misconduct. Negative emotional feelings such as anger, hatred, envy and jealousy often lead to the malevolent meddling, of kin and neighbours, resulting in sorcery and witchcraft.

The different stages of betrothal that culminate in marriage often require key members of the bride's extended family to be visited by the bridegroom and/or his family. During these visits, presentations are made by the boy's family to key members of the bride's family. These gifts, which include palm oil, salt, textiles, blankets etc. are presented in recognition of the relationship between the receiver and the bride and to introduce the new nucleus, the young couple. This is a potential source of conflict. First, for economic and other logistical reasons it might not be possible to visit all 'important' kinsmen and women. Secondly, some of the bride's kin may be unsatisfied with the quality and/or quantity of the gifts received. The distribution of the dowry poses similar problems. Thus, feelings of resentment may develop and with time be transformed into malevolent thoughts, finally giving way to curses, evil spirits, sorcery and witchcraft. Often the young couple are oblivious of these sentiments until they start experiencing problems, especially the inability of the bride to conceive or to carry a pregnancy successfully to term. Pregnancy loss sets in motion a chain of traditional investigation and prescribed treatment. Sometimes kinsmen demonstrate their displeasure openly or obliquely, thus initiating placatory actions by the couple.

The sickness of 'the water in the stomach' is considered to be particularly dangerous among the Beti, although it is also found among the Douala and Bamileke of Littoral and West Provinces respectively. As a result of this disorder, the fetus is exposed to excessive fluid in the womb which retards its growth and development. This can only be detected and successfully treated by traditional healers. Valuable time is therefore lost in consulting modern health professionals who are ill-equipped to diagnose or treat this ailment. Untimely intervention not only results in miscarriage or stillbirth but also in maternal death. The successful treatment of an episode of this illness does not preclude its subsequent reoccurrence, so that help must be sought in subsequent pregnancies to prevent it.

Children of the Rope

Among the Bakweri, miscarriages are caused by failure to perform *mondo* (see below) and by 'bad blood'. The fetal remains of a miscarriage are buried at the corner of the compound, so that another child might quickly come into the family. Thus, the newly bereaved mother is discouraged from grieving publicly but instead encouraged to get pregnant as quickly as possible to replace her loss. Traditionally, women are perceived as being incapable of digging a grave and only male members of the family are involved in the burial. Burial takes place immediately, and there is very little weeping and mourning.

The Bamileke, like the Bakweri, believe that crying over a miscarriage or stillbirth angers God, as a result of which he might not send another child or might send one after a long intervention. The remains of the first pregnancy loss are buried very quickly because it is believed that it was not a baby that came with the intention of staying or living with the family. It was a stranger who was just passing through. Since it hurried away and was not willing to stay, society is forbidden to demonstrate any attachment to it by mourning or prolonging the period before its burial. Society only mourns its members. Since babies who die due to premature or stillbirths have no names, they are not members of society and cannot be mourned. Pregnancy loss is referred to covertly, thus preventing malevolent forces from noticing when the loss occurred and causing a repeat in subsequent pregnancies. Among the Bamileke, the image of water having poured from the calabash is used to report pregnancy loss.

Traditional healers give special treatment to the special category of children who are born without any intention of living in the world of humans. This often takes the form of making an incision on the cheeks to prevent death and to facilitate easy recognition on rebirth. These are called *wana va mosinga* 'children of the rope', because they are hanging in the air on a piece of rope. They are different from ordinary children, who are born with the intention of residing in a family and growing to maturity. The children of the rope, since they are not ordinary children, possessed supernatural powers and are therefore said to have 'four eyes'.

Risk-Prevention Strategies: The *Mondo* Ritual

In cognizance of the inherent risk in reproductive morbidity, including maternal morbidity and mortality, pregnant mothers are expected to seek the services of herbalists from the first month of pregnancy. Among the Bakweri, at this visit they are given a herbal potion to be used as an enema, the object of which is to prevent miscarriage or premature birth. At about six or seven months into pregnancy, the *mondo* or bangle ritual is performed. Traditionally, a brass bangle was used for this ritual. With the coming of Christianity and the introduction of modern health facilities, especially antenatal care, the bangle was replaced by a ring as being more discrete and modern.

In the case of first pregnancies, this ritual begins with the sacrifice of a young male goat which must be uncastrated and the result of a single birth. On the chosen day, a clay pot containing herbs and a brass ring is taken to the *mondo* shrine by the expectant mother and traditional healer. The herbs and ring are boiled together. The ring signifies the marital status of the woman as well as her pregnant condition. The ring ceremony is intended to ward off witchcraft, difficult birth positions and stillbirths. For the next week the expectant mother must observe dietary restrictions which cover plantains, cocoyam, fish, wild game and huckleberry, items which constitute a considerable part of the staple diet of the Bakweri as well as other ethnic groups in Cameroon. At the end of this period of prohibition the cooked ring is removed from the pot and worn by the expectant mother. The traditional healer at the shrine then cooks for her a variety of foods which she must eat alone to ensure the potency and efficacy of the medicine. In subsequent pregnancies, she need not perform the whole ritual again but is expected to retrieve the clay pot, into which she must put boiled water. The solution from the infusion is used as an enema.

Discussion

Social Perception and the Allocation of Guilt

In traditional society, the infertile man does not exist. Men's reproductive organs are external and produce seminal fluid regardless of sperm count or motility, thereby projecting a semblance of normality even in the face of male failure. In any case society has a series of socio-cultural alternatives available to him to help protect and project his image in cases of what is often presumed to be female failure: concubinage, polygyny and the levirate. Women's organs, on the other hand, are for the most part internal and hidden, potential sites of disease (from both natural and supernatural causes), the cause of anxious surveillance and health intervention (Inhorn, 1994).

Socio-culturally, women bear the major responsibility for reproduction. They must keenly observe their menstrual cycle, know when they are fertile, bear children and control fertility when birth control is required. Since they are perceived as the prime actors in the delivery process, women also bear the brunt of any reproductive failure, morbidity as well as mortality. As a result of strong socio-cultural pressures women have internalized these norms, not only feeling a strong sense of responsibility to become pregnant and produce a live birth, but also feeling entitled to one. Women take risks to achieve this goal, sacrificing their well-being and dignity in conforming with the requests of health practitioners, both modern and traditional.

Society expects the childless woman to be persistent and relentless in her efforts to conceive and deliver a live baby. Consequently, she repeatedly consults diviners and traditional healers and, when these fail, modern health practitioners. Doing nothing to redress pregnancy loss or childlessness is tantamount to a personal admission of failure and of irresponsibility. It is also perceived as an overt admission of guilt of having sold or pledged her babies (even before conception) to supernatural forces in return for personal gratification such as longevity, wealth and success. Childless women suffer marital stress, social stigma and ostracism. Affines accuse them of a past history of sexual promiscuity and (if they are educated) indiscriminate use of contraceptives and induced abortion. Pregnancy loss affects women's socio-cultural as well as personal identity. It signifies the loss of some part of their self, a stage of life (Peretz, 1970). Their status within the household, the extended family system, their economic security, inheritance and even access to health care is influenced by their reproductive ability. Women who experience pregnancy loss are subject to personal grief, as has been well documented (see Wolff, Nelson and

Schiller, 1970; Cullberg, 1972; Benfield, Leib and Vollman, 1978; Peppers and Knapp, 1980; Forrest, Standish and Baum, 1982; Ney, Fung, Wickett and Beaman-Dodd, 1994).

Yet in many societies in Cameroon, pregnancy loss is often perceived as being self-inflicted. Wittingly or unwittingly, by acts of omission or commission, women bring it upon themselves. Women who cultivate good relationships with their co-wives in polygynous unions and with their husband's relatives as well as with their neighbours have sources of help available in times of need. This network of friends and relatives assists her in carrying out farm work, bringing back foodstuffs, cooking and looking after her younger children during the difficult phases of pregnancy. An inability to cultivate this social network is indicative of negative attributes in make-up, of malicious behaviour and a lacunae in her personal relationships. Since pregnancy loss is perceived as being self-inflicted, it attracts little or no sympathy. Thus, as has been documented elsewhere, interpersonal conflicts or social rifts within the family are important factors in the allocation of responsibility for pregnancy loss and episodes of morbidity (see Kloos, Etea and Defega, 1987; Kendall, 1990; Coppo, Pisani and Keita, 1992). Similarly in Niger, prolonged labour is indicative of a bad-tempered woman (Jaffre and Prual, 1994).

Sexual misconduct is another example of self-inflicted fetal wastage. Among the Bamileke, this even includes sexual relationships entered into before marriage, but which after marriage came into the category of affinal relationships and therefore became incestuous.

Mourning in Pregnancy Loss

For a variety of reasons, women are discouraged from grieving over lost pregnancies, a common but unfortunate practice (Rowe, Clyman, Green, Mikkleson, Haight and Ataide, 1978; Borg and Lasker, 1981; Wilson, Fenton, Stevens and Soule, 1982; Lovell, 1983; Kowalski, 1987), as this impedes recovery (Parkes, 1972; Helmrath and Steinitz, 1978; Borg and Lasker, 1981; Stierman, 1987). Rather, women are encouraged to 'let go', accept pregnancy loss with stoicism, forget the unfortunate episode and replace the dead baby by getting pregnant again as soon as possible, especially if it belonged to the category of those 'born to die' (Scheper-Hughes, 1992; Castle, 1994). The 'replacement child syndrome' has implications for the well-being of the mother and for untimely pregnancies as well as family-planning programmes.

In their study on pregnancy loss, French and Bierman (1962) observed that spontaneous abortions are most likely to happen in the second and third months. According to the World Fertility Survey, about 30 percent of women over the age of thirty had experienced fetal loss in Cameroon. Among the eight African countries studied, Cameroonian women recorded the third highest percentage of loss after Senegal and the Ivory Coast (Casterline, 1989).

As a result of the perceived spiritual and physical risks involved in pregnancy and childbirth, there is a strong cultural blanket of silence over acknowledging or affirming conception, especially in the early months, perceived as being the most vulnerable, when pregnancy loss is most likely to occur. Thus, women resolutely refuse either to admit or to deny outright that they are pregnant, even when it is obvious that they are. Early declarations of pregnancy are perceived as notifying and providing an opportunity to those who, through physical and supernatural forces, wish to hurt the expectant mother before the pregnancy becomes secure and difficult to dislodge by causing a miscarriage or stillbirth, preventing fetal growth, aspirating the fetus out[2], changing the original sex of the baby, etc. As a result, it is culturally impolite or insensitive to ask a woman if she is pregnant. Only a woman's husband or lover has the prerogative to demand an answer to such privileged and personal information.

This culture of silence on the early confirmation of pregnancy is particularly marked among the Bakossi of South-West Province. It is only after a public ceremony during which her pregnancy is officially proclaimed (even though she is visibly pregnant) that a woman may be referred to as being pregnant. Anyone who breeches this norm and calls her pregnant before the ceremony is held responsible for any adverse event that may occur to either mother or baby.

Health professionals are also conceded the right to know the pregnancy status of a woman, especially when she goes for a consultation at the hospital, the threshold of their sphere of influence. These socio-cultural beliefs are often translated into behavioural patterns and contribute to the late presentation of women at antenatal clinics. Although access to modern health-care services, especially antenatal care, is perceived by policy makers as important in reducing pregnancy loss, ensuring a successful and risk-free result, health institutions are not necessarily perceived by all women in this light. Women with a low socio-economic status especially perceive hospitals as potentially unsafe and as inadvertently contributing to the risk of pregnancy loss (Njikam Savage, 1992). For these women, the hospital environment is not conducive to the performance of the necessary traditional rites which may be prescribed for administration just before and during delivery to protect mother and child from untoward birth outcomes. In Cameroon, as in many African countries, neither spouse nor any other relative is allowed into the hospital's labour room during delivery. Thus, unlike in traditional home births, the expectant mother is often removed from the reach of her anxious relatives, who have no access to her until well after delivery and can therefore offer no help should the need arise. Consequently, although they may have attended antenatal clinics in urban centres, primiparae as well as multiparae (that is, first-time mothers as well as women who had given birth before) often return home to their villages for delivery (see Gwan, 1982; Huguet and Prual, 1988; Save The Children, Cameroon, personal communication, 1990).

Despite the unusually large size of the discussion groups, the study results cannot be extrapolated to reflect reproductive morbidity on a national level. The study did not attempt to address the prevalence of pregnancy loss among the study population or associate it with the high levels of sexually transmitted diseases found in the area. Nonetheless, the data provide meaningful insights into the subject of pregnancy loss as perceived by women, particularly in societies where the fertility level is high and largely uncontrolled, and children are highly valued, with the result that artificial contraceptive usage is low. This has implications for the use of maternal and child health services and the Safe Motherhood programme which Cameroon is trying to implement.

Acknowledgements

My sincere appreciation goes to all the women who shared personal and sometimes painful details of their lives, especially the Bamileke, Bakweri (Aunty Mary) and Beti women's groups. Partial support from the University of Yaounde and the WHO Centre for Research in Human Reproductive Health, Yaounde, is also acknowledged.

Notes

1. In Francophone Cameroon douching is an essential part of female toiletrie. Kerosene is introduced into the vagina in the hope that it will induce menarche.

2. It is widely believed in Cameroon that malevolent forces almost literally suck out fetuses, as a result of which the expectant mother experiences a miscarriage.

References

Benfield, D.G., Leib, S.A. and Vollman, J.H., 'Grief Response of Parents to Neonatal Death and Parent Participation in Deciding Care', *Pediatrics*, vol. 62, 1978, pp. 171–7

Borg, S. and Lasker, J., *When Pregnancy Fails: Families Coping With Miscarriage, Stillbirth and Infant Death*, Boston, Beacon Press, 1981

Caldwell, J.C., Caldwell, P., Ankrah, M., Anarfi, J.K., Agyeman, D., Awusabo-Asare, K., Orubuloye, K. and Orubuloye, I.O., 'African Families and AIDS: Context, Reactions and Potential Interventions', *Health Transition Review,* Sexual Networking and HIV/AIDS in West Africa Supplement, vol. 3, Canberra, 1993, pp. 1–16

Casterline, J.B., 'Collecting Data on Pregnancy Loss: A Review of Evidence from the World Fertility Survey', *Studies in Family Planning*, vol. 20. no. 2, 1989, pp. 81–95

Castle, S., 'The (Re)negotiation of Illness Diagnoses and Responsibility for Child Death in Rural Mali', *Medical Anthropology Quarterly*, vol. 8, no. 3, 1994, pp. 314–35

Coppo, P., Pisani, L. and Keita, A., 'Perceived Morbidity and Health Behaviour in a Dogon Community', *Social Science and Medicine*, vol. 34, 1992, pp. 1227–35

Cullberg, J., 'Mental Reactions of Women to Perinatal Death', in *Proceedings of Psychosomatic Medicine in Obstetrics and Gynaecology*, Third International Congress, Basel, Karger, 1972, pp. 326–9

Demo 87, Second Census, Cameroon/UNFPA

Forrest, G.C., Standish, E. and Baum, J.D., 'Support After Perinatal Death: A Study of Support and Counselling After Perinatal bereavement', *British Medical Journal*, vol. 285, 1982, pp. 1475–9

Fortes, M., *The Web of Kinship among the Tallensi: The second Part of the Analysis of the Social Structure of a Trans-Volta Tribe*, Oxford, Oxford University Press, 1949.

French, F.E. and Bierman, J.E., 'Probabilities of Fetal Mortality', *Public*

Health Report, vol. 77, no. 10, 1962, pp. 835–47

Gwan, E., 'Pregnancy Outcome in Adolescents in Cameroon', unpublished M.D. thesis, Yaounde, University Centre for Medical and Health Sciences, 1982

Helmrath, T.A. and Steinitz, E.M., 'Death of an Infant: Parental Grieving and the Failure of Social Support', *Journal of Family Practice*, vol. 6, 1978, pp. 785–90

Huguet, D. and Prual, A., *La Sante Maternelle à Niamey, Analyse de la Situation, Direction de la Santé Publique et des Affaires Sociales*, Republique du Niger, 1988

Inhorn, M.C., 'Introduction', Symposium: Interpreting Infertility: Medical Anthropological Perspectives', *Social Science and Medicine*, vol. 39, no. 4, 1994, pp. 459–61

Jaffre, Y. and Prual, A., 'Midwives in Niger: An Uncomfortable Position Between Social Behaviours and Health Care Constraints' *Social Science and Medicine*, vol. 38, no. 8, 1994, pp. 1069–73

Kendall, C., 'Public Health and the Domestic Domain: Lessons from Anthropological Research on Diarrheal Disease', in J. Coreil and J.D. Mull (eds), *Anthropology and Primary Health Care*, Boulder CO, Westview Press, 1990

Kloos, H., Etea, A. and Defega, A., 'Illness and Health Behaviour in Addis Ababa and Rural Central Ethiopia', *Social Science and Medicine*, vol. 23, 1987, pp. 1003–19

Kowalski, K., 'Perinatal Loss and Bereavement in Women's Health', in L. Sonstegard, K. Kowalski and B. Jennings (eds), *Women's Health, Vol. 3: Crisis and Illness In Childbearing*, New York, Grune and Stratton, 1987

Lovell, A., 'Some Questions of Identity: Late Miscarriage, Stillbirth and Perinatal loss', *Social Science and Medicine*, vol. 11, 1983, pp. 755–61

Mbiti, S., *African Religions and Philosophy*, (2nd edn), Oxford, Heinemann, 1989

Morton-Williams, P., 'Yoruba Responses to the Fear of Death', *Africa*, vol. 30, no. 1, 1960, pp. 34–9

Ney, P.G., Fung, T., Wickett, A.R. and Beaman-Dodd, C., 'The Effects of Pregnancy Loss on Women's Health', *Social Science and Medicine*, vol. 38, no. 9, 1994, pp. 1193–200

Njikam Savage, O.M., 'Socio-behavioural Aspects of Reproductive Health', paper presented at the National Workshop on Reproductive Health Priorities for The Cameroonian Woman, University Centre for Medical and Health Sciences, CUSS, Yaounde, 1992

——, and Tchombe, T.M., 'Anthropological Perspectives on Sexual Behaviour in Africa: Review of Literature', *Annual Review of Sex Research*, vol. 5, 1995

Parkes, C.M., *Bereavement: Studies of Grief in Adult Life*, New York, International Universities Press, 1972

Peppers, L.G. and Knapp, R.J., 'Maternal Reactions to Involuntary Fetal/Infant Death', *Psychiatry*, vol. 43, 1980, pp. 155–9

Peretz, D., 'Reaction to Loss', in B. Schoenberg, A.C. Karr, D. Peretz and A. Kutscher (eds), *Loss and Grief: Psychological Management in Medical Practice*, New York, Columbia University Press, 1970

Rowe, J., Clyman, R., Green, C., Mikkleson, C., Haight, J. and Ataide, L., 'Follow-up of Families who Experience a Perinatal Death', *Pediatrics*, vol. 62, 1978, pp. 166–170

Scheper-Hughes, N., *Death Without Weeping: The Violence of Everyday Life in Brazil*, Berkeley, University of California Press, 1992

Stefaniszyn, B., 'African Reincarnation Re-examined', *African Studies*, no. 13, 1954, pp. 131–46

Stierman, E.D., 'Emotional Aspects of Perinatal Deaths', *Clinical Obstetrics and Gynecology*, vol. 30, 1987, pp. 352–61

Taylor, C., 'Condoms and Cosmology: The Fractal Person and Sexual Risk in Uganda', *Social Science and Medicine*, vol. 31, no. 9, 1990, pp. 1023–8

Wilson, A.L., Fenton, L.J., Stevens D.C. and Soule, D.J., 'The Death of a Newborn Twin: An Analysis of Parental Bereavement', *Pediatrics*, vol. 70, 1982, pp. 587–91

Wolff, J., Nelson, P. and Schiller, P., 'The Emotional Reaction to a Stillbirth', *American Journal of Obstetrics and Gynecology*, vol. 108, 1970, pp. 73–6

Part II

Other Studies

—6—

Variation in Risk of Pregnancy Loss

Michael A. DeLuca and *Paul W. Leslie*

Introduction

Pregnancy loss can affect the pattern and level of fertility and thus the process of family formation. The actual impact of fetal loss depends on the magnitude and distribution of risk of loss within populations; its contribution to differences among populations depends on the interpopulation variation in risk. It would therefore be useful to know how variable the risk is among populations.

Until very recently information about pregnancy loss in developing populations had to rely on data collected as part of reproductive histories. Intrauterine mortality was rarely the study focus, but rates of pregnancy loss could be estimated from data collected for other purposes. These studies produced rather homogeneous rates of pregnancy loss ranging from 15–20 per cent of all pregnancies and seemed to indicate that there was little interpopulation variation in rates of spontaneous abortion. However, with the advent of better biochemical assays, researchers began to find pregnancy loss rates in the 40–60 per cent range, and evidence of greater intra- and interpopulation variation has begun to accumulate.

The purpose of this chapter is to review what is known about variation in rates of pregnancy loss. We will also touch on some of the technical and methodological problems that arise in trying to measure it. We begin with some necessary definitions and a brief review of the timing of events surrounding conception and implantation. This is followed by a discussion of clinical studies conducted in Western populations and field surveys of pregnancy loss in non-Western populations. Finally, there is a description of factors known to influence the probability of pregnancy loss.

Terminology, Physiology and Detection of Pregnancy Loss

Following fertilization of an oocyte, the conceptus travels along one of the fallopian tubes toward the uterus, dividing while it travels. When it reaches the uterus three to four days after fertilization, the conceptus, now called a blastocyst, consists of approximately eight cells. About 90 per cent of the blastocyst will become the trophoblast (placenta and other tissues) and 10 per cent will become the embryo. Cell division continues, and six to eight days after fertilization the trophoblast begins the process of implantation. This involves orienting the trophoblastic cell layer so that it faces the implantation site on the endometrial wall (apposition), formation of microvilli by the trophoblast, which join with the cells of the endometrium to establish the maternal-fetal link (adhesion), and the process whereby the embryo buries itself beneath the surface of the endometrium and lacunae of maternal blood are formed around the embryo (penetration). The lacunae provide the source of fetal nutrition (Edmonds, 1987).

There are a variety of means of detecting and tracking pregnancies, including self-reporting, physical detection (for example, ultrasound) and biochemical assays. These differ with regard to reliability and how early they can detect pregnancy. Because the risk of pregnancy loss declines rapidly with gestational age, techniques that can detect pregnancy earlier will generally yield higher estimates of the rate of loss (see Figure 6.1). Self-reporting is the simplest approach, but it fails to reveal virtually all losses occurring within two weeks of conception, and many even later. In fact, pregnancies approaching three months of gestational age sometimes go unrecognized (Braunstein, Karow, Gentry and Wade, 1977). Biochemical markers are more reliable but themselves vary in sensitivity (the minimum amount of hormone that a particular assay can detect) and specificity (the degree to which an assay cross-reacts with other substances). An assay with high sensitivity can detect smaller amounts of hormone and can therefore detect pregnancies at an earlier stage. An assay with high specificity will recognize only the target hormone and will not produce false-positive results due to cross-reaction with other substances.

Currently, the most reliable and sensitive tests for pregnancy use human chorionic gonadotropin (hCG) as a marker. HCG is a glycoprotein hormone produced by the trophoblast almost immediately after it forms which reaches detectable levels around the time of implantation (Wilcox, Weinberg, Baird, and Canfield, 1993). It plays a crucial role in the establishment of pregnancy, including maintenance of the corpus luteum during the first five to six weeks. It is also involved in other endocrinological pathways that influence the course of pregnancy and fetal development. Circulating levels of hCG peak around the twelfth week of gestation and decline slowly until parturition.

HCG has alpha- and beta-subunits. The alpha-subunit is nearly

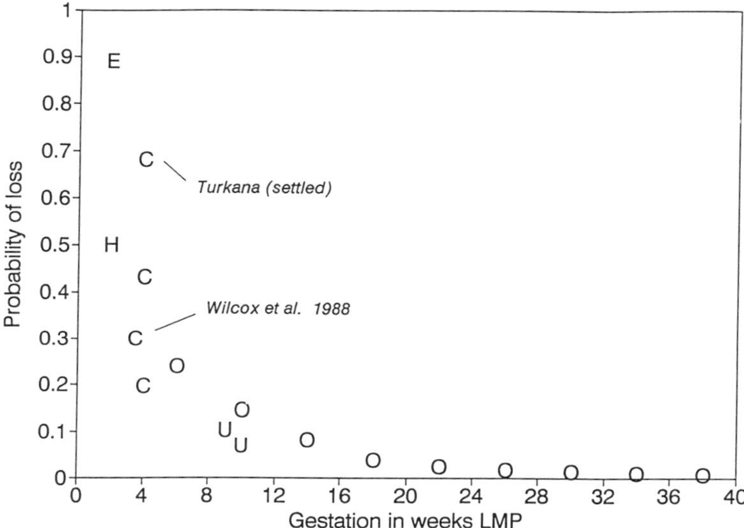

Figure 6.1. Estimates of the probability of pregnancy loss, to term, by gestational age (in weeks since last menstruation). Estimates are labelled to indicate the method of pregnancy detection used; sources of the estimates are: **E**, "Early Pregnancy Factor" (Rolfe, 1982); **H**, development of fertilized ova recovered from hysterectomies (Hertig et al., 1959); **C**, hCG assays (Miller et al., 1980; Whittaker et al., 1983; Wilcox et al., 1988; Leslie et al., 1993); **U**, ultrasound (Gilmore and McNay, 1985; Cashner et al., 1987); **O**, obstetric records (French and Bierman, 1962).

identical to the alpha-subunits of other human glycoproteins (for example, luteinizing hormone, follicle stimulating hormone). Because of this, early hCG assays cross-reacted with other hormones (for example, Udry, Keovichit, Burnwright, Cowgill, Morris and Yamarat, 1971). The lack of specificity meant that a degree of sensitivity had to be sacrificed in order to avoid false positive tests. However, the beta-subunit of hCG has a terminal sequence of 32 amino acids that is unique to hCG. This allows for the improved specificity of the current generation of pregnancy tests.

The time-frame used to date the products of conception varies among researchers and is a source of confusion. Some researchers date the products of conception from the last menstrual period (LMP), some from the time of conception (gestational age, GA) and others by stage of development. For example, a conceptus which is six weeks LMP is the same age as one that is four weeks GA and both are equivalent to a two-week embryo. In a field situation it is usually easiest to obtain information on the last menstrual period, though it is often feasible to assay urine samples for the hormones needed to estimate gestational age.

A distinction is made between clinical and sub-clinical pregnancy and pregnancy loss. Sub-clinical refers to the approximately two-week period after conception and before the next expected menstrual period. Losses occurring during this period often go unrecognized by the woman and usually manifest themselves as bleeding around the expected time of menstruation. Sub-clinical pregnancies and losses are only detectable through biochemical means such as assays for hCG. The most sensitive of these assays can only detect pregnancies that survive until the time of implantation, so the first week after conception remains unobservable with current techniques. Some researchers claim to have detected a pregnancy marker less than forty-eight hours after fertilization (for example, Smart, Roberts, Clancy and Cripps, 1981). This 'Early Pregnancy Factor' is controversial because it has not been isolated and the assay is difficult (Wilcox et al., 1993). Clinical pregnancies refer to pregnancies in the time-frame after the first missed menstrual period, about two weeks after conception. Spontaneous abortions occurring in the clinical phase are generally recognized as pregnancy losses.

Fetal demise refers to death of the fetus prior to its being aborted. This is sometimes called a 'missed abortion' because a woman may continue to carry a fetus for several weeks after it has died. Fetal demise may be determined quite easily in a clinical setting with the use of hormone assays. In a field situation one may have to rely on a woman's report of non-movement or on listening for a fetal heartbeat. However, quickening occurs about fifteen weeks GA and fetal heartbeats cannot be detected by doppler until ten weeks GA. These techniques are not able to detect fetal demise in the majority of spontaneous abortions which occur earlier in gestation.

Risk of Pregnancy Loss: Clinical Studies

An early and unique study of pregnancy loss was conducted by Hertig and co-workers (Hertig, Rock, Adams and Menkin, 1959), who examined uteri from 210 women who were having therapeutic hysterectomies and who had had at least one live birth. Over the course of seventeen years they recovered thirty-four fertilized eggs. Microscopic examination, without the benefit of karyotyping to detect chromosomal anomalies, showed twenty-four of the zygotes to be morphologically normal and ten to be abnormal. It was assumed that all morphologically abnormal conceptuses would have aborted and that only the abnormal zygotes would have aborted. Hertig et al. estimated that 40 per cent of all pregnancies ended before the next expected menses. There are a number of problems with accepting this estimate at face value, including likely selectivity of the sample, but the study did establish the possibility that the overall rate of pregnancy loss might be much higher than had been believed.

The first epidemiological study of pregnancy loss to utilize radioimmunoassay (RIA) of hCG was conducted by Miller and colleagues (Miller, Williamson, Glue, Gordon, Grudzinskas and Sykes, 1980). They collected urine samples from 197 women beginning on day twenty-one of the menstrual cycle and then on alternate days until menstruation or until biochemical detection of pregnancy by standard pregnancy tests. The RIA showed some cross-reactivity with luteinizing hormone, so the pregnancy threshold levels were raised in order to avoid false positives. Using these criteria they detected 152 conceptions in 623 cycles, with an overall pregnancy loss rate of 43 per cent. More than three-quarters of these losses occurred during the sub-clinical stage. Of the pregnancies that were clinically recognized, about 14 per cent ended in spontaneous abortion, which is similar to rates reported from other studies utilizing reproductive histories.

Subsequent studies utilized hCG assays with greater specificity. Edmonds, Lindsay, Miller, Williamson and Wood (1982) reported that 62 per cent of all detected pregnancies ended before twelve weeks gestation and that 92 per cent of the losses occurred in the sub-clinical stage. Whittaker and co-workers (Whittaker, Taylor and Lind, 1983) reported that 12 per cent of the clinically observable pregnancies in their sample aborted before term, a figure that agrees with earlier estimates, but the rate of sub-clinical loss was an unexpectedly low 8 per cent. It is not clear how much the discrepancies in these results are due to differences in risk among the women in these clinical samples and how much to differences in procedures (Wilcox et al., 1993).

The *Early Pregnancy Study* conducted by the National Institute of Environmental Health Science (Wilcox, Weinberg, O'Connor, Baird, Schlatterer, Canfield, Armstrong and Nisula, 1988) has provided what is generally recognized as the most robust estimate of the probability of pregnancy loss per conception. The sample included 221 healthy women attempting to conceive and a control group of twenty-eight women who had been sterilized by tubal ligation. Pregnancies were tracked using an immunoradiometric assay (IRMA) for urinary hCG which is both more specific and more sensitive than the RIAs used in the earlier studies. The overall pregnancy loss rate was 31 per cent of the 198 detected pregnancies. About 70 per cent of the losses occurred sub-clinically.

Risk of Pregnancy Loss: Field Studies and Interpopulation Variation

The studies described above were all conducted in modern, Western populations. Indeed, the samples generally do not even reflect the socioeconomic heterogeneity in the populations from which they were drawn, so it is natural to ask whether their results are representative of non-Western populations. As most anthropologists are keenly aware, it is practically impossible to attain clinical conditions in a field situation. For this reason, clinical studies and field studies have differed in their techniques. With few exceptions, field studies of pregnancy loss have been retrospective and rely almost exclusively on reproductive histories.

Casterline (1989) examined the probability of pregnancy loss in eight developing countries from reproductive histories collected by the World Fertility Survey. The proportions of pregnancies lost varied more than two-fold among these populations (see Table 6.1). Because they are based on retrospective interviews, these figures exclude subclinical, early pregnancy loss, and suffer from an unknown degree of recall error or reluctance to discuss miscarriages. Differential ascertainment might contribute to the apparent differences in risk.

Table 6.1. Pregnancy loss rates for several countries

Country	% of pregnancies lost	Source
Retrospective studies:		
Ivory Coast	9.6	Casterline, 1989
Tunisia	7.7	Casterline, 1989
Syria*	11.0	Casterline, 1989
Korea	7.1	Casterline, 1989
Philippines	8.7	Casterline, 1989
Costa Rica	12.6	Casterline, 1989
Mexico	9.4	Casterline, 1989
Guyana*	17.4	Casterline, 1989
Prospective studies:		
Punjab, India	13.6	Potter et al., 1965
Bangladesh*	17.6	Ford et al., 1989
Turkana Nomads, Kenya	0.0	Leslie et al., 1993
Turkana Settled, Kenya	45.0	Leslie et al., 1993

* Induced losses not distinguished from spontaneous losses

Prospective studies avoid some of the difficulties inherent in retrospective studies, and a few have been done in non-Western contexts. Potter and colleagues (Potter, Wyon, New and Gordon, 1965) investigated pregnancy loss prospectively among women in eleven villages in the state of Punjab, India. The women kept menstrual diaries and were interviewed weekly. Based on nearly 1,800 pregnancies, the total rate of pregnancy wastage was 13.6 per cent, with about 77 per cent of all losses occurring before twenty-eight weeks gestation. Although it is prospective, this approach still depends on women recognizing early symptoms of pregnancy. Reproductive histories were also collected; recalled pregnancy losses were less than one-fifth of those detected by monthly household visits.

Intrauterine mortality was one of the birth-interval components considered by Ford, Huffman, Chowdhury, Becker, Allen and Menken (1989) in an investigation of the relationship between maternal weight and birth-interval dynamics in rural Bangladesh. Pregnancies were detected by interview at least two weeks after conception. The reported pregnancy loss rate was 17.6 per cent, but in this case the authors believe that this may be an over estimate because spontaneous and induced abortions were not distinguished.

The first prospective study of pregnancy wastage in a non-Western population to utilize urinary hormone assays rather than self-reporting or clinical detection was conducted among the Turkana of northwestern Kenya (Leslie, Campbell and Little, 1993). This study compared pregnancy loss rates between Turkana living as traditional nomadic pastoralists and Turkana who have settled on an irrigation scheme. Eighteen pregnancies in the nomadic women and thirty-one pregnancies in the settled women were detected and followed. All of the nomadic pregnancies terminated in live births, whereas fourteen of the settled pregnancies did not reach term. Overall, the pregnancy loss rate for the settled sample was 45 per cent, 0 per cent for the nomadic sample (95 per cent confidence intervals were 27–64 per cent and 0–15 per cent respectively). Because these were cross-sectional surveys, many of the pregnancies had already survived the period of greatest risk by the time they were detected. If only pregnancies detected in the first trimester are considered, the rate of loss jumps to 68 per cent among the settled women. Because of the small sample sizes, the results should be interpreted with caution. However, a number of factors, such as conservative criteria for attributing pregnancy and the cross-sectional nature of the study, should produce results that underestimate actual pregnancy loss. Furthermore, one of us (MAD) recently completed the fieldwork in a longitudinal study of pregnancy loss in the same Turkana settlement, and preliminary results confirm the high rate of loss found in the first study. We cannot yet explain the observed rates. Increased disease stress in the settled community (for example, malaria) is a likely explanation, but further epidemiological research is needed. The elevated risk of pregnancy loss among the settled Turkana, along with the contrast between the nomadic and settled sub-populations, suggest that there may be a lot more variation in pregnancy loss to be found if only it were looked for.

Causes of Pregnancy Loss

In the absence of adequate information about the actual interpopulation variation in pregnancy loss, we are left to consider the *potential* for such variation arising from the causes of intrauterine mortality. To the extent that these vary among populations, so may pregnancy loss.

There are myriad factors in the physical environment that may influence the risk of fetal wastage. The effects of many, such as radiation or exposure to specific toxic chemicals, are likely to be restricted to specific areas or sub-populations. Others, such as alcohol consumption or tobacco-smoking, may be more widespread. These factors are too numerous and too population-specific to permit discussion here. Kline, Stein and Susser (1989) provide a useful review. We consider here some of the factors associated with pregnancy loss that are known to be especially important or that are well documented and are likely to affect many or all populations. Some of these factors are likely to vary across populations, resulting in different intrauterine mortality rates.

Genetic Causes

Chromosomal abnormalities such as trisomies, monosomies and translocations are known to increase the risk of spontaneous abortion. Fifty per cent or more of clinically recognized first trimester pregnancy losses result from chromosomal anomalies (Simpson and Carson, 1993). Autosomal trisomies are the largest single class of genetic abnormality implicated in pregnancy loss. The contrast between the frequency of specific chromosomal anomalies in spontaneously aborted fetuses and in live births, as shown in Table 6.2, indicates the impact of these anomalies on fetal viability. Clearly, chromosomal anomalies are a major cause of pregnancy loss. Such aberrations often vary with age of mother (and sometimes with age of father as well), but we have been unable to find any evidence that their frequency varies among populations.

Immune Factors

A mother's immunological system may respond to a fetus as though it were a foreign organism; genetically it is. It is well known that Rhesus sensitization can result in late second or third trimester losses (Simpson and Carson, 1993). There is also evidence that ABO incompatibility

Table 6.2. Frequency of chromosomal anomalies in spontaneous abortions and live births

Anomaly	Spont. abortion	Live born	Source
Monosomy X	18%	1/7,500 females	Cummings, 1994
Trisomy 8	1/331	1/14,500	McKusick, 1969
Trisomy 13	9%	1/15,000	Cummings, 1994
Trisomy 16	15%	almost zero	McKusick, 1969
Trisomy 18	9%	1/11,000	Cummings, 1994
Trisomy 21	9%	1/900	Cummings, 1994
XXY	1%	1/1,000 males	Cummings, 1994
XYY	1%	1/1,100 males	Cummings, 1994
XXX	1%	1/1,200 females	Cummings, 1994
Triploidy	17%	1/10,000	Cummings, 1994
Tetraploidy	6%	almost zero	Cummings, 1994

increases the risk of fetal loss (Hook and Porter, 1980). However, having both Rh and ABO incompatibility appears to mitigate the risk (Harrison, Tanner, Pilbeam and Baker, 1988). Auto-immune diseases such as systemic lupus erythmatosis have also been associated with increased risk of fetal loss (Beer, Quebbeman and Semprini, 1987). One noteworthy point is that *protection* of the fetus from the maternal immune system may be stimulated by histo-incompatibility. Many repeated aborters share HLA antigens with their partner (Schacter, Weitkamp and Johnson, 1984). The increased risk of spontaneous abortion among such couples is believed to be related to the lack of stimulation of the maternal immune blocking factor, due to the parents sharing too many antigens.

The incidence of incompatibility is a function of gene frequencies and also of marriage patterns (frequency of consanguineous matings). Since these vary considerably among human populations, the impact of immune factors on pregnancy loss may also be expected to vary.

Luteal Phase Deficiency

Luteal phase deficiency (LPD) describes the condition in which the endometrium does not respond to progesterone to the degree necessary for implantation and the maintenance of pregnancy. This may result from insufficient progesterone production or from a problem with the progesterone receptors of the endometrium. There is now ample evidence that nutritional stress and work loads affect reproductive function and, more specifically, progesterone levels. Studies of well-nourished women on weight-loss programmes show that dieting women who experience moderate weight loss have reduced levels of progesterone and subsequent luteal insufficiency compared to non-dieting women (Lager and Ellison, 1990). Ellison and Lager (1986) also showed that moderate exercise can lower progesterone levels in women.

Dieting is in some ways analogous to 'natural' situations entailing food shortage. Efe and Lese women in the Ituri Forest of northeastern Zaire were found to have salivary progesterone levels indicative of shortened luteal phases and luteal insufficiency (Ellison, Peacock and Lager, 1986). Neither population was chronically malnourished, but both groups experience periods of food shortage and the women had lost 7–8 per cent of their body weight during the preceding six months. Van der Walt, Wilmsen and Jenkins (1978) found that !Kung San women of Botswana had suppressed levels of gonadal steroids and reduced luteal activity. A peak in San birth rates occurred nine months after women achieved their annual peak weight, and these authors postulated that seasonal nutritional stress suppresses steroid production and interferes with successful pregnancy.

Although low progesterone profiles have been documented in several populations and are associated with negative energy balance, it is not known whether the implied luteal deficiency does translate into increased risk of pregnancy loss. Such an effect is reasonable and there is some clinical evidence in its support (Daily, Walters, Soto-Albers and Riddick, 1983), but at least one study suggests that it may be unimportant (Baird, Weinber, Wilcox, McConnaughey, Musey and Collins, 1991).

Infectious Disease

A wide variety of infectious diseases have been associated with increased rates of spontaneous abortion. Table 6.3 provides an extensive but surely not exhaustive list of implicated organisms. McFalls and McFalls (1984) describe the evidence linking the more common of these to pregnancy wastage. Infectious agents may lead to pregnancy loss in a number of ways. The placenta is an effective barrier to many substances and microbes, but some pathogens (for example, rubella, toxoplasma) can cross it, infect the fetus, and cause fetal demise and subsequent abortion. The placenta itself may be infected and its ability to transfer nutrients to the fetus compromised, resulting in fetal growth retardation or fetal demise. Uterine adhesions and scarring from disease processes (or from surgical procedures) that cause endometritis or trauma to the uterine wall may interfere with implantation. Side-effects of maternal illnesses, such as high fever, independently increase the risk of spontaneous abortion (Douglas, 1980; Kline et al., 1989). Furthermore, drugs used to treat some maternal illnesses may have teratogenic effects and result in pregnancy loss (Simpson and Carson, 1993).

Table 6.3. Infectious agents associated with increased risk of spontaneous abortion

Infectious agent	Source
Borrelia spp.	2
Brucella toxoplasmosis	1
Campylobacter	2
Chlamydia trachomatis	1
Cytomegalovirus	1
ECHO viruses	3
Haemophilus	2
Hepatitis	2
Herpes I	3
Herpes II	3
Influenza	2
Laptospira spp.	2
Plasmodium spp. (malaria)	1
Mycobacterium tuberculosis	2
Mycoplasma hominus	1,2
Pyelonephritis	2
Rubella (German measles)	3
Rubeola (measles)	3
Salmonella typhi (typhoid fever)	1,2
Staphylococci	2
Streptococci	2
Treponema pallidum (syphilis)	3
Toxoplasma gondii (toxoplasmosis)	3
Ureaplasma urealyticum	1
Vaccina	1
Variola (smallpox)	1
Venezuelan equine encephalitis	3
Vibrio cholerae (cholera)	2
Vibrio foetus (vibriosos)	1

1. Simpson and Carson, 1993
2. Charles and Larsen, 1987
3. Sever, 1980

One example of a disease that can be transmitted across the placenta and affect the fetus directly is syphilis (*Treponema pallidum*). In its primary or secondary stages, syphilitic infection elevates the risk of spontaneous abortion, especially during the second trimester, and the incidence of stillbirths (WHO, 1975). Syphilis is common in many developing countries, especially in Africa, but its prevalence varies greatly among regions, even within the same country (Belsey, 1976; Willcox 1977). In at least some populations, syphilis may contribute to low fertility (for example, Retel-Laurentin, 1973), but the effects of syphilis are often difficult to separate from those of concomitant gonorrhoea (World Health Organization, 1975; Romaniuk, 1968), and it is not clear how much of the fertility effect is attributable to fetal loss and how much to secondary sterility. The risk of pregnancy loss decreases during later stages of the infection as partial immunity to the disease is acquired, so its impact on both individual reproductive histories and fertility at the population level is limited.

The more virulent forms of malaria (associated with *Plasmodium falciparum*) are of particular interest. Malaria has long been one of the most common and most serious of human diseases (Livingston, 1971). It remains widespread, and strains that are resistant to the most common anti-malarial drugs are proliferating. Where it is prevalent, even a moderate effect on the risk of pregnancy loss could have a significant demographic impact. Malarial infection can result in pregnancy loss through both its effect on the placenta and its side-effects. The side-effects include anaemia, hemolytic crises and high fever, all of which can increase the risk of spontaneous abortion (McFalls and McFalls, 1984). *P. falciparum* can parasitize the placenta and thereby interfere with the transfer across the placenta of oxygen and nutrients from the mother and metabolic waste products from the fetus. It is well accepted that placental parasitization can retard fetal growth and lead to low birth weights and prematurity (Macgregor and Avery, 1974), which itself contributes to perinatal mortality. The extent of further effects of placental infection on intrauterine mortality are unclear. One interesting but indirect indication that malaria can have a significant impact on pregnancy loss rates is the shift in the seasonal distribution of births in Ceylon (now Sri Lanka) reported by Newman (1970; cited in Gray 1979). Births occurring in the months with the lowest births rates would have been conceived during the peak malaria months. The birth trough largely disappeared as malaria control was achieved, which suggests that the earlier pattern of birth seasonality was at least in part a product of malaria-induced intrauterine mortality.

Maternal Factors

Age is probably the most widely recognized maternal factor influencing the risk of pregnancy loss. The graph of risk of spontaneous abortion by maternal age is roughly a J-shaped curve with women less than twenty years old having a slightly elevated risk and twenty to thirty year olds having the lowest risk. There is a substantial increase in risk after the mid-thirties (Simpson and Carson, 1993; Harlap, Shiono and Ramcharan, 1980; Alberman, 1987). This pattern has also been documented in several non-Western populations (Leridon, 1976; Casterline, 1989; Ford et al., 1989). A number of factors may be involved in the age effect. Certain chromosomal anomalies, such as trisomies, occur more frequently in the zygotes of older women (Kline et al., 1989). Advancing age may be associated with poor vascularization of the endometrium or longer exposure to toxins and chronic infections. It is also possible that some of the age effect is due to women with recurrent losses attempting to achieve a desired family size, especially in controlled fertility populations. Another interesting possibility is presented by Peacock (1991), who reports some contested evidence indicating that older women are less likely to abort a compromised pregnancy spontaneously than younger women. If this is the case, then older women might be more likely to maintain a compromised pregnancy to clinical recognition and to have any losses detected.

In addition to the age effect, Casterline (1989) found that gravidity, length of birth interval and previous pregnancy loss were associated with risk of fetal wastage in most of the eight countries he examined. First pregnancies were slightly more likely to end in spontaneous loss than second ones, and the risk for third, fourth, fifth and sixth pregnancies was higher than that for the first two pregnancies in all countries except Costa Rica. Interestingly, there is an apparent decrease in risk of pregnancy wastage for the seventh and higher order pregnancies. This may reflect a bias for ending the reproductive career with a live birth, or perhaps it is an artefact of more 'competent' reproducers attaining higher gravidity. Age and gravidity are strongly correlated, but statistical analysis suggests that the effect of age on pregnancy loss is stronger than that of gravidity. Casterline also found that pregnancies conceived sixteen to thirty-five months after the termination of the last pregnancy were at lower risk than conceptions occurring after shorter or longer intervals, whether or not the previous pregnancy resulted in a live birth. A pregnancy following a loss was approximately three times more likely to terminate in a loss in most of the countries; the risk of loss following two spontaneous abortions was substantially greater than the risk after only one pregnancy loss. This apparent effect of previous outcome is likely to be an artefact of heterogeneity in risk among women rather than an effect of previous outcome – that is, women who are at higher risk are more likely to experience multiple losses (Wood, 1994).

Age at menarche has also been associated with increased risk of spontaneous abortion. In Limón, Costa Rica, Madrigal (1991) found that women who reported at least one miscarriage had a significantly earlier age of menarche than women who had not had miscarriages. She also found that early maturers had an earlier age at first pregnancy and had significantly more pregnancies than women who were late maturers. It remains to be determined if the greater number of miscarriages was a result of the greater number of pregnancies or if the greater number of pregnancies was a result of having more pregnancy losses.

Conclusions

At the beginning of this chapter, we posed the question, 'How much variation is there among populations in the risk of pregnancy loss?' At this time, the answer must be, 'We don't know.' Certainly, the investigations cited here have produced a range of estimates of the overall risk of loss, but much of this variation is surely due to differences in techniques used to detect pregnancy and loss, and to measurement error (for example, selection bias, under-reporting).

Most early pregnancy loss appears to arise from defects in the zygote, especially chromosomal anomalies, but there is little evidence that their frequency varies among populations. The hormonal environment, especially luteal progesterone deficiency, is another potential contributor to pregnancy loss. Recent advances in the study of human reproductive ecology have revealed previously unsuspected variation in ovarian function and impressive sensitivity of aspects of ovarian function to activity patterns and environmental conditions. Such variation could contribute to variation in early pregnancy loss, but its actual impact is not yet clear.

In contrast, some factors that are associated with late pregnancy loss, especially infectious diseases, do vary markedly among populations, and it is reasonable to expect the associated risk of pregnancy loss to vary in the same way. As pointed out by Wood (1994), rates of third-trimester pregnancy loss have decreased in Western countries during this century, and also vary with ethnicity and education. Secular trend and sub-population differences constitute evidence for an effect of environmental factors that vary in time and space.

Loss of more advanced pregnancies will be of greater significance to the women and families involved; they also obviously have a greater bearing on a given birth interval than does a single early pregnancy loss. For some research questions, then, failure to detect early pregnancy loss is not a problem. However, the much greater frequency of early losses, coupled with the possibility of women experiencing repeated early losses, increases the potential impact of early loss on fertility levels and patterns in a population and on individual reproductive histories.

In sum, there are indications of real interpopulation variation in risk of pregnancy loss, but the magnitude of that variation remains poorly characterized. The range of populations in which pregnancy loss, especially early loss, has been studied is narrow. It seems likely that more variation in risk will be uncovered as well-designed studies are carried out in contexts more fully representative of the range of human experience. Consequently, there is a need for more thorough investigation of both the rates and timing of pregnancy loss in a variety of populations, to complement the growing understanding of its environmental and physiological causes and its social and psychological consequences.

References

Alberman, E., 'Maternal Age and Spontaneous Abortion', in M.J. Bennett and D.K. Edmonds (eds), *Spontaneous and Recurrent Abortion*, Oxford, Blackwell Scientific Publications, 1987

Baird, D., Weinber, C., Wilcox, A., McConnaughey, D., Musey, P. and Collins, D., 'Hormonal Profiles of Natural Conception Cycles Ending in Early, Unrecognized Pregnancy Loss', *Journal of Clinical Endocrinology and Metabolism*, vol. 72, 1991, pp. 793–800

Beer, A.E., Quebbeman, J.F. and Semprini, A.E., 'Immunopathological Factors Contributing to Recurrent and Spontaneous Abortion in Humans', in M.J. Bennett and D.K. Edmonds (eds), *Spontaneous and Recurrent Abortion*, Oxford, Blackwell Scientific Publications, 1987

Belsey, M.A., 'The Epidemiology of Infertility: A Review with Particular Reference to Sub-Saharan Africa', *Bulletin of the World Health Organization*, vol. 554, 1976, pp. 319–41

Braunstein, G., Karow, W., Gentry, W. and Wade, M., 'Subclinical Spontaneous Abortion', *Obstetrics and Gynecology*, vol. 50 (suppl.), 1977, pp. 41s–44s

Cashner, K.A., Christopher, C.R. and Dysert, G.A., 'Spontaneous Fetal Loss After Demonstration of a Live Fetus in the First Trimester', *Obstetrics and Gynecology*, vol. 70, 1987, pp. 827–30

Casterline, J.B., 'Maternal Age, Gravidity, and Pregnancy Spacing Effects on Spontaneous Fetal Mortality', *Social Biology*, vol. 36, 1989, pp. 186–212

Charles, D. and Larsen, B., 'Infectious Agents as a Cause of Spontaneous Abortion', in M.J. Bennett and D.K. Edmonds (eds), *Spontaneous and Recurrent Abortion*, Oxford, Blackwell Scientific Publications, 1987

Cummings, M.R., *Human Heredity: Principles and Issues*, (3rd edn) New York, West, 1994

Daly, D., Walters, C., Soto-Albers, C. and Riddick, D., 'Endometrial Biopsy During Treatment of Luteal Phase Defects is Predictive of Therapeutic Outcome' *Fertility and Sterility*, vol. 40, 1983, pp. 305–10

Douglas, C.P., 'Perinatal Implications of Maternal Disorders', in S. Aladjem, A.K. Brown and C. Sureau (eds), *Clinical Perinatology*, St. Louis, C.V. Mosby, 1980

Edmonds, D.K., 'Early Embryonic Mortality' in M.J. Bennett and D.K. Edmonds (eds), *Spontaneous and Recurrent Abortion*, Oxford, Blackwell Scientific Publications, 1987

——, Lindsay, K.S., Miller, J., Williamson, E. and Wood, P.J., 'Early Embryonic Mortality in Women', *Fertility Sterility*, vol. 38, 1982, pp. 447–53

Ellison, P.T. and Lager, C., 'Moderate Recreational Running is Associated with Lowered Salivary Progesterone Profiles in Women', *American Journal of Obstetrics and Gynecology*, vol. 154, no. 5, 1986, pp. 1000–3

——, Peacock, N. and Lager, C., 'Salivary Progesterone and Luteal Function in Two Low-fertility Populations of Northeast Zaire', *Human Biology*, vol. 58, 1986, pp. 473–83

Ford, K., Huffman, S.L., Chowdhury, A.K.M.A., Becker, S., Allen, H. and Menken, J., 'Birth-interval Dynamics in Rural Bangladesh and Maternal Weight', *Demography*, vol. 26, 1989, pp. 425–37

French, F.E. and Bierman, J.M., 'Probabilities of Fetal Mortality', *Public Health Reports*, vol. 77, 1962, pp. 835–47

Gilmore, D.H. and McNay, M.B., 'Spontaneous Fetal Loss Rate in Early Pregnancy', *Lancet*, vol. 1, 1985, p. 107

Gray, R.H., 'Biological Factors Other than Nutrition and Lactation which may Influence Natural Fertility: A Review', in H. Leridon and J. Menken (eds), *Natural Fertility*, Liège, Ordina Editions, 1979

Harlap, S., Shiono, P.H. and Ramcharan, S., 'A Life Table of Spontaneous Abortions and the Effects of Age, Parity, and Other Variables', in I.H. Porter and E.B. Hook (eds), *Human embryonic and fetal death*, New York, Academic Press, 1980, pp. 145–58

Harrison, G.A., Tanner, J.M., Pilbeam, D.R. and Baker, P.T., *Human Biology: An Introduction to Human Evolution, Variation, Growth, and Adaptability*, (3rd edn), Oxford, Oxford University Press, 1988

Hertig, A.T., Rock, J., Adams, E.C. and Menkin, M.C., 'Thirty-four Human Ova, Good, Bad and Indifferent, Recovered from 210 Women of Known Fertility: A Study of Biologic Wastage in Early Human Pregnancy', *Pediatrics*, vol. 23, 1959, pp. 202–11

Hook, E.B. and Porter, I.H., 'Terminological Conventions, Methodological Considerations, Temporal Trends, Specific Genes, Environmental

Hazards, and Some Other Factors Pertaining to Embryonic and Fetal Death', in I.H. Porter and E.B. Hook (eds), *Human Embryonic and Fetal Death*, New York, Academic Press, 1980

Kline, J., Stein, Z. and Susser, M., *Conception to Birth: Epidemiology of Prenatal Development*, New York, Oxford University Press, 1989

Lager, C. and Ellison, P.T., 'Effect of Moderate Weight Loss on Ovarian Function Assessed by Salivary Progesterone Measurements', *American Journal of Human Biology*, vol. 2, 1990, pp. 303–12

Leridon, H., 'Facts and Artifacts in the Study of Intrauterine Mortality: A Reconsideration from Pregnancy Histories', *Population Studies*, vol. 30, 1976, pp. 319–35

Leslie, P.W., Campbell, K.L. and Little, M.A., 'Pregnancy Loss in Nomadic and Settled Women in Turkana, Kenya: A Prospective Study', *Human Biology*, vol. 65, no. 2, 1993, pp. 237–54

Livingston, F., 'Malaria and Human Polymorphisms', *Annual Review of Genetics*, vol. 5, 1971, p. 33

McFalls, J.A. and McFalls, M.H., *Disease and Fertility*, New York, Academic Press, 1984

Macgregor J. and Avery, J., 'Malaria Transmission and Fetal Growth', *British Medical Journal*, vol. 3, 1974, pp. 433–6

McKusick, V.A., *Human Genetics*, (2nd edn), Englewood Cliffs, Prentice-Hall, 1969

Madrigal, L., 'Menarcheal Age and Spontaneous Abortion: Further Evidence for a Connection', *American Journal of Human Biology*, vol. 3, 1991, pp. 625–8

Miller, J., Williamson, E., Glue, J., Gordon, Y.B., Grudzinskas, J.G. and Sykes, A., 'Fetal Loss After Implantation: A Prospective Study', *Lancet*, vol. 2, 1980, pp. 554–6

Newman, P., 'Malaria Control and Population Growth', *Journal of Development Studies*, vol. 6, 1970, pp. 133–58

Peacock, N., 'An Evolutionary Perspective on the Patterning of Maternal Investment in Pregnancy', *Human Nature*, vol. 2, no. 4, 1991, pp. 351–85

Potter, R.G., Wyon, J.B., New, M. and Gordon, J.E., 'Fetal Wastage in Eleven Punjab Villages', *Human Biology*, vol. 37, no. 2, 1965, pp. 262–73

Retel-Laurentin, A., 'Fécondité et syphilis dans la région de la Volta Noire', *Population*, vol. 28, 1973, pp. 793–815

Rolfe, B.E., 'Detection of Fetal Wastage', *Fertility and Sterility*, vol. 37, no. 5, 1982, pp. 655–60

Romaniuk, A., 'Infertility in Tropical Africa', in J.C. Caldwell and C. Okonjo (eds), *The Population of Tropical Africa*, New York, The Population Council, 1968

Schacter, B., Weitkamp, L.R. and Johnson, W.E., 'Paternal HLA Compatibility, Fetal Wastage, and Neural Tube Defects: Evidence for a T/t-like Locus in Humans', *American Journal of Human Genetics*, vol. 36, 1984, pp. 1082–91

Sever, J.L., 'Infectious Causes of Human Reproductive Loss', in I.H. Porter and E.B. Hook (eds), *Human Embryonic and Fetal Death*, New York, Academic Press, 1980, pp. 169–75

Simpson, J.L. and Carson, S., 'Biological Causes of Foetal Loss' in R. Gray, H. Leridon, and A. Spira (eds), *Biomedical and Demographic Determinants of Reproduction*, Oxford, Clarendon Press, 1993

Smart, Y., Roberts, R., Clancy, R. and Cripps, A.,'Early Pregnancy Factor: Its Role in Mammalian Reproduction – Research Review', *Fertility and Sterility*, vol. 35, 1981, pp. 397–402

Udry, J.R., Keovichit, S., Burnright, R., Cowgill, D., Morris, N. and Yamarat, C., 'Pregnancy Testing as a Fertility Measurement Technique: A Preliminary Report on Field Results', *American Journal of Public Health*, vol. 61, 1971, pp. 344–52

Van der Walt, L.A., Wilmsen, E.N. and Jenkins, T., 'Unusual Sex Hormone Patterns Among Desert-dwelling Hunter-gatherers', *Journal of Clinical Endocrinology and Metabolism*, vol. 16, 1978, pp. 658–63

Whittaker, P.G., Taylor, A. and Lind, T., 'Unsuspected Pregnancy Loss in Healthy Women', *Lancet*, vol. 1, 1983, pp. 1126–7

Wilcox, A.J., Weinberg, C., O'Connor, J.F., Baird, D., Schlatterer, J.P., Canfield, R., Armstrong, E.G. and Nisula, B.C., 'Incidence of Early Loss of Pregnancy', *New England Journal of Medicine*, vol. 319, no. 4, 1988, pp. 189–94

——, Weinberg, C., Baird, D. and Canfield, R., 'Endocrine Detection of Conception and Early Foetal Loss', in R. Gray, H. Leridon and A. Spira (eds), *Biomedical and Demographic Determinants of Reproduction*, Oxford, Oxford University Press, 1993

Willcox, R., 'Venereal Diseases', in G. Howe (ed.), *A World Geography of Human Diseases*, New York, Academic Press, 1977

Wood, J.W., 'Dynamics of Human Reproduction', *Biology, Biometry, Demography*, New York, Aldine de Gruyter, 1994

World Health Organization, *The Epidemiology of Infertility*, Technical Report Series 582, 1975

–7–

'Never Such Innocence Again': Irony, Nature and Technoscience in Narratives of Pregnancy Loss

Linda L. Layne

> I'll never hear those words again ['You are pregnant'] with the same naive joy, the same innocence of spirit. I know that in future pregnancies, there will be a cloud over the news and I'll wonder if it is going to happen again. (Davis, 1988, p. 25)

I take my title 'Never such innocence again' from the concluding line of one of the poems on which Paul Fussell based his account of the Great War as a critical turning point in the way we think about the world and engage in the art of memory (Fussell, 1975, p. 19).[1] In this chapter I examine the discursive production of pregnancy loss in the newsletters of two of the over nine hundred pregnancy-loss support organizations which have sprung up in the United States during the last fifteen years, noting a striking similarity between the way that the World War I soldiers described by Fussell and the would-have-been parents I have studied confront, and come to terms with, senseless death through their use of irony.[2]

The ironies which feature in narratives of pregnancy loss, like those explored by Fussell's memoirists,[3] are 'ironies of circumstance'. Such ironies are of the type Booth, the primary literary theorist on irony, describes as stable and overt. Unlike covert ironies, which require an act of ironic reconstruction (the reader must figure out what the author really meant), the ironies of pregnancy loss described in support-group newsletters 'require no special act of reconstitution or translation. They simply assert an irony in things or events that the speaker has observed and wants to share' (Booth, 1974, p. 236). Such ironies hinge on the fact that things did not turn out as expected. The depth of irony corresponds to the extent of the gap between what one expects will happen and what actually happens. Thus if, as Fussell suggests, 'every war is ironic because every war is worse than expected' (1975, p. 7), a pregnancy that ends in a miscarriage or stillbirth also lends itself to ironic treatment, for the outcome is certainly worse, far worse, than what the would-have-been parents anticipated.

Although conventional literary theory on irony focuses on this gap between what is expected and what happens, of at least equal phenomenological importance is the depth of conviction with which the expected is expected and the extent to which the expected mattered. For most members of pregnancy-loss support groups, a pregnancy loss is experienced as an abrupt, unthinkable deviation from the natural, normal biological and social progression that pregnancies are expected to entail. Both the social transformation of 'would-be parents' to 'parents' that wanted pregnancies normally achieve and the 'natural' biological progression of a pregnancy over a period of nine months (now commonly understood in terms of a popularized medical model of fetal development) that such pregnancies ordinarily enact are suddenly and unexpectedly abrogated and annulled.

Such a challenge to deeply held beliefs about the order or nature of things is, as Fussell observes, often associated with an 'ironic mode of understanding'. For instance, continuing with our World War I example, according to Fussell the world before the war was 'a different world', a world in which 'the certainties were intact' (1975, p. 21); with these certainties gone, 'the dominating form of understanding' has been 'essentially ironic' (ibid., p. 35). Similarly, for many members of pregnancy-loss support groups the loss of a wished-for baby is a watershed event after which they will never experience the world or think about their lives in the same way. Their life narratives become punctuated by the loss, and other experiences come to be understood as having occurred either before or after this pivotal event. This appears to be the case, at least for some, even after the successful birth of a subsequent child.

In other words, for many it is not just the pregnancy that is lost, but innocence as well. This is a recurrent theme in narratives of loss published in support-group newsletters: Kristen Ingel, a facilitator for a subsequent pregnancy support group, writes of her pregnancy following the stillbirth of her daughter (1989): 'Gone is one's innocence. Gone is the thought that pregnancy means you will have a baby', and Mary Cushing Doherty observes (1991), 'Never again will I capture the innocent joy'. Another contributor, Susan Erling (1988), writes, following a stillbirth: 'My spiritual, trusting innocence or naivete is gone now, never to be recaptured.'[4] Because such a loss of innocence stems from the disruption of profoundly held beliefs about the nature of things, narratives of loss offer a rich source for examining fundamental elements of contemporary culture, including beliefs about life, God nature and science.

According to Fussell, the thing that made 'the Great War. . .more ironic than any before or since' was the fact that 'it was a hideous embarrassment to the prevailing Meliorist myth which had dominated the public consciousness for a century' (1975, p. 8). But the myth of never-ending progress which Fussell claims was irreparably shattered by the Great War is, at least in the realm of biomedicine, still very much alive and well. This is, I will argue, at least partially because of the myth of biomedical progress that so many members of pregnancy-loss support groups find irony such an appropriate interpretive means. Yet, despite their belief in a technologically improved and improvable nature, members of pregnancy-loss support groups also appear to hold views of nature very much like those of the nineteenth-century Romantics, that is of a sacred nature which reflects God's glory.[5] This alternative concept of nature, rather than counteracting the effects of the myth of biomedical progress, compounds the discrepancy between expectation and reality and thus, like the myth of biomedical progress, also contributes to the adoption of an ironic form of understanding. But ultimately (and perhaps ironically), many would-have-been parents find the means for negotiating the challenge that a pregnancy loss poses to a view of nature as the work of a just and providential God in the Christian conception of redemptive nature.[6] By locating the ironies of their situation in the context of the ironic reversals of Christian dogma, many bereaved parents are able to reconcile the gap between their expectations and reality, thus making their loss a meaningful one.

This chapter is based on an analysis of the six annual issues of the SHARE (Source of Help in Airing and Resolving Experiences) newsletter from 1984 to 1991 and the quarterly newsletters of Unite (not an acronym) from 1981 (starting with their first issue) to 1991. SHARE is the largest pregnancy-loss support organization in the United States, and their newsletter includes contributions from members throughout the country. Unite is a regional group with several support groups serving Pennsylvania and New Jersey. The newsletters of both groups feature poems, narrative accounts, excerpts from personal journals and letters from bereaved parents describing their experiences. They also typically include articles by professionals on topics of interest; reviews of new publications and films on pregnancy loss; announcements of successful births and adoptions by members; and sometimes patterns for making commemorative items.

The membership of these two organizations (and the other groups I have worked with) is predominately white and middle class. Most support-group meetings are attended by couples, but some women and an occasional man attend on their own. Women, mostly would-have-been mothers but also sometimes other female relatives and friends, and nurses, write most of the newsletter items. Men (again, mostly would-have-been fathers but also occasionally would-have-been grandfathers or brothers) contribute about one-fifth of the personal items.

Members vary in religious backgrounds, representing the three major traditions in the United States (Protestantism, Catholicism and Judaism), and although SHARE was founded by a Catholic nun and many SHARE groups are based at Catholic hospitals, both groups are ecumenical and the degree of religious commitment among the members varies substantially. The same can probably be said for the membership's attitudes towards abortion.

Textual analysis of the newsletters was supplemented by participant observation with Unite, SHARE and the New York Section of the National Council of Jewish Women (NCJW) at support-group meetings in New Jersey and New York, national and regional conferences and events, interviews with the founding members of several groups, the analysis of scholarly and other popular texts on the subject and my personal experience of five miscarriages.

Improving on Mother Nature: The Meliorist Myth and Reproductive Medicine

Fussell asserts that the Great War was 'the last to be conceived as taking place within a seamless, purposeful "history" involving a coherent stream of time running from past through present to future' (1975, p. 21). While this view of a linear, ever-improving history may no longer prevail in terms of ideas about global, civilizational or national progress, many social critics of science would argue that the Meliorist vision continues to inform the myth of techno-scientific progress.

Certainly within the realm of biomedicine, critics like Illich who not only deny that medical services have made a significant contribution to the changes in life expectancy that have occurred, but believe that the medical establishment is, in fact, 'a major threat to health' (Illich, 1976, p. 3), are the exception rather than the rule. Although physicians in the United States have come under increasing attack since mid-century, most criticism of medicine has focused not on the efficacy of medical treatment but rather on the economics of medicine – unequal access, excessive medical costs, greed – and on the increasing impersonality of medical care (Burnham, 1985; Starr, 1982).[7] In the 1970s, a noted philosopher of medicine asserted that 'No disorder, however complex or intractable, is beyond the possibility of conquest. Man's Promethean hope of removing the restraints of disease on history seem less illusory than ever before' (Pellegrino, 1979, p. 245). By and large, this notion still prevails.

This vision of the triumphant march of medical progress is perhaps nowhere more apparent than in the fields of neonatal and reproductive medicine. Sociologists of neonatology have remarked upon the 'conviction' of practitioners in the field 'that [its methods] are constantly improving' (Guillemin and Holmstrom, 1986, p. 26). 'Over the last twenty years, the adaptation of many adult therapies to the treatment of full-term infants has been successful. The presumption in neonatology is that progress will continue undiminished at the same rate and prove as equal to the challenge of saving very low birth weight neonates as it has to saving more developed newborns' (ibid., emphasis mine). Other excellent examples of this triumphalist attitude are provided in the cover stories of the December 1993 *Life* magazine entitled 'Miracles of Birth: The Blessings of a Medical Revolution' and the September 30th, 1991 issue of *Time* magazine entitled 'How a dazzling array of medical breakthroughs has made curing infertility more than just a dream.'[8]

The *Life* article declares, 'not so long ago, nature was in control. . .. Since then, year by year, doctors have learned to manipulate the mechanics of pregnancy and birth' (1993, p. 75). In a similar fashion, the *Time* article describes a 'reproductive revolution' – 'a series of remarkable advances' through which scientists 'have opened a new window on the mysteries of fertilization' which enables them to 'manipulate virtually every aspect of the reproductive cycle' (1991, p. 58). This article is interspersed with a series of three-part illustrative boxes which give a one-sentence description of an aspect of the reproductive cycle followed by a one-sentence explanation of 'What can go wrong' and completed in the final segment with a sentence explaining 'How to fix it'. Not only do these boxes reinforce the view of reproduction as a mechanical process which can easily be fixed by a physician/technician, they exaggerate and distort actual medical competence.[9]

As I have described elsewhere (Layne 1992a), the combination of the under-reporting of pregnancy losses and the over-reporting of technology's 'miracle babies' has led to a situation in which expectations concerning reproductive outcomes are higher than the level of medical competence.[10] The impact of unrealistic expectations generated by the widespread belief that if there is a problem during a pregnancy doctors will be able to fix it, is poignantly expressed in the words of one would-have-been father. Even having gone through one miscarriage he retained his faith in biomedicine's power. When, during the last months of his wife's subsequent pregnancy, an electronic stethoscope used to amplify fetal heartbeats (which he described as an 'electronic wizard') revealed that the baby had died, he explains 'I didn't want to accept it. Not with modern technology. . .' (Friedrich, 1984). Another would-have-been father describes his similar feelings of disbelief: 'Surely this cannot be serious. Babies don't die nowadays' (Jones, 1987).[11]

She was Born/She Died: The Terrible Irony of Pregnancy Loss

Though the discrepancy between the expectation that 'modern technology' can now fix all problem pregnancies and the actuality of pregnancy loss certainly creates the potential for ironic understanding, the primary irony of pregnancy loss is the conflation of birth and death, of the beginning of life with the end of it. Contributors to support-group newsletters capture this irony in their poems with lines like 'I gave birth to death once' (Heil, 1982); 'Two years since I never met you' (Hoch, 1988); 'A little boy of no days old' (Aunt Debbie 1991).

This primary irony is compounded and reinforced in many narratives by the memory of other minor ironic details, as in the case of the woman who recalled that her mother had prepared her favourite dish the night that she went into premature labour. Another woman writes:

> The baby wasn't due until August, but we enrolled in childbirth classes in May, as they didn't give the classes in the summer. The first class was a trip through the labor and delivery floors at the hospital. It was on a Sunday afternoon and while we leisurely strolled around, little did we know that the very next day I would be using all these facilities, 12 weeks too soon. (Iacono 1982, p. 4)

The organization of their memory into 'a series of little ironic vignettes' (Fussell, 1975, p. 32)[12] provides these individuals (much as it did for World War I soldiers) with a structure by which to remember and give shape to events which have challenged the certainties of their world.

A number of contributors to support-group newsletters openly declare the irony of their situations; for example, one woman wrote: 'It really seemed ironic, although the baby was dead it wasn't ready to be born', (Iacono, 1982). Another woman describes her feelings about the stillbirth of her daughter six and a half years earlier as 'the lifelong sorrow of a catastrophe whose misery is only matched by its irony' (Donato, 1988).

Like other ironies of circumstance, the ironies of pregnancy loss derive largely from the fact that things did not turn out as expected. In a poem entitled 'Dead, Instead', one woman indexes a number of such discrepancies:

I bought birth announcements,
I used death announcements.
I bought dresses and dolls,
I used casket and plot.
I wanted congratulations and baby gifts,
I got sympathy cards and flowers.
I wanted a beautiful new life,
I got ugly death.
I wanted a new beginning,
I got an old ending.
I wanted mornings filled with joy,
I got mornings filled with mourning.
(Daniels, 1988)

Clearly, in these cases, it is not just that things did not turn out as expected but that things did not turn out as they *should* have. Even after the loss, many would-have-been parents insist that their expectations were justified and reasonable: 'I am a woman who longs for what should have been but isn't' (Chiffens, 1991). Or:

> Today I celebrate my baby's first birthday, without my baby. I'm sitting on the rocking chair in her room holding her stuffed musical lamb, lamb chop, who is wearing her pink hat from the hospital. I should be holding my baby. It is so quiet. This is not supposed to be. It should be loud and noisy with cries, laughter and baby babbling. (Murphy 1991)

The sense of 'how things are supposed to be' expressed in these texts reflects a conviction in a natural order of things in which pregnancies progress in a unidirectional, inalterable and inevitable way over a nine-month period until the baby is ready to be born – a benign nature takes its course.[13] Despite the medicalization of pregnancy and childbirth and the associated mechanistic approach to women's bodies and the birth process that have been so well documented in recent years,[14] the narratives of support-group members suggest that, for these would-have-been parents at least, the idea that a pregnancy results in the birth of a baby remains a great incontrovertible fact of nature.

Mother Nature and the Cruel Irony of Spring

The nature portrayed in these narratives of loss is not the wild, chaotic, unruly nature needing to be subdued by science which Merchant describes (1980), but rather a Romantic vision of nature more akin to that normally associated with Wordsworth, Turner and Ruskin.[15] These same nineteenth-century figures informed the way that British soldiers experienced and portrayed the Great War. But whereas many of the British officers of Fussell's study were aware of the literary and artistic origins of this Romantic view of nature, contributors to pregnancy-loss support-group newsletters are most probably not. (I have found no equivalent to the British soldier who wrote 'Was it Ruskin who said. . .?' (Fussell, 1975, p. 54).) Yet contributors to these newsletters use the Romantically freighted significance of nature to many of the same effects. Where sunrise and sunset were the primary images of nature used by British officers recalling the Great War (ibid., 1975, pp. 52–63), in narratives of pregnancy loss it is the annual cycle of the changing seasons which is most typically employed.[16] Where World War I authors achieved an ironic effect by 'juxtaposing a sunrise or sunset with the unlovely physical details of the war' (ibid., 1975, p. 55), pregnancy-loss support-group members achieve a similar effect by juxtaposing the traditional meanings associated with the seasons, particularly spring, with the details of their loss:

> Our son was born in April just as the trees budded and the birds began to sing with joy as Spring arrived. . .after having our bundle of joy home only one week, our son was hospitalized. . ..Our son never did come home (Abel, 1984).

Another would-have-been mother develops this theme in a poem entitled 'Spring':

> Spring is a cruel irony:
> So much life-
> While one is missing.
> A spring sun,
> Drying the tears of winter,
> Makes sport of sadness.
> Birds ridicule the silence
> Of a season of grief. . ..
> (Wallace, 1991)

In a spring issue of the Unite newsletter Janis Heil, one of the founders of Unite, writes 'The sights and smells of Spring remind us of newness and life. Yet often in our grief we feel rotted and dead inside'. In another poem she asks God to 'Help me face the harsh reality of sunshine and renewed life' (Heil, 1984).

Weather and seasons were used in nineteenth-century American poetry on infant loss in ways similar to those found in these late twentieth-century texts. In their analysis of nineteenth-century narratives of loss, Simonds and Rothman (1992, p. 59) found 'pleasant weather serves as a foil to a mother's distress and indicates that she feels at odds with nature and with the God who created living things'.[17]

Feelings of isolation are a frequent theme at pregnancy-loss support-group meetings. Participants repeatedly comment on their fear that they were going crazy because no one seemed to understand or find appropriate the feelings they were experiencing. Another frequent topic is how they feel unable to take part in holidays (Christmas, Mother's Day, etc.) and other celebrations (especially baby showers, parties given in the United States for expectant mothers and now increasingly their partners as well, at which gifts are given for the anticipated baby). The isolation of an individual from society is the defining characteristic of tragedy according to Frye (1973 [1957], p. 41). But in addition to feeling isolated and excluded from society, accounts like those discussed above, which contrast the new life and hope of spring with death and feelings of despair, portray subjects who feel isolated from, and out of step with, nature too. This feeling is also expressed, though in a somewhat different way, by contributors who liken their loss to freaks of nature.

For example, one woman writes:

> The funeral was on Veteran's day. . ..Rain had been forecast that day but instead, there was a freak snowstorm, totally uncharacteristic for early November. But then everything about Clare's birth and death seemed unreal, from her unexpected birth on Halloween night to her deformed face, caused by a condition called Trisomy 13. (Brown, 1988)

Another woman refers to abnormal weather in describing her daughter's funeral: she 'was buried on a bright, sunny day (uncharacteristic of winter in Chicago)' (Casimer, 1987). And a would-have-been father remarks on the fact that his son was born on the day that Halley's Comet appeared and explains how Mark Twain, who was apparently also born on the same day as an appearance by Halley's comet, used to refer to himself and the comet as 'two uncommon freaks of nature'. He goes on to note the additional irony that whereas Twain had 'planned to go out the same way,' that is seventy-six years later, their son 'came and left with Halley's comet. . .the very same year' (Jones, 1987).[18]

Both of these literary devices (juxtaposing spring and death, and the association of an abnormal birth experience with other abnormal natural occurrences) make ironic use of the standard techniques of the pathetic fallacy where nature is attributed with sentiments in keeping with the dramatic action (as in Ruskin's famous example from a ballad by

Kingsley of 'the cruel, crawling foam' over which men retrieve the body of a young woman who had drowned (Ruskin, 1890, p. 176)). In the case of the juxtaposition of spring with death, the standard portrayal of nature in 'solemn sympathy' with human endeavours is inverted. The association of abnormal weather and other unusual natural occurrences with the contributors' abnormal birth experience, on the other hand, constructs a parallelism between the actors and nature but does so by making freaks of both.

Redemptive Nature

Despite the challenges that a pregnancy loss poses to these individuals' beliefs about mother nature (and God and the relationship between the two), nature continues to function as a spiritually healing force for many would-have-been parents. Accounts of pregnancy loss frequently portray the bereaved parents turning to nature as a source of comfort in their loss. For example, one woman writes of how, after the burial of their daughter (born at twenty-four weeks gestation), she asked her husband 'if we could go to the beach to talk. . ..We sat on a large log, watched the waves roll upon the sand and cried our hearts out' (McGinness, 1988). Another woman tells of how, in response to the return of profound grief eleven months after the loss of her daughter, she 'wanted to run somewhere, far away, to a tree, a beautiful green meadow. . .' (Gana, 1984). While these self-representations of would-have-been parents communing with nature depict an important connection between these individuals and nature (a connection which may have been threatened by the loss), nature is portrayed here as it was so often in eighteenth- and nineteenth-century British poetry as 'a retreat and solace from human society and ordinary human consciousness' (Williams, 1973, p. 129).[19] In other words, although these individuals may feel at one with nature, they still feel isolated from society. Given the lack of social support for such losses, one may ask, as Williams (1973, p. 130) does of Wordsworth's poem 'Michael', whether the narratives of these mourners can be interpreted as a form of social criticism – of evidence of the lack of community, and of social life as a life of pain.

Eventually, though, most would-have-been parents deal with their losses in a way which enables them to take up their everyday lives and to feel once more a part of their communities. The Unite and SHARE newsletters suggest that the Christian narrative of redemption helps many to achieve this sense of reintegration.[20] In many of the accounts that are written some time after the loss, the feelings of isolation and despair expressed in earlier accounts become transformed into one moment in a spiritual journey – a journey from certainty to doubt and then ultimately to renewed and strengthened certainty.

This journey of salvation and rebirth is frequently portrayed as one both paralleled in and learned from nature. As Frye noted, in literature, sheep and pleasant pastures have been closely associated with the idyllic mode (a mode which normally portrays the incorporation of the central character into society), such pastoral imagery being often used in literature, 'as it is in the Bible, for the theme of salvation' (1973, p. 43). We find pastoral imagery employed in just such a way in the following account of the memorial services one couple held for their stillborn daughter four and a half months after her birth/death:

> On a sunny September morning we drove out to the valley, passing the strawberry fields and cow pastures. We went to a state park that had an open field surrounded by a swiftly flowing river and towering cliffs. We walked to the centre of the field and stood there in the wet grass with the sun warming our bodies. In a circle we celebrated the life we had. (Cruickshank-Chase, 1988)

The redemptive capacity of nature is even clearer in poems which relate the transformation of the seasons:

> We must live through the weary winter,
> If we would value the spring
> And the woods must be cold and silent,
> Before the robins sing.
>
> The flowers must be buried in darkness,
> Before they can bud and bloom.
> And the sweetest and warmest sunshine,
> Comes after the storm and gloom.
>
> So the heart, from the hardest trial,
> Gains the purest joy of all.
> And from the lips that have tasted sadness,
> The sweetest songs will fall.
>
> For as peace comes after suffering
> And love is reward of pain
> So, after earth, comes heaven
> And out of our loss, the gain.
> (Unknown, 1988)

Another contributor writes:

> You have to believe the buds will grow,
> Believe in the grass in the days of snow.
> Ah, that's the reason a bird can sing
> On his darkest day he believes in Spring.
> (Mallock, 1985)

Margaret Donato writes in an open letter six and a half years after the stillbirth of her daughter:

> Lessons to be learned when birth turns into death, just as death turns to birth, as these trees here shedding the last of their spring and summer life will bloom again. Mothers who suffer those losses stand in the shade of an actuality where hurt and anguish can turn itself into love. (Donato, 1988)

In other words, in these later narratives, the ironic distance between how things ought to be and how they are, which had been expressed through the jarring juxtaposition of spring and death, is bridged through the portrayal of death (even such an untimely one) as an essential part of nature. By situating death in nature in this way, and by defining nature as essentially a reflection of God's triumph over death, the loss becomes both intelligible and tolerable. In this Christian concept of redemption, Christ redeems humankind from the senseless cycles of death and rebirth that belong to the realm of a fallen nature. Indeed, in the narratives of loss examined here, the seasonal cycle is in fact routinely transformed into a linear narrative always culminating in spring (and implicitly the resurrection).

The symbolism of redemptive nature is also used in a common pregnancy-loss support-group ritual, the planting of a tree as a living memorial.[21] In a handbook on organizing pregnancy loss rituals compiled by the founder of SHARE, Sister Jane Marie Lamb offers suggested scripts for tree planting ceremonies which make explicit use of this symbolism:

> We are aware of the symbolism of the tree's life and death cycle according to the seasons. In spring new life follows the death evident in winter, summer bears fruit and autumn again brings colourful beauty. Each season has its own gift. We accept the gift of each season, just as we appreciate the gift of each child, however short his or her life may have been. (Lamb, 1988b)[22]

This imagery does more than suggest an acceptance of life as it comes, 'to every thing there is a season'; it offers the hope of death defeated and transformed:

> May we come to know more fully in visiting this place and our tree, that nothing dies, rather life is transformed into new life. . ..We have placed their names within the soil around our tree. As the paper degrades and becomes one with the soil, our tree will be nourished to grow and bring forth new life. (Lamb, 1988b)

In addition to the seasons (and trees portrayed therein), images of rainbows and butterflies frequently appear in narratives of loss, no doubt because their transformative character makes them particularly appropriate symbols of redemptive nature.[23]

Irony Vanquished and the Myths Restored

According to Booth, 'irony is usually seen as something that undermines clarities, opens up vistas of chaos, and either liberates by destroying all dogma or destroys by revealing the inescapable canker of negation at the heart of every affirmation' (1974, p. ix). As we have seen, for many support-group members, the irony of pregnancy loss does appear to have 'undermined clarities, opened vistas of chaos' in challenging deeply held beliefs about the power of biomedicine and the order of a benign nature. But the narratives of loss published in support-group newsletters indicate that many would-have-been parents have found an alternative to the two subsequent scenarios sketched by Booth. Christian dogma presents ready-made a framework for dealing with discrepancies between our cultural models of nature, of science, of a normal life-course, and the often harsh reality of lived experience. As Sontag has observed, there is no Christian tragedy. 'In a world envisaged by. . .Christianity, there are no free-standing arbitrary events. . .every crucifixion must be topped by a resurrection. Every disaster or calamity must be seen. . .as leading to a greater good. . .' (Sontag, 1966, p. 137).

As I have remarked elsewhere (1990a, p. 83), the compulsion to find or make something good come from these calamities is striking. Fussell (1975, p. 115), following Frye (1973, p. 42), was correct, then, in positing a close connection between ironic and mythic modes of understanding, even though Frye's rationale for doing so (a theory of cyclical history) is ill-conceived. The relationship, at least when it comes to ironic tragedy like that explored here, lies in the very preconditions for ironic understanding. It is precisely because of deeply held beliefs, beliefs that are not confirmed in life, that irony comes about in the first place. As Abel (1963) noted, 'one cannot create tragedy without accepting some implacable values as true' (quoted in Sontag, 1966, p. 136). But as Sontag so rightly observes: 'It is not the implacability of values which is demonstrated by tragedy, but the implacability of the world' (ibid.). These tragic-ironic texts successfully mediate the incongruity or exceptionalness of tragic events with the inevitability of human suffering (cf. Frye 1973, p. 42).

But if the notion of redemptive nature (whether explicitly Christian or a secularized version of the same) can help people emerge from the crisis of pregnancy loss with their beliefs in the goodness of nature and of God intact (if somewhat revised), how does biomedicine fare? Is there an equivalent model of redemptive medicine as well? Narratives published in pregnancy-loss newsletters shed only limited light on this issue because as I have described elsewhere (Layne, 1992a), other than setting the stage for disappointment, the primary role that biomedical knowledge plays in narratives of loss is to lend authority to the claim that a 'baby' existed. The more difficult and chronologically later questions as to what such an existence means are normally addressed via alternative discourses (including Christianity). In order to answer this intriguing question, one would have to look elsewhere – not to narratives of loss but to the narratives of subsequent pregnancies. Following a loss, many would-have-been parents turn to medicine not only for answers concerning what caused their loss but for help in assuring that such a loss will never take place again. For some, this involves hormone therapy, for others surgical procedures, and for nearly all a close medical monitoring of any subsequent pregnancy. Since most women who suffer a loss do go on to have a successful pregnancy, perhaps biomedicine is both redeemed and redeeming.

Acknowledgements

The research on which this essay is based was funded by a grant-in-aid from the Wenner Gren Foundation for Anthropological Research and a Paul Beer Minigrant Award. Earlier versions of this essay were presented at the annual meeting of the Society for Social Studies of Science, 1991, and the International Conference on Narrative, 1993, and I am grateful for the feedback I received on those occasions. My attention was drawn to the subject of irony and to Fussell's book by Mary Taylor Huber's excellent treatment of irony in her *The Bishops' Progress: A Historical Ethnography of Catholic Missionary Experience on the Sepik Frontier* (Washington DC, Smithsonian Institution Press,

1988). I profited from discussing this contribution with her and with a number of the members of Rensselaer Polytechnic Institute's Language, Literature, and Communication Department: Carol Colatrella, Michael Halloran, and Alan Nadel. Thanks also go to Andrea Rusnock for sharing her knowledge about the myth of medical progress.

Notes

1. The poem is 'MCMXIV' by Philip Larkin, written in the early 1960s in contemplation of 'a photograph of the patient and sincere lined up in early August outside a recruiting station' (Fussell, 1975, p. 19).
2. I have been struck by a number of similarities between the 'discourses of remembrance' (White, 1992) found in these narratives of loss and those relating to twentieth-century Euro-American war dead. Points of comparison include the importance of naming and other memorializing practices (Laqueur, 1994); rituals of redemption, including letters to the dead (Carlson and Hocking, 1988, and Kennedy, 1990); and the moral charge never to forget (White, 1992 and Kennedy, 1990).
3. And like those found in the poems of Thomas Hardy described by Booth (1974) and Fussell (1975).
4. See Sandelowski (1993) for a description of similar feelings by couples in her study who achieved a pregnancy after struggling with infertility.
5. In Sandelowski's sample of infertile women, the socio-economically advantaged women and couples placed their faith in physicians, sometimes likening them to 'God almighty,' while the less advantaged women were more likely to believe that conception was in 'God's hands' (1993, pp. 92–3).
6. Although SHARE and Unite groups discussed here provide services to people with diverse religious backgrounds, and contributors to the two newsletters refer to various religious traditions, overall the SHARE newsletter tends to be more Catholic and the Unite newsletter more Protestant in approach. The frequency with which religious beliefs and imagery figure in narratives published in the two newsletters is notable. As I describe in my paper 'Of Fetuses and Angels' (Layne, 1992a), I had started out to write a piece on the impact of new reproductive technologies on pregnancy loss but in

searching the newsletters for references to obstetrical technologies, as often as not I found angels. It is difficult to know whether participants in these groups are typical of the American middle classes in terms of religious beliefs. A 1988 report by the Office of Technology Assessment (1988, p. 364) estimated that 60 per cent of Americans belong to some established religious community, and religion may play a part in life crises, even for individuals who otherwise lead relatively secular lives.

7. Even though the amount of trust invested in physicians declined substantially from that which they enjoyed during what Burnham (1985) refers to as the 'golden era of American medicine' in the first half of the twentieth century, public opinion polls conducted in the 1960s and 1970s showed that more Americans said they trusted the medical profession than any other American institution including higher education, government and organized religion (*Newsweek*, 1973).
8. According to Brown (1980, p. 77), popular magazines and newspapers in the United States have praised the accomplishments of medicine 'and prophesiz[ed] the future success of medical science' since the 1890s.
9. For example, the third block begins 'a two-day-old, 16–cell embryo heads for the uterus'. The 'what can go wrong' segment explains that 'its DNA may contain genes that lead to cystic fibrosis and other problems' and the final section reports that 'scientists will soon be able to screen for abnormalities and possibly correct them' (*Time*, 1991, p. 59). While the article does report on the ability to perform genetic screening on embryos of this size before implantation, there is, to my knowledge, no indication that this would be possible for the embryo pictured in the illustration, that is one in a fallopian tube on its way to the uterus. From my point of view the most interesting and troubling aspect of the entire article is the final box which declares 'the ultimate goal' to be 'a healthy six-month fetus' (sic). Under the heading 'what can go wrong', it states that 'miscarriage can occur at any stage, though at this point the baby borders on viability' (p. 63). Not only does this assertion overlook the fact that the vast majority of miscarriages occur during the first trimester of pregnancy, it gives the false impression that the only reason for fetal demise is prematurity. There are no 'how to fix it' boxes between those of an 8–day-old embryo and the last one on a 6–month-fetus, precisely the period during which pregnancy loss is most likely to occur. The *Life* magazine article also replicates the mechanistic view of reproduction, but it is marginally more realistic in terms of outcomes. It claims to present the 'exclusive stories of people who needed miracles

– and found them', but the fifth and final story is about 'the woman who tried and tried' but ultimately failed to have a baby via embryo transfer to a surrogate.

10. According to Brown (1980), there has been a discrepancy between public expectations and actual medical competence ever since the early part of this century, when allopaths adopted a new scientific approach to medicine. 'By embracing science the medical profession gained. . .technical credibility beyond the actual medical value of contemporary scientific progress in medicine' (1980, p. xii).
11. Would-have-been fathers seem to be particularly articulate on this point.
12. The example Fussell (1975, p. 32) gives is from Blunden's 'Undertones of War', in which the author tells of passing a 'young and cheerful lance-corporal making tea' in a trench: a moment later a single shell is dropped in the trench, which blows the young man to bits. 'Irony engenders worse irony: At this moment, while we looked with dreadful fixity at so isolated a horror, the lance-corporal's brother came round.'
13. Of course, contributors to these newsletters know that many pregnancies are voluntarily terminated, but regardless of their personal stance *vis-à-vis* abortion (and this probably varies as much within these groups as it does nationwide), the possibility of abortion does not appear to contradict this sense of the naturalness of pregnancies culminating in the birth of a healthy baby. I discuss the dilemma that pregnancy loss and the pregnancy-loss support-movement poses for feminists in my paper, 'Breaking the Silence' (Layne, 1990b).
14. Excellent examples include Martin (1987), Rothman (1982, 1989) and Davis-Floyd (1992).
15. Of course, these Romantic figures were not in perfect agreement about the meaning of nature. See, for example, Helsinger (1982), on how Ruskin's views departed from those of Wordsworth.
16. It would be interesting to know how frequently the seasons are used in thinking about successful pregnancies. One would-have-been mother makes use of this imagery in describing her experience of the pregnancy before its loss: 'July was such a long long time away. . .. Finally the seasons began to change and the anticipation grew. . .' (Fitzgerald, 1988, p. 23).
17. Simonds and Rothman also noted (ibid.) how in the nineteenth-century precursors to these texts, 'winter and stormy weather' were sometimes used to 'emphasize women's depression and passion', much as they are in the description of a Unite newsletter contributor of her feelings during the burial of her would-have-been child on a

'bleak hillside in November. I feel the cold, bone-chilling and penetrating, like death, so appropriate for the day' (Brown, 1988, p. 1).

18. According to Fiedler (1978), in our not too distant history, all feti were considered as freakish. (See Layne, 1992b for more on the notion of 'freak of nature' in the context of pregnancy loss.)
19. See my review (1988) of the film *Some Babies Die* (1986) for other examples.
20. The prevalence in these newsletters of this view of nature and the meta-narrative of healing and reintegration it supports may at least partially be an outcome of editorial control. When one of the former editors of the Unite Newsletter was queried on this subject, she explained that not everything submitted is published; pieces that strike the editor as too graphic or too abstract are sometimes not included. When I asked about a piece that expressed great anger, she said that it might not be included if the editor thought 'it might be too scary for some people, the extremes are shaved off.'
21. One of the activities of the October 1989 Pregnancy and Infant Loss Awareness Weekend in Washington DC was a tree-planting ceremony. In addition to such collective rituals of tree plantings, many contributors tell of planting some sort of living memorial in their yards.
22. In addition to the analogy between the survivor's journey and evolving understanding of his/her loss, analogies are made between the tree and the child. Lamb suggests that the Bradford Pear is a particularly appropriate tree. 'Each tree, also, has its own gift. The Bradford Pear tree was chosen for its special qualities and gifts: The Bradford pear remains small, does not produce fruit, has blossoms which are pure and sweet and remind us of innocence, requires little care just as 'the children who had died cannot receive the care you longed to give them'. (1988a)
23. See Layne, 1992b for details.

References

Abel, H., 'A Father's Loss, Too', *Unite Notes*, vol. 3, no. 4, 1984, p. 4

Abel, L., *Metatheatre: A New View of Dramatic Form*, New York, Hill and Wang, 1963

Aunt Debbie, 'Dear Little One. . .', *Unite Notes*, vol. 10, no. 3, 1991, p. 5
Booth, W.C., *A Rhetoric of Irony*, Chicago, University of Chicago Press, 1974
Brown, D., 'Photographs of a Funeral', *Unite Notes*, vol. 7, no. 4, 1988, p. 1
Brown, E.R., *Rockefeller Medicine Men: Medicine & Capitalism in America*, Berkeley, University of California Press, 1980
Burnham, J.C., 'American Medicine's Golden Age: What Happened to it?', in J.W. Leavitt and R.L. Numbers (eds), *Sickness and Health in America: Readings in the History of Medicine and Public Health*, Madison, WI, University of Wisconsin Press, 1985
Carlson, A.C. and Hocking, J.E., 'Strategies of Redemption at the Vietnam Veterans' Memorial', *Western Journal of Speech*, vol. 52, 1988, pp. 203–15
Casimer, L.A., 'Sarah's Story – With Love', *SHARE Pregnancy and Infant Loss Support Newsletter*, vol. 10, no. 3, 1987, pp. 11–13
Chiffens, M. 'Sorrow and Hope', *Unite Notes*, vol. 10, no. 2, 1991, p. 1
Cruickshank-Chase, R., 'Family Farewell', in Sister J.M. Lamb (ed.), *Bittersweet. . .Hellogoodbye*, Section 2, Belleville, Ill.: Charis Communications, 1988, p. 14
Daniels, B.A., 'Dead, Instead', in Sister J.M. Lamb (ed.), *Bittersweet. . .Hellogoodbye*, Section 4, Belleville, Ill.: Charis Communications, 1988, p. 29
Davis, M., 'Miscarriage: Remnants of a Life', in Sister J.M. Lamb (ed.), *Bittersweet. . .Hellogoodbye*, Section 1, Belleville, Ill.: Charis Communications, 1988, p. 25
Davis-Floyd, R., *Birth as an American Rite of Passage*, Berkeley, University of California Press, 1992
Doherty, M.C., 'Please', *Unite Notes*, vol. 10, no. 2, 1991, p. 5
Donato, M., A Letter Published in Sister J.M. Lamb (ed.), *Bitter-sweet. . . Hellogoodbye*, Section 1, Belleville, Ill.: Charis Communications, 1988, pp. 32–3
Erling, S., 'Change in Self–After the Loss of a Baby', *Unite Notes*, vol. 8, no. 1, 1988, p. 2
Fiedler, L.A., *Freaks: Myths and Images of the Secret Self*, New York, Simon and Schuster, 1978
Fitzgerald, D., 'To my Special Friend', in Sister J.M. Lamb (ed.), *Bittersweet. . .Hellogoodbye*, Section 1, Belleville, Ill.: Charis Communications, 1988, p. 23
Friedrich, J., 'Reflections Without Mirrors', *SHARE Pregnancy and Infant Loss Support Newsletter*, vol. 7, no. 3, 1984, p. 2
Frye, N., *Anatomy of Criticism: Four Essays*, Princeton, Princeton University Press, 1973 [1957]

Fussell, P., *The Great War and Modern Memory*, London, Oxford University Press, 1975
Gana, K., 'Recoil. . .and Growth', *Unite Notes*, vol. 4, no. 1, 1984, p. 3
Guillemin, J.H. and Holmstrom, L.L., *Mixed Blessings: Intensive Care for Newborns*, Oxford, Oxford University Press, 1986
Heil, J., 'Giving Birth to Death', *Unite Notes*, vol. 2, no. 1, 1982, p. 2
——, 'A Prayer for Spring', *Unite Notes*, vol. 3, no. 3, 1984, p. 1
Helsinger, E.K., *Ruskin and the Art of the Beholder*, Cambridge, Harvard University Press, 1982
Hoch, M., 'Two Years', *Unite Notes*, vol. 7, no. 3, 1988, p. 4
Huber, M.T., *The Bishops' Progress: A Historical Ethnography of Catholic Missionary Experience on the Sepik Frontier*, Washington DC, Smithsonian Institution Press, 1988
Iacono, L., 'Faith', *Unite Notes*, vol. 2, no. 1, 1982, pp. 4–6
Illich, I., *Medical Nemesis: The Expropriation of Health*, New York, Pantheon Books, 1976
Ingel, K., 'Subsequent Pregnancy', *Unite Notes*, vol. 8, no. 2, 1989, p. 1
Jones, C.L., 'A Fiery Tale', *SHARE Pregnancy and Infant Loss Support Newsletter*, vol. 10, no. 2, 1987, p. 3
Kennedy, K., 'The Moving Wall: Construction of Ephemeral Place', paper delivered at the annual meeting of the American Ethnological Association, 1990
Lamb, Sister J.M., 'Symbolism of the Tree', in Sister J.M. Lamb (ed.), *Bittersweet. . .Hellogoodbye*, Section 3, Belleville, Ill., Charis Communications, 1988a, p. 7
——, 'A Blessing and Dedication of the Tree', in Sister J.M. Lamb (ed.), *Bittersweet. . .Hellogoodbye*, Section 3, Belleville, Ill., Charis Communications, 1988b, p. 8
Laqueur, T.W., 'Memory and Naming in the Great War', in John Gillis (ed.), *Commemoration: The Politics of National Identity*, Princeton, Princeton University Press, 1994
Layne, L.L., 'Review of Some Babies Die: A Film by Martyn Langdon Down, 1986', *Visual Anthropology*, vol. 1, no. 3, 1988, pp. 491–7
——, 'Motherhood Lost: Cultural Dimensions of Miscarriage and Stillbirth in America', *Women and Health*, vol. 16, no. 3, 1990a, pp. 75–104
——, 'Breaking the Silence: Pregnancy Loss and the Problem of Language', paper presented at the American Anthropological Associations's Annual Meeting, New Orleans, 1990b
——, 'Of Fetuses and Angels: Fragmentation and Integration in Narratives of Pregnancy Loss', in D. Hess and L. Layne (eds), *Knowledge and Society*, Greenwich, Conn., JAI Press, 1992a
——, 'Mother Nature/Freaks of Nature: Constructing Motherhood and

Nature in Narratives of Pregnancy Loss', paper delivered at the Society for Literature and Science's annual meeting, Atlanta, 1992b

Life, 'Miracles of Birth: The Blessings of a Medical Revolution, Healthy Babies who 10 Years Ago would Never have Been Born', December 1993, pp. 75–84

Mallock, D., 'Untitled', *SHARE Pregnancy and Infant Loss Support Newsletter*, vol. 8, no. 3, 1985, p. 1

Martin, E., *The Woman in the Body*, Boston, Beacon Press, 1987

McGinness, P., 'Reflections and Regrets', in Sister J.M. Lamb, (ed.), *Bittersweet. . .Hellogoodbye*, Section 1, Belleville, Ill., Charis Communications, 1988, pp. 27–8

Merchant, C., *The Death of Nature: Women, Ecology and the Scientific Revolution*, New York, Harper & Row, 1980

Murphy, J., 'Remembering. . .Looking Forward', *Unite Notes*, vol. 10, no. 2, 1991, pp. 2–3

Newsweek, 'What America Thinks of Itself', 10 December 1973, pp. 40–8

Office of Technology, *Infertility: Medical and Social Choices*, Washington D.C., Congress of the United States, 1988

Pellegrino, E.D., 'The Sociocultural Impact of Twentieth-century Therapeutics', in M.J. Vogel and C.E. Rosenberg (eds), *The Therapeutic Revolution: Essays in the Social History of American Medicine*, Philadelphia, University of Pennsylvania Press, 1979

Rothman, B.K., *Labor: Women and Power in the Birthplace*, New York, W.W. Norton, 1982

——, *Recreating Motherhood: Ideology and Technology in a Patriarchal Society*, New York, W. W. Norton & Company, 1989

Ruskin, J., *Modern Painters*, vol. III, New York, Lovell, Coryell & Company, 1890

Sandelowski, M., *With Child in Mind: Studies of the Personal Encounter with Infertility*, Philadelphia, University of Pennsylvania Press, 1993

Simonds, W. and Rothman, B.K., *Centuries of Solace: Expressions of Maternal Grief in Popular Literature*, Philadelphia, Temple University Press, 1992

Sontag, S., 'The Death of Tragedy', in *Against Interpretation and Other Essays*, New York, Anchor Books, 1966

Starr, P., *The Social Transformation of American Medicine: The Rise of a Sovereign Profession and the Making of a Vast Industry*, New York, Basic Books, 1982

Time, 'How a Dazzling Array of Medical Breakthroughs has made Curing Infertility more than just a Dream', 30 September 1991, pp. 56–63

Unknown, 'A Poem', in Sister J.M. Lamb (ed.) *Bittersweet. . . Hellogoodbye*, Section 4, Belleville, Ill., Charis Communications, 1988, p. 60

Wallace, M., 'Spring', *Unite Notes*, vol. 10, no. 2, 1991, p. 1

White, G.M., '"Remember Pearl Harbor": National Memory in the (Re)making', paper delivered at the annual meeting of the American Anthropological Association, 1992

Williams, R., *The Country and the City*, Oxford, Oxford University Press, 1973

—8—

Cultural Variations in South African Women's Experiences of Miscarriage: Implications for Clinical Care

Beverley Chalmers

Introduction

There is a truth universally acknowledged that every young wife who willingly embarks on a pregnancy must be in want of a successful outcome (with apologies and appreciation to Jane Austen). Unfortunately this is not always achieved and a surprisingly large number of women experience a miscarriage. Estimates of known pregnancy loss vary from a conservative one-in-six ratio (Chalmers and Hofmeyr, 1989) to a more radical one-in-three (Beck, Winkelgren, Quade and Wingert, 1988).

The medical management of miscarriage is complicated by the wide-ranging emotional reactions of both the women involved and their attending physicians. Common human failings, in particular of 'Pride' and 'Prejudice', occurring on both sides, tend to confound the management of this event. Women's pride in their pregnancies and in their ability to fulfil a woman's physiological role leads to disappointment, shock, shame, guilt, anger, helplessness, and feelings of inadequacy and a loss of social identity when pregnancy fails (Brown, 1979; Lewis, 1980; Herz, 1983; Graves, 1987; Chalmers, 1990a). Prejudice against admitting to such 'failure' may lead to an unwillingness to talk about the event and a consequent inability to mourn and thereby adjust to the experience.

On the attending physician's part, an unwillingness to deal with the difficult emotions being experienced by women and their families at this time may lead to an emphasis on the medical management of the event and a neglect of psychologically important issues. Pride, arising from the popular image of the physician's medical ability to save rather than lose lives, and prejudice against the unknown and daunting arena of the patient's emotional turmoil may well result in a reluctance to engage with this component of women's experiences. The latter characteristic of obstetricians, at least, appears to arise from a lack of training in the management of psychological issues in their professional education (Chalmers and McIntyre, 1991).

From a psychosocial perspective, three areas in the management of a spontaneous abortion which appear to have implications for the adjustment of women are addressed in this chapter. These are the events surrounding the physical experience of the fetal loss; the understanding, exploration and discussion of the possible cause of the miscarriage; and advice regarding the immediate and longer term future activities of the women during recovery from the experience and with regard to future pregnancies.

Much has been written about the typical emotional reactions of women to the loss of a wanted pregnancy (Brown, 1979; Lewis, 1980; Siebel and Graves, 1980; Stack, 1980; Borg and Lasker, 1982; Jiminez, 1982; Herz, 1983; Oakley, McPherson and Roberts, 1984; Pizer and Palinski, 1986; Graves, 1987; Leroy, 1988; Chalmers and Hofmeyr, 1989). As can be expected, feelings of failure, shame, anger, guilt, longing, dependency, insecurity and depression are possible and likely. Sometimes, in keeping with theories of the stress-reducing effects of social support, these feelings are alleviated by the availability of emotionally supportive companions either during the experience or in the days, weeks and months that follow (Kennell and Klauss, 1982). On other occasions the solicitations of others, though usually well meant, may be hurtful and serve to deepen the emotional trauma (Lewis, 1980; Chalmers and Hofmeyr, 1989). Who helps, what kind of support is valued and when it should be given are questions addressed in this chapter. Another central concern is the generalizability of womens' responses to pregnancy loss. The types of support available to women in different cultural groups, as well as those in various stages of urbanization or Westernization, could affect perceptions and reactions to loss. Major events such as life and death are universal: reactions to them may or may not be similar and may be influenced by the social, emotional, spiritual and cognitive resources available.

Much that has been written about miscarriage has been derived from explorations of Western women and health-care systems in the first world. Little, at least in terms of the psychosocial management of pregnancy loss, has been written about cultural influences on women's experiences. The present chapter therefore also explores the influence of cultural expectations on the management of miscarriage among four major cultural groups in South Africa. The groups examined represent a range of experiences from first-world, urbanized, White, Western approaches through to rural, developing community health-care services among African women. Asian (Indian) women as well as women of mixed cultural origin experiencing a predominantly first-world, Western approach to the management of miscarriage are also examined. While these four groups are representative of the major cultural groupings found in this country, they are by no means homogeneous groups and almost as much intra-group variation exists as variation between groups. For clarity, some basic characteristics of the groups studied are reported here.

Cultural Characteristics

The term 'African' as used here requires clarification. In southern Africa there are a number of peoples variously referred to as White, Black, 'Coloured', Indian or African. In current times, at least in southern Africa, the term 'Black' has come to describe all peoples who are not White, including Indian, 'Coloured' and African. The term African is commonly used to describe people of negroid lineage. 'African' as used here does not apply to all the peoples of the African continent. Rather, it is intended to refer to those people of the south of the African continent who share a philosophy of life termed 'African' as opposed to, for example, 'Western' or 'Eastern'.

The use of the term 'African' is further complicated by the complexities of the peoples to which it refers and requires illustration. In South Africa more than nine-tenths of these peoples are accounted for by two loose linguistic groupings: the Nguni and the Sotho/Tswana peoples. The two groups can be further broken down into dozens of sub-groups of related, traditional political units numbering from only a few hundreds to hundreds of thousands.

Many differences also exist among peoples commonly termed 'Indian' in South Africa. Based on religious, language and other distinctions, there are groups variously termed Hindu, Muslim and Christian in terms of religion, speaking Hindi, Tamil, Gujarati, Urdu, Telugu and other languages. According to Rosenthal (1976), approximately half the Indian population living in the study area are Muslims, a third Hindu and the remainder follow other religions such as Christianity. Most of the Muslims speak Gujarati, some Urdu. The Hindus are primarily associated with the Tamil, Hindi and Telugu languages, with a smaller proportion speaking Gujarati. The majority of Christians are converts from the Tamil Hindu group. Despite the apparent diversity inherent in these groupings, inter-religious and inter-linguistic marriages as well as the use of English as the official medium of school instruction have led to a decline in traditional language use and a mingling of customs (Rosenthal, 1976; Kuppusami, 1985).

Among White groups the major languages are English and Afrikaans and the primary religious groups are Christian (Catholic and Protestant) and Jewish.

People of mixed racial or cultural origin may present any combination of the above distinctions as well as characteristics of the African culture.

The complexity and variability of the samples studied raises issues of generalizability. Most groups, as is in fact universal, practice rituals to mark or celebrate similar events occurring throughout life. Some variation in how these events are recognized is, however, acknowledged.

Methods

Subjects

In all, 106 women who had experienced a first fetal loss before the 28th week of pregnancy within a year prior to the study were asked to participate. Women from four culturally different groups living in Johannesburg were sought out, namely, White (N=20), Asian (N=23), mixed culture (N=20) and African (N=43). African women were subdivided into those living in the urban area of Johannesburg (N=20) and those living in a rural area near Pietersburg in the Transvaal (N=23). The mean age of the total sample was 28.9 years and women had experienced an average of 2.7 pregnancies. The mean duration of pregnancy in the sample was 13.2 weeks.

Only women reporting miscarriages (that is spontaneous abortions) as opposed to induced abortions were asked to participate. Because abortion is illegal in South Africa except under restricted conditions such as rape, there is a possibility that some women who had managed to obtain 'illegal abortions' and who concealed this from the interviewers were included in the sample.

The pregnancy was reported as having been planned by 52.8 per cent of the sample (56 women) with 74.0 per cent (77) reporting being happy about it. This latter figure is relatively low and may reflect an element of self-induced abortion in the sample. On the other hand, many women report an initial disappointment with pregnancy which later converts to adjustment and satisfaction. Findings from similar White (Chalmers, 1979) and African (Chalmers, 1988) samples showed that 53 per cent and 54 per cent respectively of pregnancies had been planned, with 89 per cent of women in both cultural groups reporting being happy about their pregnancy when asked during the second or third trimester. In the present sample, and particularly in the light of the similarity in numbers of women reporting their pregnancies as planned as compared to previous research findings, pregnancy loss may have occurred before the conversion of unhappy reactions to more accepting ones. There were no differences between the groups with respect to either the planned nature of the pregnancy or women's feelings of happiness about it.

Procedure

Women were recruited into the study by obtaining the names of all women presenting at the Johannesburg, Coronation, Baragwanath, and Groothoek Hospitals and Morningside and Lenmed Clinics during the last few months of 1988 and the first few months of 1989 with a miscarriage. The hospitals are all state-owned health care services which, while now open to people of all cultural origins, were, at the time of the study, largely restricted to White, mixed origin, urban African and rural African groups respectively. The two clinics are privately owned institutions, with the Lenmed providing facilities for a primarily Asian population and the Morningside serving a multiracial but predominantly white group. Women were initially approached by means of a letter of explanation about the study and a request for an interview to be arranged telephonically shortly after. Interviews were conducted by qualified midwives of the same racial group as the woman at a time and place convenient for the woman; in all cases, this proved to be her own home. Although women were free to terminate the interview at any time should the recall of the events prove to be distressing, none did so. The study was approved by the Ethics Committee for Research into Human Subjects of the University of the Witwatersrand before its commencement.

Interviews were not conducted until at least twenty women in each group were obtained. Difficulties in obtaining each of the samples were experienced. The reasons for these difficulties differed in each group and reflect cross-cultural aspects of the experience of miscarriage. For instance, many in the White sample proved impossible to trace, as false names or addresses had been given to hospital authorities. These may reflect women who had attempted to obtain, or had obtained, 'illegal abortions' and who did not wish to be traced after discharge. Similar problems emerged with the mixed-origin sample.

Asian women, while more readily traceable, proved reluctant to be interviewed. Strong censure towards women who fail to bear live offspring is expressed and readily acknowledged by the Asian community, with resulting embarrassment and shame being experienced by women who miscarry. These women may have been hesitant to participate in the study. In addition, Asian women's roles are more restricted to the home and to their family commitments. In keeping with this, a number of the women's husbands refused to allow their wives to be interviewed. These problems were largely overcome through the employment of an approachable, respected and qualified midwife to conduct interviews. Nevertheless, the possibility of some bias, favouring the inclusion of more 'liberal'-minded Asian women in the final sample than is truly representative, must be considered.

Interviewing African women, particularly in rural areas, without readily available telephone or transport facilities provided a further difficulty. Fear of witchcraft proved to be a further problem. This concern existed among both urban (15 per cent; 3 women) and rural (21.7 per cent; 5) women. Miscarriage is traditionally associated with bewitchment by others (Chalmers, 1990b) and giving knowledge to others of one's pregnancy or even of pregnancy loss is avoided. As a visit from a health worker to one's home is an event of communal interest to, and readily observable by, the surrounding villagers or neighbours, caution regarding the reason for the visit had to be adopted until such time as the target woman could be approached in private. In addition, it was not always certain that family members were aware of the recent miscarriage, and care was taken by the interviewer not to reveal this knowledge to others. To overcome these difficulties, the visit to the home was made part of a general health-care visit to the family and to any other neighbours who needed nursing advice at the same time. In many instances the interviewer (a qualified nurse and midwife) was required to administer health advice to everyone in the area for a day or even more before obtaining an opportunity to address the issue of miscarriage with the woman selected for interview.

Interviews were conducted following a standard sixty-item interview schedule exploring psychosocial issues relating to miscarriage. The interview schedule was assessed by various professionals, including obstetricians, psychologists and childbirth educators, as well as by mothers before use. All women were interviewed according to the same schedule, which was fixed, with no 'open-ended' items being included. Possible answers were not suggested to the women; rather, their own responses were coded according to pre-determined categories. Any deviations from these categories were recorded in full and coded later. A few additional questions relating to beliefs in witchcraft as they pertained to miscarriages were asked of African women only. Copies of the interview schedule are available from the author.

Statistical Analyses

All statistical analyses of difference between groups were conducted using a Likelihood Ratio Chi Square for comparison of K independent samples. Issues with regard to the adequacy of this test in the case of small samples, which sometimes occurred in the sub-sample analyses in this study, have not yet been fully resolved, although Feinberg (1977) suggests that this test should still be applied. Certainly for the size of the total sample considered here (N=106), the chi square assumption appears reasonable. N has not been reported in the text for each chi square analysis. This was not deemed essential to the interpretation of p values, as N is subsumed in the calculation of chi square. Only group differences that are significant at the 1 per cent level ($p<0.01$) are reported in the text.

Results

Here, the results will be examined in a number of sections covering biographical characteristics of the sample; the physical experience of miscarriage; the issue of causality; the behavioural implications of miscarriage during recovery and after; the emotions experienced by women and their partners; the sources and effectiveness of available social support; and the women's ability to cope with their loss experiences.

Biographical Characteristics of the Sample

There were significant differences in marital status between the groups, reflecting current differences in the society. Of the total sample, 59.4 per cent (63 women) were married, 1.9 per cent (2 women) were divorced, 2.8 per cent (3 women) were separated, 25.5 per cent (27 women) had never been married and were either living alone or with their parents, and 10.4 per cent (11 women) had never been married but were living with their partner. The majority of White and Asian women were married, while relatively high numbers of mixed origin and African women had never been married. Educational levels also differed between the groups, reflecting the impact of apartheid as well as the commonly accepted Asian bias against the higher education of women. The majority of White women had completed 12 years of schooling and 88.9 per cent (16 women) had obtained post-school education. Amongst Asian women, 52.6 per cent (10 women) had completed their schooling, with only one woman receiving post-school training. Fewer mixed-origin (20 per cent; 4 women), urban African (25 per cent; 5 women) and rural African (27.3 per cent; 6 women) had completed school, with a small number achieving some post-school education (mixed-origin 0; urban African, 2 women; rural African, 1 woman).

While occupational activities also varied across the sample, there appeared to be greater similarities between cultural groups on this issue. Similar numbers of White, Asian or mixed origin women described themselves as either housewives (White 30 per cent; 6 women: Asian 34.8 per cent; 8 women: and mixed origin 26.3 per cent; 5 women) or clerical workers (White 30 per cent; 6 women: Asian 30.4 per cent; 7 women: and mixed-origin 21.1 per cent; 4 women). Less than 13 per cent of African women (3) fell into these categories. Among African women unemployment was, however, reported as high (urban 50 per cent; 10 women: rural 39.1 per cent; 9 women), with 21.1 per cent of mixed-origin women (4 women) regarding themselves as unemployed. Only one Asian woman and none of the White women reported being unemployed. When women did work outside the home, occupations reported (in addition to clerical positions) were teaching, professional (for example nursing), and factory (all occurring in less than 13 per cent of the sample (3 women) in any one category).

The Physical Experience of Miscarriage

While the average pregnancy ended at 13.2 weeks, women reported realizing that something was wrong approximately one week earlier than this, at 12.9 weeks on average. In general White (X=9.8 weeks) and Asian (X=11.9 weeks) women miscarried earlier than mixed-origin (X=14.5 weeks), urban African (X=14.2 weeks) and rural African women (X=15.3 weeks). It is not known whether these differences reflect medical variations between cultural groups. It is, however, more likely that cross-cultural differences in women's reactions to events, and the varying resources available to physicians assisting the different groups, contributed to the differences observed.

The most commonly reported signs of an impending complication were bleeding (71.1 per cent; 76 women) and pain (55.7 per cent; 59 women). Having a 'feeling' that something was wrong was reported by 46.2 per cent (49 women) of the total sample, with no fetal heart (23.6 per cent; 25 women) and no movement (17.9 per cent; 19 women) being diagnosed quite often. Significant differences between the groups regarding the signs of an impending problem were obtained. Bleeding was reported most often by urban African women (90 per cent; 19 women) and least often by rural African women (52.2 per cent; 12 women). Pain was regarded as symptomatic of problems by more urban African (75 per cent; 15 women), rural African (69.6 per cent; 16 women) and mixed-origin (65 per cent; 13 women) than Asian (47.8 per cent; 11 women) or White women (20.0 per cent; 4 women). Interestingly all African women reported having a 'feeling' that something was wrong, while only 2 Asian women, 4 White women and none of the mixed-origin women admitted to this.

In general most women (83.3 per cent; 75 women) told a close family member such as their partner about their suspicions on the same day rather than a few days later. The exceptions to this were some urban (26.3 per cent; 5 women) and rural (42.9 per cent; 5 women) African women, who were possibly unable to communicate with their partners or other family through a lack of communication facilities. While most women consulted their doctors on the same day (73.2 per cent; 71 women), both rural (52.2 per cent; 12 women) and urban (60 per cent; 12 women) African groups as well as White women (64.3 per cent; 9 women) were slower to communicate with their physicians than either Asian (95.2 per cent; 20 women) or mixed-origin women (94.7 per cent; 18 women).

For some women (13.3 per cent; 14 women), mostly Asian (34.8 per cent; 8 women) and White (15.8 per cent; 3 women), the pregnancy finally terminated at home. By far the majority of women experienced a dilatation of the cervix and curettage of the uterine contents (D & C) preceded by discomfort or other signs (58.1 per cent; 61 women), while 22.9 per cent (24 women) had D & C's without obvious previous symptomatology.

Almost half the women (47) saw the expelled fetus. Most of these women reported seeing 'clots of blood' or 'tissue' (28 women) while some reported seeing fully formed fetuses (19 women). About half the women who did see the dispelled products were sorry to have done so (21 women), but 16 were pleased. The appearance of the delivery seems to have contributed to women's reactions to the sight, with significantly more women expressing contentment with seeing a fully formed fetus than expelled tissue. It must be noted that only womens' perceptions of the dispelled products of conception were studied: actual medical diagnoses, for example, of a blighted ovum, were not available. While for most women the pregnancy ended too early to tell the baby's gender (52.4 per cent; 55 women) a small number (17.1 per cent; 18 women) of women of mostly African origin (15 women) who generally miscarried later were able to learn the sex of the fetus. In contrast, 59.2 per cent of women (61) expressed a strong need to know their baby's gender and others would quite like to have known (11.7 per cent; 12 women). This need was greatest for urban African women (95 per cent; 19 women) and to a lesser extent for rural African (86.9 per cent; 20 women), mixed-origin (63.1 per cent; 12 women) and Asian women (65.2 per cent; 15 women). Interestingly only 3 White women expressed a strong desire to know their baby's gender, while 4 more were quite interested.

Women were also asked about their reactions to the use of the medical term 'spontaneous abortion'. While 24.5 per cent (25 women) expressed a preference for it, 31.4 per cent (32 women) reported an aversion to it because of its connotations of an induced abortion. A further 36.3 per cent (37 women), however, were indifferent to its use. Significant inter-group differences regarding this issue did arise, with both urban (60 per cent; 12 women) and rural (57.1 per cent; 12 women) African women preferring the medical term and many mixed-origin women (45 per cent; 9 women) disliking it. Many White (61.1 per cent; 11 women), Asian (60.9 per cent; 14 women) and mixed-origin (55 per cent; 11) women expressed indifference to its use.

Causality

Cross-cultural differences occurred in explanations given by the women. Most women (70 per cent; 70 women) in all groups and all urban African women reported not knowing why the miscarriage had occurred. Some ascribed the cause to hard work (8 per cent; 8 women) or to stress (6 per cent; 6 women). Almost a quarter of the White sample (23.5 per cent; 4 women) reported the cause as a blighted ovum and others to a septic intra-uterine device (11.8 per cent; 2 women). None of the women in the remaining groups did so.

According to most women, reasons for the miscarriage were not often given by the doctor attending them (67 per cent; 69 women), although more mixed-origin (68.4 per cent; 13 women), Asian (73.9 per cent; 17 women) and urban African women (95 per cent; 19 women) were not given an explanation than rural African (13.6 per cent; 14 women) or White women (33.3 per cent; 6 women). Reasons given differed with the various groups. Reasons may reflect reality, physicians' perceptions of what women would find acceptable, or the reasons available for diagnosis. The most commonly reported reason given to White women was a blighted ovum (27.8 per cent; 5 women) or a chromosomal abnormality (16.7 per cent; 3 women). The latter reason was also given to two women of mixed-origin while two Asian women were told that the loss was due to abnormality and two others that it was due to their 'psychological imbalance'. The one urban African woman who was given an explanation was told that her miscarriage was due to weak or thin blood. Some rural African women were also offered this explanation (3 women) as well as 'ectopic pregnancies' (4 women) and an 'open' or 'weak' uterus (1 woman). For many women (67.4 per cent; 33 women), particularly White women (76.5 per cent; 13 women), the reason given by the doctor was acceptable. The physicians' actual diagnosis of aetiology is not known; only womens' reports of the reasons given to them for their miscarriages were available for analysis.

Almost all women in all groups wished to know the cause of their miscarriage (88.5 per cent; 85 women). About a quarter (23.8 per cent; 25 women) blamed themselves for the loss, although cross-cultural differences were evident. Whites, mixed-origin women and Asians were more likely to blame themselves, with African women doing so far less often (15 per cent; 3 urban women) or not at all (rural).

Medical exploration for a cause was done infrequently, except for White women (55 per cent; 11 women). Figures obtained were distorted by the reply from 75 per cent (15 women) of the urban African sample that tests (in reality routine haemoglobin tests) had been performed to ascertain causality. This finding reveals a lack of any clear explanation for procedures being given to some women. Most women expressed a wish for tests for causality to be performed (81.5 per cent; 58 women).

Some African women in both groups had consulted a traditional healer (*sangoma*) to ascertain the cause of their loss. Of the 20 per cent of urban women (four) who sought this advice, two were told the cause was ancestral displeasure and the other two that the miscarriage was due to bewitching by other persons. Of the rural African women who consulted a *sangoma*, one was told that the herbal medication she had taken during pregnancy (*isihlambezo*) was bewitched, another woman that the placenta from a previous birth had fallen into the wrong hands and had been used to cause her or her baby harm, and the remaining woman that she had revealed her pregnancy to others too early, leading to misuse of this information. All these reasons are in keeping with traditional beliefs (Chalmers, 1990b).

Treatments prescribed by *sangoma*s for the prevention of future losses included traditional medicines, rituals to appease the ancestors and bodily massage. Rural women also reported receiving other sorts of ritual treatment.

Behavioural Implications of Miscarriage

The discussion of a number of topics relating to behavioural changes following the miscarriage was considered desirable by almost all women. In reality, rather few women had had discussions on these issues with their doctor. The topics explored, ratings of their desirability and actual discussion rates are given in Table 8.1.

Topics raised most often were those relating to the duration of bleeding, the resumption of intercourse, the type of contraceptive to use and the possibility of falling pregnant again. Discussed less often were issues of when to bath again, whether breast milk would be produced and the use of tampons.

Table 8.1. Frequency and desirability of discussion topics

Topics	Total	White	Coloured	Asian	Urb.Afr	Rur.Afr	P
When to plan another pregnancy	49.5(51)	83.3(15)	36.8(7)	56.5(13)	55.0(11)	21.7(5)	0.001
Desirability of discussion	99.0(91)	100.0(13)	100.0(13)	95.7(22)	100.0(20)	100.0(23)	NS
Duration of bleeding	46.6(48)	84.2(16)	15.8(3)	59.1(13)	55.0(11)	21.7(5)	0.0001
Desirability of discussion	98.0(96)	92.3(12)	100.0(19)	95.7(22)	100.0(20)	100.0(23)	NS
Resumption of intercourse	44.2(46)	79.0(15)	15.8(3)	43.5(10)	55.0(11)	30.4(7)	0.001
Desirability of discussion	93.9(93)	85.7(12)	94.7(18)	91.3(21)	100.0(20)	95.7(22)	NS
Contraceptive use	40.4(42)	42.1(8)	31.6(6)	43.5(10)	55.0(11)	30.4(7)	NS
Desirability of discussion	93.9(93)	71.4(10)	94.7(18)	95.7(22)	100.0(20)	100.0(23)	0.01
Possibility of pregnancy	51.5(53)	77.8(14)	26.3(5)	78.3(18)	55.0(11)	21.7(5)	0.0001
Desirability of discussion	100.0(96)	100.0(12)	100.0(19)	100.0(22)	100.0(20)	100.0(23)	NS
Use of tampons	21.8(22)	23.5(4)	0	9.1(2)	55.0(11)	21.7(5)	0.04
Desirability of discussion	78.6(77)	28.6(4)	79.0(15)	68.2(15)	100.0(20)	100.0(23)	0.0001
Production of breast milk	9.1(30)	11.1(2)	26.3(5)	30.4(7)	55.0(11)	21.7(5)	0.04
Desirability of discussion	90.8(89)	50.0(7)	100.0(19)	90.9(20)	100.0(20)	100.0(23)	0.0001
Bathing	28.0(28)	27.8(5)	10.5(2)	25.0(5)	55.0(11)	21.7(5)	0.03
Desirability of discussion	78.2(79)	25.0(4)	89.5(17)	65.2(15)	100.0(20)	100.0(23)	NS

Percentages of women who discussed each topic and considered it desirable (N in brackets). Final column gives probability values for chi square tests (NS: not significant)

Significant differences occurred between groups on the frequency with which various topics were discussed (see Table 8.1). The duration of bleeding, when to plan another pregnancy, when to resume intercourse, what contraceptive to use and the possibility of conceiving again were discussed with White women most often and with rural African and mixed-origin women least often.

Emotional Reactions

Thirty-seven possible emotional reactions were explored. The most commonly reported feelings (occurring in at least a third of the sample) were disappointment (41.5 per cent; 44 women), loss (34.9 per cent; 37 women) and sadness (33 per cent; 35 women). Feelings also expressed quite often were a longing for a baby (27.4 per cent; 29 women), that others did not understand one's feelings (26.4 per cent; 28 women), feeling unable to express one's grief (23.6 per cent; 25 women), needing to have another baby quickly (23.6 per cent; 25 women) and bitterness (22.6 per cent; 24 women). Noticeable, however, is the lack of unanimity in the feelings experienced. This relatively low per centage of congruence suggests either a wide range of emotional reactions to miscarriage among women or a differential ability to admit to such feelings.

Cross-cultural analysis of differences in the feelings experienced by women supports the argument that women's reactions to a pregnancy loss differ widely between cultural groups. There were significant differences between the five groups studied with regard to each of the thirty-seven different emotional reactions explored. The emotional reactions most common among White women were general feelings of anxiety and nervousness (5 women), disappointment (8 women), asking 'Why Me?' (8 women) and a feeling of emptiness (7 women). Asian and mixed-origin women admitted to extremely few emotional reactions and these often differed from those experienced by White women. Mixed-origin women occasionally admitted to disappointment (7 women).

In contrast, African women, whether urban or rural dwellers, admitted experiencing many emotions. At least one-third of both groups of African women reported feeling sad, bitter, disappointed, a feeling of loss, a wish to avoid another pregnancy in the near future, an inability to express their grief, disbelief, a need to be loved, a feeling that others did not understand them and a longing for a baby. Interestingly, more rural African women reported feelings of acceptance (8 women) than any other group of women. Almost all women of all cultural groups (94.2 per cent; 97 women) reported not ever thinking, prior to the event, that they might experience a miscarriage. In agreement with this finding, very few women admitted to having read books (4 women) or magazine articles on pregnancy loss (5 women) before their miscarriage. In fact, most women reported never having read any books (65.7 per cent; 67 women) or magazine articles (57.3 per cent; 59 women) on miscarriage either before or after their experience. There were no cross-cultural differences regarding the reading of books. White women, however, reported reading magazine articles on miscarriage more often than women in the remaining groups. These findings suggest that cultural differences in attitudes occur towards miscarriages and to the expression of feelings surrounding the event.

Women were asked whether their partners had experienced feelings as, more, or less intensely than themselves. Almost half the total sample reported that their partners had had similarly intense feelings, while about a quarter were reported as having even more intense feelings, and the remainder somewhat less. There were no cultural differences with regard to this issue. The reasons commonly given for this difference were that the partner was more pleased than themselves about the pregnancy (5 mixed-origin women: 10 rural African women), or that he hid his feelings in order to provide support for the woman (5 mixed-origin women).

Social Support

There were significant cross-cultural differences in the amount of time spent by doctors or nurses discussing the miscarriage with the women either before or after it occurred (see Table 8.2).

In contrast to expectations, and with the exception of the rural African women, nurses were more likely than doctors to spend no time at all with women both before and after the loss. Differences between the groups were, however, most noticeable with regard to the opposite end of the time-scale. While no doctors or nurses spent more than an hour with urban or rural African women, 61.1 per cent (11 women) of both categories of health-care professional spent this length of time with mixed-origin women before the final stages of the miscarriage and almost as many (doctors: 52.7 per cent; 10 women: and nurses: 63.1 per cent; 12 women) talked with women after the event. White women as well as both urban and rural African women were likely to obtain little support from nurses before the loss, with this trend continuing for White women into the post-miscarriage stage. Both groups of African women were likely to receive little emotional support from doctors either before or after the event. Differences probably reflect variations in hospital policies regarding the counselling of women after loss.

Table 8.2. Percentage time spent by health-care professionals discussing the miscarriage before and after it occurred*

		Total		White		Coloured		Asian		Urb. Afr		Rur. Afr.	
		Dr	Ns	Dr	Ns	Dr	Ns	Dr	Ns	Dr	Ns	Dr	Ns
Before													
No time	%	33.3	52.5	22.2	70.6	0	0	17.4	26.1	50.0	83.3	69.6	82.6
At all	N	34	52	4	12	0	0	4	6	10	15	16	19
Less than	%	30.4	18.2	44.4	5.9	11.1	16.7	30.4	34.8	45.0	16.7	21.7	13.0
1 hour	N	31	18	8	1	2	3	7	8	9	3	5	3
About	%	16.7	13.1	16.7	17.7	27.8	22.2	26.1	21.7	5.0	0	8.7	4.4
1 hour	N	17	13	3	3	5	4	6	5	1	0	2	1
More than	%	19.6	16.2	16.7	5.8	61.1	61.1	32.1	17.4	0	0	0	0
1 hour	N	20	16	3	1	11	11	6	4	0	0	0	0
After													
No time	%	28.2	38.2	10.5	70.6	0	0	4.4	21.7	73.7	40.0	52.2	60.9
At all	N	29	39	2	12	0	0	1	5	14	8	12	14
Lessthan	%	32.0	29.4	47.4	11.8	10.5	15.8	43.5	30.4	26.3	60.0	30.4	26.1
1 hour	N	33	30	9	2	2	3	10	7	5	12	7	6
About	%	23.3	14.7	31.6	11.8	36.8	21.1	30.4	26.1	0	0	17.4	13.0
1 hour	N	24	15	6	2	7	4	7	6	0	0	4	3
More than	%	16.5	17.7	10.5	5.8	52.7	63.1	21.7	21.8	0	0	0	0
1 hour	N	17	18	2	1	10	12	5	5	0	0	0	0

* All cross-cultural comparisons significant at $p<0.0001$

While the actual presence of a supportive person is important, the perceived helpfulness of this person may play a larger role in assisting one to cope with an event of this nature (Chalmers, 1979). Despite the low proportion of time spent with most groups of women by health care professionals, feelings of satisfaction with the time spent with them were expressed by all except rural African women (see Table 8.3). Nevertheless, many women would have appreciated more time being spent with them by doctors than by nurses, despite the finding that doctors did in fact spend more time with them. Rural African women expressed by far the most dissatisfaction with the time spent with them by both kinds of professionals as well as more desire for additional time to be devoted to them (Table 8.3).

Table 8.3. Perceptions of time spent with women by health-care professionals before and after their miscarriage

Percentages of women satisfied with time spent with them*

Professional		Total	White	Coloured	Asian	Urb. Afr.	Rural Afr.
Doctor:	%	72.4	62.4	84.2	77.3	100.0	37.5
	N	63	13	16	17	11	6
Nurses:	%	67.5	53.3	88.2	69.6	100.0	25.0
	N	52	8	15	16	10	3

Percentage of women who would have appreciated more time being spent with them*

Professional		Total		White		Coloured		Asian		Urb. Afr.		Rural Afr.	
		Before	After	B.	A.	B.	A.	B.	A.	B.	A.	B.	A.
Doctor	%	46.2	46.9	38.5	37.5	16.7	21.1	36.4	40.9	50.0	47.1	81.1	81.1
	N	56	45	15	6	6	4	8	9	9	8	18	18
Nurses	%	44.4	44.2	30.0	50.0	11.1	10.5	33.3	33.3	36.4	26.3	95.2	95.5
	N	36	42	3	7	2	2	7	7	4	5	20	21

* All cross-cultural comparisons significant at $p<.0001$

Husbands (59.2 per cent; 58 women) and mothers (59.1 per cent; 52 women) were rated as extremely supportive in the weeks following the miscarriage (see Table 8.4). Husbands were seen as more supportive by both White (70 per cent; 14 women) and urban African women (70 per cent; 14 women), while mothers were rated particularly highly by rural African women (82.6 per cent; 19 women). Common to all groups, however, were the low per centages of women who rated members of the health-care professions as extremely supportive in the weeks after the miscarriage.

Table 8.4. Sources of support in the weeks after the miscarriage

	Percentage rated as 'extremely' supportive*						
	Total	White	Coloured	Asian	Urban Afr.	Rural Afr.	P
Husband	59.2(58)	70.0(14)	56.3(9)	54.6(12)	70.0(14)	45.0(9)	NS
Mother	59.1(52)	61.1(11)	36.4(4)	42.1(8)	58.8(10)	82.6(19)	NS
Other family	26.8(15)	33.3(2)	100.0(3)	44.4(4)	12.5(2)	18.2(4)	<.008
Sibling	80.0(12)	83.3(5)	83.3(5)	100.0(1)	50.0(1)	0(0)	NS
In-laws	50.0(8)	66.7(4)	37.5(3)	50.0(1)	0(0)	0(0)	NS
Obstetrician	12.7(9)	22.2(4)	9.1(1)	21.1(4)	0(0)	0(0)	NS
General Practitioner	19.1(4)	25.0(2)	0(0)	25.0(2)	0(0)	0(0)	NS
Other medical professions	14.3(2)	50.0(2)	0(0)	0(0)	0(0)	0(0)	-
Nurses	7.4(5)	35.7(5)	0(0)	0(0)	0(0)	0(0)	-
Friends	20.8(15)	55.6(10)	0(0)	29.4(5)	0(0)	0(0)	.0001
Religious	6.3(1)	0(0)	20.0(1)	0(0)	0(0)	0(0)	-

* (N in brackets)
Final column gives P values for chi square tests (NS: not significant)

Coping After the Loss

After the miscarriage, women found it hard to cope with feeling generally emotional (41.9 per cent; 41 women), with their partner's feelings (36.3 per cent; 37 women), with not knowing the cause of the miscarriage (35.7 per cent; 35 women) and with fearing a repeat experience (35 per cent; 35 women). Some cross-cultural differences in perceived difficulties with coping did emerge, although no clear patterns of response within the sub-groups were evident.

It is often suggested that well-intentioned but nevertheless hurtful statements by others make coping with a miscarriage experience difficult (Lewis, 1980; Chalmers and Hofmeyr, 1989). Findings suggest that this occurs more often among White and Asian women than in the other groups studied. All White women and the majority of Asian women (65.2 per cent; 15 women) were told not to worry, as they could have another baby. White women were also advised not to feel bad, as they already had other children (66.7 per cent; 18 women). White women felt that these statements were made through a lack of understanding in others (71.1 per cent; 10 women) and that they were inconsiderate (60 per cent; 6 women). In contrast, half (9 women) of the Asian women felt encouraged by such comments.

Women's concerns about their miscarriage experience clearly persist for some time after the event. The majority of women reported being either excessively (24.8 per cent; 26 women) or quite (51.4 per cent; 54 women) concerned about pregnancy since the miscarriage. Events surrounding their miscarriage are described as exceptionally clearly (47.2 per cent; 50 women) or quite clearly (45.3 per cent; 48 women) recalled. As many as 26.4 per cent (28 women) reported dreaming about their miscarriage, although this occurred more often among White and Asian women. The majority of women (81.8 per cent; 81 women) admitted needing someone to talk to about their experience, and practically all (94.9 per cent; 93 women) reported having a confidant available.

While some women did report emotional 'recovery' from the miscarriage within two (14.3 per cent; 14 women) or four (11.2 per cent; 11 women) weeks of it, more (39.8 per cent; 39 women) reported still not having recovered over three months later. Many White (9 women), mixed-origin (6 women) and Asian (5) women who worked returned to work within one week of the miscarriage but none of the African women returned to work before two weeks had elapsed, probably in accordance with cultural taboos (Chalmers, 1990b). For most women who worked, going back to work made them feel better (76.1 per cent; 35 women).

Women were asked what they thought would have made it easier for them to cope with their loss. Although cross-cultural differences emerged, all women, except the urban African group, regarded knowing the cause of the miscarriage as the most important factor in easing their adjustment. Additional desires included having more supportive doctors (3 White women), taking it easy (3 urban African women) and having a loving and supportive husband (5 Asian women).

Discussion

The findings presented suggest that the management of a miscarriage could be enhanced by attention to psychosocial issues. In particular, discussions of causality and the behavioural changes concomitant with a miscarriage are valued by women. The apparent hesitancy of doctors in discussing such topics is in keeping with findings from recent research into stresses experienced by obstetricians, which revealed difficulties in handling issues relating to psychosocial matters (Hayward and Chalmers, 1990). Such difficulties appear to stem from a lack of medical training in dealing with this aspect of women's experiences.

Causality, and the lack of information about it in particular, results in anxiety for women. Most women in this study did not know the reason for their miscarriage. While this is not unreasonable, as cause is usually difficult to determine, as many as half the women claimed that this was not even discussed. White women were given possible reasons for their pregnancy failure most often. Mixed-origin and White women were given 'medical' reasons most often (for example, blighted ovum, chromosomal abnormality) and expressed most acceptance of these reasons. Other groups were given some 'medical' reasons as well as some rather nebulous reasons (for example, mental imbalance, weak blood) more often and expressed least satisfaction with this type of explanation. It appears that accuracy of information is valued.

Discussion of behavioural changes linked to the current miscarriage experience as well as planning for future pregnancies was desired by women far more often than it was actually received. Cultural differences in discussion frequency occurred, with White women receiving most benefits and rural African and mixed-origin women having discussions of this nature least often. While language barriers may have been an issue, particularly with regard to rural African women, this probably did not apply to mixed-origin women. The different educational backgrounds of women in the groups studied might have influenced the nature and depth of discussion entered into with them by doctors. The findings of this study, however, suggest that doctors need to reassess the quality of information given to women of all cultural groups regarding their miscarriage.

There is some question in clinical practice as to whether or not to show women the expelled fetus. The findings of this study suggest that women who see a fully formed fetus regard this positively in retrospect. If the conceptus resembles a collection of tissue, then women tend to regret having seen it.

A unique cultural difference emerged from this study. All African women, without exception, expressed a 'feeling' that something was wrong with their pregnancies before the onset of any obvious symptoms. Few women in any of the other groups did so. It has been suggested that in Africa, in contrast to the West, there is a greater subjective awareness of bodily processes (Holdstock, 1981; Chalmers, 1990b). Western women, who rely largely on physiological and biological explanations, may relegate feelings about well-being to the background. While the retrospective nature of this study may have influenced the recall or reporting of such issues, it is unlikely to have done so differentially between the groups.

In the interpretation of the findings of this study, it must be remembered that sub-sample sizes were often small and that interpretations must be made with caution. Nevertheless the findings suggest that while most women experience the unwanted loss of a pregnancy with difficulty, as could be expected, cultural differences do influence the specific reactions and experiences of women. The wide range of feelings expressed by women indicate the very different emotional reactions that can occur.

Alternatively, cultural differences in the ability to express, rather than to experience, feelings may have occurred. The results of this study suggest that at least Asian and mixed-origin women experienced greater difficulty admitting to feelings than women in other groups. In contrast, African women reported many more emotional reactions than women of other cultural groups. Whether this freedom to express disappointment, frustration and grief is causally related to the greater frequency of feelings of acceptance of the miscarriage amongst African women remains to be explored further. It is, however, in keeping with psychotherapeutic principles.

In contrast to previous research on health-care professionals' roles (Hayward and Chalmers, 1990), an examination of the support received from these sources in this study revealed that doctors were far more helpful than nurses. Rural African women were least satisfied with the support received from doctors and nurses.

Comments made by others, often with good intentions, may actually be hurtful. The findings suggest, however, that care must be taken not to generalize the possible effects of these comments across cultural groups, since while some are seen as hurtful by women of one cultural group, they may be viewed as encouraging by women of another. This finding in particular, as well as the wide variations evident in women's responses to miscarriage in this study, highlight the importance of providing social support that is appropriate to the cultural group in question. Care must be taken not to generalize concepts obtained from Western samples to all other groups. While this point has been made frequently in social science literature, it bears stressing, due to the difficulties involved in its practical implementation.

It is possible that other psychosocial factors, not explored in this study, could influence womens' perceptions of their miscarriage experiences. Certainly the influence of having other children should be explored. In the present study all women experienced an early pregnancy loss (on average at 13.2 weeks), all were interviewed within a few months of this experience and none had had a previous miscarriage. In addition, womens' reactions were no doubt influenced by availability of and access to medical care, as well as by their attitudes to such care. Discrepancies in this regard, in the various cultural groups in Southern Africa, are well known (Chalmers, 1990b). Despite these differences, the findings of this study point to the greater need for medical professionals to recognize and attend to the psychosocial needs of women during their care. While this need is common to all women, regardless of racial orientation, specific preferences with regard to aspects of their care did occur among the various groups studied. These findings are of importance for the multivariate, multi-level health-care approach being proposed for the new South Africa (Chalmers, 1990b).

Implications for Clinical Care

Some years ago, Beard, Pinker and Mowbray (1985) appealed for attention to be directed to the psychological meaning of the term 'abortion' for mothers who experience a pregnancy loss without wanting it. It appears that writers and researchers took heed of this appeal. A count of the titles of papers published in the *British Journal of Obstetrics and Gynaecology* referring to unwanted early pregnancy loss in 1981–2 and 1989–90 revealed a change in the terminology used before and after this editorial (Chalmers, 1992). While almost all the papers at the start of the decade used the term 'abortion' in their titles, none of those published later did so.

While this change in orientation is welcome, particularly from a psychological perspective, it may be limited in its value to some culturally distinct groups of women. The present research indicates that mothers from different cultural backgrounds are not equally concerned about medical terminology, with its possible negative emotional overtones. The results suggest that women express mixed views regarding their preferences for terminology, with almost equal numbers being opposed to, in agreement with and indifferent to the formal term 'spontaneous abortion'. Cultural differences occurred in this regard, with more African women preferring the medical term, more mixed-origin women disliking it, and White and Asian women being fairly indifferent to its use.

Research and comment on this issue has concentrated on the use of the term 'abortion' for describing early pregnancy loss. There are, however, other phrases used when caring for women who lose babies which may also have emotionally negative connotations. Terms such as 'failed pregnancy', 'incompetent cervix', 'inadequate germ plasm', 'abnormal chromosomal material' and 'blighted ovum' (not sperm) are reasonably commonly used. While these have objective medical meanings for the physician, their meaning for the mother may be different. Women may focus on the words 'failed, incompetent, inadequate, abnormal' and 'blighted', all of which are part of everyday English, and apply them not to their physiological functioning but to themselves as persons. Feelings of failure, shame, guilt, insecurity and depression are recognized reactions to an unwanted miscarriage (Oakley et al., 1984; Pizer and Palinski, 1986; Graves, 1987; Leroy,

1988). The use of medical terminology which carries negative connotations for the lay person may contribute to the development of negative self-perceptions, particularly in those already predisposed to think ill of their miscarriage experience.

Womens' difficulties in adjusting to an unwanted loss of a pregnancy (Oakley et al., 1984; Chalmers and Hofmeyr, 1989) may be compounded by the procedure followed with regard to the lost baby. The medical and nursing professions commonly refer to the 'products of conception'. Women, in contrast, tend to think of their loss as a 'baby'. In addition, the outcome of the pregnancy is not usually buried but 'disposed of' by sluicing or incineration. Contradictions such as these emphasize a discrepancy between some womens' views of their pregnancy loss and those of the professionals attending them: for the women the pregnancy is real and they may wish for the lost baby to be buried, while for the medical profession the conceptus does not warrant such 'human' recognition.

It is possible that recent developments in technology may have exacerbated the difficulty of adjusting to an early pregnancy loss. In societies such as the Zulu (Larsen, Msane and Monkhe, 1983), women traditionally did not acknowledge conception until four to six months into pregnancy. Today women are aware of their pregnancies far earlier, with a mean knowledge of gestational age occurring at 2.1 months among white South African women (Chalmers, 1984). This trend towards earlier acknowledgement of conception follows the encouragement of women to seek antenatal care earlier. In addition the application of technology, like sonography, allows for early diagnosis of conception. The psychological consequences of these medical developments may well be an earlier identification with the 'baby' on the mother's or parents' parts, facilitated by visual and auditory images of the unborn baby. It would not be unreasonable to hypothesize, therefore, that loss of a baby might result in disappointment even if it occurs early in the pregnancy.

Many women in the present study reported not having recovered emotionally from their miscarriage experience months after the event. The absence of clear 'rites of passage' may contribute to this inability to adjust. The lack of recognition of the loss as a baby, particularly if the miscarriage takes place in very early pregnancy; the absence of any burial ceremony to mark the recognition of the lost life; the inability to identify any place of remembrance, such as a burial site; the lack of social recognition of the woman as a mother, even if only of a baby that has died, and the expectation that mourning is not needed or is inappropriate in the event of early pregnancy loss, all may make mourning more difficult.

Recent recommendations regarding the management of a stillbirth recognize the importance of having something to remember about the baby to facilitate mourning and acceptance of the experience (Barr 1989; Bourne & Lewis 1991). Simply seeing and holding the baby at birth helps: this is further aided by having a photograph or sonography print for remembrance. It may be that these ideas can be applied to earlier pregnancy loss as well, particularly when this loss is stressful to the woman. The present research indicates that seeing the outcome of the early pregnancy loss, so long as this resembles a fetus and not a mass of tissue, is regarded positively by the women. Further research is needed to confirm the possible benefit of this approach among women of differing cultures.

Changes in practice, including those of language and behaviour, are worthy of consideration in the process of providing medical and emotional care for women who miscarry unwillingly. Variations in cross-cultural perceptions, as well as individual differences in the meaning of a miscarriage experience, must always be acknowledged, explored and understood when caring for the individual woman.

Acknowledgements

The financial assistance of the Institute for Research and Development of the Human Sciences Research Council towards this research is hereby acknowledged. The opinions expressed in this publication and conclusions arrived at are those of the author and do not necessarily represent the views of the Institute for Research Development or the Human Sciences Research Council.

The assistance and co-operation of the hospital authorities of the Johannesburg Hospital, Baragwanath Hospital, Groothoek Hospital, Coronation Hospital, Lenmed Clinic and Morningside Clinic in obtaining subjects for this study is gratefully acknowledged, as is the assistance of Sisters Stephanie Oboler, Francis Malatji, Feroza Judgbhay and Andronika August for conducting the interviews.

References

Barr, P., *Some Babies Die*, Langdon Films, Australia, 1989

Beard, R.W., Pinker, G.D. and Mowbray, J.R., 'Miscarriage or Abortion', *Lancet*, vol. 2, 1985, pp. 1122–3

Beck, M., Winkelgren, I., Quade, V. and Wingert, P., 'Miscarriages', *Newsweek*, 15 August 1988

Borg, S. and Lasker, J., *When Pregnancy Fails*, London, Routledge & Kegan Paul, 1982

Bourne, S. and Lewis, E., 'Perinatal Bereavement: A Milestone and Some New Dangers', *British Medical Journal*, vol. 302, 1991, pp. 1167–8

Brown, W.A., *Psychological Care during Pregnancy and the Post-Partum Period*, New York, Raven Press, 1979

Chalmers, B., 'The Role of "Stressful" Life Events in the Development of Complications of Pregnancy', unpublished doctoral dissertation, Johannesburg, University of the Witwatersrand, 1979

——, 'Behavioural Associations of Pregnancy Complications', *Journal of Psychosomatic Obstetrics and Gynecology*, vol. 3, 1984, pp. 27–35

——, 'The Pedi Woman's Experience of Childbirth and Early Parenthood: A Survey of Major Findings', *Curationis*, vol. 11, 1988, pp. 12–19

——, *Pregnancy and Parenthood: Heaven or Hell*, Sandton, Berev Publications, 1990a

——, *African Birth: Childbirth in Cultural Transition*, Sandton, Berev Publications, 1990b

——, 'Terminology used in Spontaneous Pregnancy Loss', *British Medical Journal*, vol. 99, 1992, pp. 357–8

—— and Hofmeyr, G.J., *Miscarriage: A Crisis Discarded*, Johannesburg, Central Television Services, University of the Witwatersrand, 1989

——, and McIntyre, J., 'Spreading the Heresy: Psycho- Obstetric Teaching in the Labour Ward', paper presented to the 10th Priorities in Perinatal Care Conference, Malaga, April 1991

Feinberg, S.E., *The Analysis of Cross Classified Categorical Data*, Cambridge MA, MIT Press, 1977

Graves, W.L., 'Psychological Aspects of Spontaneous Abortion', in M.J. Bennett and D.K. Edmonds (eds), *Spontaneous and Recurrent Abortion*, Oxford, Blackwell Scientific Publications, 1987

Hayward, J. and Chalmers, B., 'Obstetricians' and Mothers' Perceptions of Obstetric Events', *Journal of Psychosomatic Obstetrics and Gynaecology*, vol. 11, 1990, pp. 57–71

Herz, E.K., 'Psychological Repercussions of Pregnancy Loss', in L. Dennerstein and M. De Senarclens (eds), *The Young Woman: Psychosomatic Aspects of Obstetrics and Gynaecology*, Amsterdam, Exerpta Medica, 1983

Holdstock, T.L., 'Indigenous Healing in South Africa: A Neglected Potential', *South African Medical Journal*, vol. 4, 1981, pp. 31–46

Jiminez, S.L.M., *The Other Side of Pregnancy*, Englewood Cliffs, Prentice Hall, 1982

Kennell, J. and Klaus, M., 'Cariñg for the Parents of a Stillborn or an Infant who Dies', in M.H. Klaus and J.H. Kennell (eds), *Parent-Infant Bonding*, St Louis, C.V. Mosby, 1982

Kuppasami, C., *Religions, Practices and Customs of South African Indians*, Durban, Sunray Publications, 1985

Larsen J., Msane, C. and Monkhe, H., 'The Zulu Traditional Birth Attendant', *South African Medical Journal*, vol. 63, 1983, pp. 540–2

Leroy, M., *Miscarriage*, London, McDonald Optima, 1988

Lewis, H., 'Effects and Implications of a Stillbirth or Other Perinatal Death', in B.L. Blum (ed.), *Psychological Aspects of Pregnancy, Birthing and Bonding*, New York, Human Sciences Press, 1980

Oakley, A., McPherson, A. and Roberts, H., *Miscarriage*, Glasgow, Fontana, 1984

Pizer, H. and Palinski, C., *Coping with a Miscarriage*, New York, New American Library, 1986

Rosenthal, L.N., 'Marriage, the Family and Social Change among the Gudgerati speaking Indians of Johannesburg', Johannesburg, unpublished doctoral dissertation, 1976

Siebel, M. and Graves, W.L., 'The Psychological Implications of Spontaneous Abortions', *Journal of Reproductive Medicine*, vol. 25, 1980, pp. 161–5

Stack, J.M., 'Spontaneous Abortion and Grieving', *American Family Physician*, vol. 21, 1980, pp. 99–102

—9—

Memories of Pregnancy Loss: Recollections of Elderly Women in Northern Ireland

Rosanne Cecil

Introduction

This chapter reports on a study into elderly women's recollections of pregnancy loss. The events recalled occurred during the 1940s, 1950s and beginning of the 1960s, a period of considerable change throughout the United Kingdom in terms of maternal mortality rates, perinatal death rates and family size. While this general pattern of change was evident in Northern Ireland, family size remained (and remains) generally larger there than in the rest of the United Kingdom, and maternal mortality and perinatal mortality rates have only recently begun to converge with those of Britain. In this context, how the loss of a pregnancy was viewed, how the woman herself felt about her loss, and how those in her social milieu reacted to the loss have been the main focus of my study, an integral aspect of which has been how the memories of such events are expressed.

It is a truism to observe that the lives of ordinary women have been largely hidden from history. Women's lives have also escaped full documentation within biographies and autobiographies. Data on many aspects of the everyday experiences of women in the recent past can very easily remain uncollected, unanalysed and lost to documentation. Certainly, everyday occurrences such as pregnancy losses have rarely been recorded. This small study records some of the experiences of a small group of rural women which might otherwise be lost, for there is little evidence to suggest that information about pregnancy losses is even passed on from one generation of women to another. On the contrary, none of the women in the study had talked at any length (if at all) to a daughter or other younger female relative. It seems that many elderly women have a tendency to undervalue their own worth and the value of their personal experiences. The reticence which some women expressed in discussing pregnancy and pregnancy loss (see below) was sometimes difficult to distinguish from their general belief that nothing in their lives would be of any great interest to a researcher.

Birth and Death in Ireland

Among the many subjects which have been the focus of study by ethnographers and folklorists in Ireland, death and funerary rites have attracted a considerable amount of attention. Birth has attracted rather less attention, although some of the traditional beliefs and practices associated with pregnancy and childbirth were referred to by Scheper-Hughes (1979) in her work on a community in Kerry, and documented systematically by Ballard (1985) and Nic Suibhne (1992).

Scheper-Hughes (1979) reported on some of the beliefs surrounding pregnancy and childbirth held by older villagers in Ballybran, Co. Kerry, such as the prohibition on a pregnant woman seeing animals born or slaughtered. Despite a number of proscriptions and prohibitions regarding the behaviour of the pregnant woman it was also felt, somewhat paradoxically, that a pregnant woman should not 'pamper' herself and that a woman who did so, even if she was attempting to avert a threatened miscarriage, would be liable to the scorn of others.

Using the archives of the Ulster Folk and Transport Museum, Ballard (1985) discussed a number of aspects of childbirth and early childcare prior to the establishment of the National Health Service (NHS) in 1948. Remarking on the 'aura of secrecy surrounding the subject. . . there is a need to keep secret, and to be seen to be keeping secret, information relating to childbirth' (p. 59) she discussed the role of the handywoman (the untrained local woman who was experienced in delivering babies and caring for expectant and newly delivered mothers), illegitimacy, and the ritual of churching following childbirth, which took place within both the Church of Ireland and the Catholic Church.

The archives of the Irish Folklore Commission, which Nic Suibhne (1992) drew on in her investigation into pregnancy and childbirth, included material which had a bearing upon pregnancy loss. The material on which she worked was collected in counties Donegal, Tyrone and Antrim between 1935 and 1970. Nic Suibhne found records of a number of customs and beliefs among the predominantly Catholic respondents concerning the pregnant woman's state of vulnerability. In particular, a pregnant woman was to avoid having anything to do with 'the supernatural otherworld' and its association with birth and death (1992, p. 15). Thus a pregnant woman should avoid entering a graveyard or attending a wake and also should avoid contact with new-born children through, for example, sponsoring a child in baptism. Similarly, a number of customs and practices were to do with the vulnerability of the new-born child, such as the use of iron to protect it from supernatural forces. Most important was the protection given the child by early baptism.

The ritual of baptism not only gives a child a name but also marks its entry into society as a full member. If a child died before baptism it was believed to have gone to limbo, a place where the light of God never shone. Until the 1960s, unbaptized and illegitimate children in Ireland were not usually buried in the consecrated ground of churchyards because the Catholic Church did not regard them as part of its community (Nic Suibhne, 1992). In some parts of Ireland such children were buried in *ceallunaigh* or *cillini*, that is, children's burial grounds (Ó Súilleabháin, 1939; Mytum, 1992; Sugrue, 1993). According to Sugrue (1993), church sites which had been abandoned (due to the Church being reorganized along episcopal instead of monastic lines) commonly came over time to be used as *cillini*, and Ó Súilleabháin observed that *cillini* were often in, or near, old forts. Sugrue (1993), who worked on the Iveragh peninsula of southwest Kerry (where there are reportedly 103 *cillini*), tells of an informant who had buried stillborn twins in a *cillin* in 1939. These were apparently among the last children to be buried there; a few years later, when the same woman lost another set of twins, they were buried in the chapel yard, although in a special corner away from other burials.

It seems that children were buried in a *cillin* with little or no ceremony. Burials usually took place during daylight; though 'if the child was illegitimate or if it was an early miscarriage, then it would be buried at night so that no one would know' (Sugrue, 1993, p. 40). No wake was held for these children, neither was the house of the bereaved full of visitors, as is still customary today at the time of a death, for 'it is not for the community to mourn those whom they did not know' (Sugrue, 1993, p. 64). *Cillini* were in some cases also used for the burial of any child aged around six months or less. This suggests that full membership of the community was not necessarily achieved at the point of baptism (although it could not be achieved *without* baptism) but had been a more gradual process taking a period of months or years. As far as the community was concerned, according to Sugrue (1993, p. 69) 'a dead infant did not differ much in status from the child in the womb'.

No equivalent study has been undertaken into the place of burial or disposal of miscarried fetuses, stillbirths and infants in the area in which my study took place. It is not clear whether, in the more religiously mixed area of north-east Ulster, such sites existed and were put to the same use as in the west of Ireland. Ó Súilleabháin (1939) reported *cillini* in the north-west of Ireland, in County Donegal, as well as many counties further south, but did not report any in the north-eastern counties. In some places, according to Ó Súilleabháin, boundary fences, crossroads, isolated bushes and the vicinity of wells were used as burial sites for fetuses and infants. A report of a small village in Co. Antrim from the nineteenth century stated that a special plot attached to a graveyard would have been used for the burial of unbaptized children and the stillborn, as well as for strangers (Day and McWilliams, 1992). By the middle of the twentieth century it seems that unbaptized and stillborn children would have been buried in the family plot but without a funeral service, according to an informant from another small village in the county. An older, baptized child would have been buried with a funeral service, although there would have been no wake for a very young child. The burials of infants usually took place between the hours of sunset and sunrise. In the more remote rural areas, such as in this case, different denominations would have been buried in the one graveyard; thus Catholics and Presbyterians were buried in the Church of Ireland graveyard in this north-coast village.

Within the Irish literature on death and funerary rites, the Irish wake in particular has achieved a degree of notoriety (see, for example, Ó Súilleabháin, 1967; Crozier, 1989 and O Crualaoich, 1990, 1993, and also Sheehy, 1994), and the role of the Banshee at the time of a death has had an enduring place within Irish folk tradition (Lysaght, 1986). Largely missing from these accounts, however, has been specific data on how stillbirths and miscarried fetuses and the deaths of new-born infants were dealt with.[1] Little is known as to which rituals, if any, were associated with such deaths or how the parents, family and wider community acknowledged the loss. In contrast, the work of Prior (1989) into the social organization of death provides information on the management of the death of infants and stillbirths in Belfast.

Prior argued that the perceived social worth of different groups of the deceased is expressed symbolically in the spatial organization of cemeteries and graveyards. Of one cemetery, situated significantly on the periphery of the city, Prior observed that the public plot which had at one time been for the burial of the poor was now only used for the burial of the stillborn: 'in their unmarked graves is symbolized their social value' (Prior, 1989, p. 117). Some stillborn babies would be buried in individual plots and according to Christian ritual, but these would be rare. It would be more common for their burials to be 'contracted out' to a firm of undertakers who would bury the bodies of the infants in common plots without religious ritual.

That attitudes to pregnancy loss may now be changing rapidly is indicated by the recent opening of a garden of remembrance in Belfast, mostly for the remains of miscarried babies, but also for stillborn babies and those that lived for a very short time (White, 1994). Also, a small number of Catholic churches in Northern Ireland now hold a special Mass of Remembrance at the Feast of the Holy Innocents for such infants.

Memories of Twelve Women

The loss of a pregnancy through miscarriage is an experience many women have had. To lose a child at a later stage, through a stillbirth or a neonatal death, is rather less common but nevertheless it was not rare among women in Ireland in the middle of the century. It cannot be claimed that the experiences of the women presented here are typical or in any way representative of the experiences of other women of their generation, yet neither is there any reason to think that they are necessarily untypical. Nevertheless, the fact that they were willing to talk about their experiences of pregnancy loss (while others who were approached were not) must be acknowledged, as it may indicate significant differences between these women and others. The different ways in which women view their loss may depend on a number of factors. Even within this small sample, the range of experiences of pregnancy loss was considerable. There was considerable diversity in terms of the stage of the loss (pre- or post-partum); the number of losses experienced; the size of any existing family; and factors such as religious affiliation and age.

At the time of being interviewed the women's ages ranged from sixty-five to eighty-nine. Their ages at the time of the events they were recalling ranged from twenty-four to forty-four. Seven of the women were Catholics and five were Protestant (of the five Protestant women, three were Presbyterian, one was a member of the Church of Ireland and one attended a Gospel Hall). All the women were from rural areas of Northern Ireland and ten of them were either from farming backgrounds or had married into a farming family. Not all the women had known financial hardship in their childhood or early adulthood, although a number of them had. Nevertheless, all spoke of the lack of facilities, amenities and opportunities that existed in Ireland at that time, particularly with regard to information about, and access to, health care, including contraception. All the women had been married (two still were, the remainder were widows) and their age at marriage ranged from twenty-one to thirty-two. Nine of them had had at least one miscarriage, two had had one or more stillbirths and five had lost at least one child in infancy. For five women the losses occurred at home, the remainder being hospitalized for at least some stage in the process. The average size of the women's families (that is, the number of children who had lived to adulthood) was five, with a range from one woman who had no child who had survived longer than a month, to two women who had had ten children (see Appendix).

When asking women to recall events that occurred between thirty and fifty years earlier it is pertinent to ask how accurate those memories could be. Memories of events which happened to one personally, known as autobiographical memories, are not literal representations of the past, but 'can best be characterized as inaccurate in detail but truthful. Truth in an autobiographical memory is preserved as one conveys the meaning of life events through plausible reconstructions of those events' (Barclay, 1988). Memories are not entities which can be retrieved intact at will. Rather, they may constantly be subject to modifications through the changing life experiences of the individual and the specific contexts in which events are recalled.

It is commonly thought that the elderly remember events from the distant past, such as childhood events, more easily than they remember recent events. That is, it is thought that their long-term memory is stronger than their short-term memory. Experimental studies into memory suggest, however, that one of the factors critical in the retention of an event is the frequency of recall. There may, for example, be a number of favourite memories which are preserved through frequent recall and through discussion (Cohen and Faulkner, 1988).

It was clear, from the interviews which I conducted with the women, that their memories of pregnancy loss had not been recounted many times over the years. For each woman, her memories were, on the whole, a very personal and private account of a personal and private event which had occurred many years earlier. With some exceptions, they had not been shared to any great extent with others. For some women, however, they had clearly been rehearsed in private many times, particularly in the weeks and months following the loss. The women had struggled to make personal sense of their loss and to form an explanatory framework of the event. As Rabbitt and Winthorpe have noted: 'We do not passively rehearse our memories, but rather use them to try to understand and control our lives. . .' (1988, p. 306).

At the time of the pregnancy loss, some women had a sympathetic response from their husband and were able to talk a little about their feelings. More frequently, however, the husband had not offered any support. For example, the comments of two women were: 'Not a bit worried about me. . .the husbands weren't worried about their wives then. Mine wasn't anyway' (05),[2] and: 'He never thought of me to tell you the God's honest truth' (06). One woman even thought that her husband's violent behaviour may have been the cause of her many miscarriages: 'Maybe that's what caused the miscarriages. . .you daren't say anything, maybe it could have been avoided' (07). In a number of cases the husband barely spoke about the loss: 'He was never a man who showed what he felt' (11); 'He never liked to talk about it, somehow or other' (12), which inevitably limited the possibility of shared discussion between husband and wife. In one case, the husband, in his concern for his wife, effectively restricted any discussion within the family about what had happened. This was apparently appreciated by his wife, who said: 'Oh, he was very good to me. He tried to protect me from people prying and asking questions. . ..He told his mother and sister that whenever I came home (from hospital) they were not to start asking questions as to what he looked like or what happened or anything else.' She then went on to say: 'It was just we tried to forget about it, but you don't forget. . ..On a farm you don't get time to sit and brood. You have your thoughts to yourself, like many a time afterwards, when I was washing the milker and no one was around, I cried to myself but nobody knew I did it.'

If discussion within the family was limited, beyond the bounds of the family it was very rare indeed. One woman (11) remarked: 'Definitely nobody ever said "we are sorry you lost the baby". No, it just wasn't mentioned.' Another said, 'In them days there were very little time, very little talk or very little thought, do you know what I mean? In the old days, that's fifty years ago, nobody ever talked about it' (13).

The women I approached for the study were thus being asked to speak to a stranger of something which was not only a very private event which had occurred many years earlier, but of something about which they had rarely spoken. Their memories had, by and large, not been shared with others and had thus not been reinforced by repetition. While for some women it appeared that the importance of the event led to some aspects being recalled in detail, for others (perhaps for those for whom the event was of less significance) the recollections were not so vivid.[3]

The actual experience of the loss of the pregnancy was, in many cases, rather difficult or traumatic for a number of reasons. With the present level of antenatal care (and especially the use of ultrasound), it is unlikely that today a woman would carry a dead fetus within the womb (i.e. a missed abortion) for as long as some of the women in the sample. One woman (01) who thought that she was six months pregnant was told when she miscarried that the fetus had only been of about six weeks gestation. Recalling her pregnancy, she said, 'I just assumed I was keeping my figure well. . .I had no idea that there was anything wrong. . .you didn't run to the doctor all the time.' Another woman who, in contrast, had realized that she had lost her pregnancy at two months gestation, carried it for a further five months until it came away of its own accord. Her doctor had refused to 'do a curette', for her bones were 'too strong and firm'. For some women the lack of amenities, such as a telephone or a car, meant that summoning help was not easy. The distance from the woman's home to the nearest doctor, hospital or even road presented problems. (One woman recalled walking a mile in labour to meet the ambulance which could not reach their hillside farm; on this occasion the child was delivered safely.) For all women, the experiences of pregnancy, pregnancy loss and childbirth took place, if not actually under a veil of secrecy, then in an atmospherē in which such matters were not freely discussed and experiences shared.

Ceremonies and Memories

The event which the women were asked to recall and speak of not only did not form part of a shared social memory (such as the second world war or, for an earlier generation in Ireland, the famine) nor was it an event which, although private (such as a wedding, birth or death), would have a significance understood and shared with others. A pregnancy loss, being largely unspoken of, was not acknowledged or recognized by others to be an event of any great significance. Connerton (1989, p. 4) has noted: 'If there is such a thing as social memory. . .we are likely to find it in commemorative ceremonies.' As noted earlier, until very recently, no commemorative ceremonies were held for miscarried and stillborn babies (nor, in some cases, for older children). There was, in Irish society, no vehicle for the shared expression of these sorts of loss, bereavement and remembrance. For some women this was a source of regret: a woman who had miscarried at three months said she felt that the fact that there had been no burial was 'awful' (09).

In the cases where there was a funeral no women would have attended. Usually only the father of the child, perhaps with a small number of male relations, would have been present. As one woman who had lost four babies shortly after birth (as well as having a miscarriage) said: 'I never was at any funeral. I never knew where them wee ones was buried 'till the morning my husband was buried. . .. I just knew they were buried somewhere in the graveyard' (12). An awareness that things have changed in this respect was apparent for a number of women. A woman who had had a stillbirth said, 'You never named it or nothing. The man that looked after the graves just came and took it and buried it and there was a wee plot in the graveyard. There were no things like they do nowadays, they have wee funerals and that now.

There were nothing like that then. I think it is nicer now' (02). One woman who (as well as having had a miscarriage) had lost a two-year-old child, remained distressed, more than thirty years after the event, that her daughter had not been given a proper funeral. Speaking of her daughter's burial, she said: 'Compared to how a child of her age is buried now. They are buried like an ordinary human being. . ..She was took up to the graveyard there and buried on a Monday evening, just like a dog' (03). The local community responded to her death as they would have to the death of an adult in the sense that the neighbours visited the home: 'I mind the people coming to the house and all, you know, they came steady to the house and all, but there was no funeral as such' (03). Although this case of the death of a two-year-old child takes us far beyond the time bounded by the term 'pregnancy loss', it has been included as it highlights so clearly the issue of commemorative ceremonies. As Connerton (1989, p. 44) has observed:

> Rites are not limited in their effect to the ritual occasion . . .. Although demarcated in time and space, rites are also as it were porous. They are held to be meaningful because rites have significance with respect to a set of further non-ritual actions, to the whole life of a community. Rites have the capacity to give value and meaning to the life of those who perform them.

A funeral rite may be considered to be the formal expression of the community's loss of one of its members. It affirms the worth of the deceased in the eyes of all those who participate. If no ceremony takes place, then no such message is expressed. However, a wake, or the visiting of the house of the bereaved by kin and neighbours, can be considered to be a less formal expression of the same thing. Unlike the funeral, a wake is attended by women. It is an event which stands apart from, and may even be opposed to, the institution of the church and the role of its clergy (see the comments of Cooper Foster, 1951, pp. 20–1 and Ó Crualaoich, 1990, p. 154). While it is clear that little was done to mark a miscarriage or stillbirth, another woman, the mother of four infants who had died shortly after birth, also remarked on the visiting that took place between the time of death and the burial: 'the house was full when the wee children died, when they were brought home, oh aye' (12). This was a time when words or actions of comfort could be given to the bereaved. She recalled an elderly woman who had visited after the death of one of the children. The elderly woman had checked to see whether the child's legs were tied; 'she came over and loosed their legs, their wee legs. . .she says "You know they wouldn't get into heaven if their legs were tied". But that was maybe just a saying, you know' (12). Nevertheless, by expressing a belief and taking an action which was considered to be for the spiritual good of the dead child, the elderly woman had remained in her mind for nearly fifty years.

For some women, the fact that a pregnancy loss was not marked in any way did not disturb them. Thus one woman, speaking of her miscarriage, said: 'I didn't want anyone to see it. It was just (not comparing one with the other) but it was just the size of a mouse in a wee bag. I don't know, I never looked what was in it. I buried it in the garden. . .well I mean to say, that was dead and dead to the world and everything and it never cost me no thoughts after it' (05).

As the lack of a proper burial or funeral rites was an important issue for some women, so too, for some, was the issue of the rite of baptism. For the predominantly Catholic group of women discussed by Nic Suibhne (1992), baptism had been of critical importance. For the mixed group of women in my sample, its significance varied. For example, a Presbyterian woman whose premature son had died shortly after birth said of him: 'He had a proper funeral, a proper burial. But the thing was he was never baptized, but then my Minister said that a little baby that came into the world like that and just lived half an hour. . .they were special cases' (09). Conversely, a Catholic woman recounted how her priest was very annoyed that the midwife had not baptized her miscarried fetus, and how he had stressed to her that 'the Lord only comes the one time to put life into a child'. (06)

The Role of Religion

It is well known that religious observance in Northern Ireland is considerably more widespread than in most other parts of the United Kingdom. Both the membership of churches and the extent of religious practice are much greater than in Britain and much more closely entwined with politics.[4] All of the women in this small sample identified herself as being a member of a particular denomination within Christianity.

The role which religion plays for women in the context of pregnancy loss does not appear to be straightforward for either Protestants or Catholics. A Catholic woman recounted how she had once been asked by a friend whether she had ever confessed to having had a miscarriage. Until that point it had not occurred to her to view miscarriage as a sin. She took the opportunity of meeting a new priest to clarify the matter for herself: 'I'll say till him just to see. And I said, "Father, I had a miscarriage and I never confessed it." "My goodness woman, you're a saint," like as much to say that's nothing, like it was no sin' (05). Women did not appear to bear a sense of guilt regarding their pregnancy loss. The causal explanations which women suggested tended to be very straightforward, such as a fall, or becoming pregnant too quickly following an earlier pregnancy. One woman suggested that boys are miscarried more easily than girls: ‘A girl will stick to the mother’s dirt, that’s the womb. . .the boys go away just like that. They go away from the mother but the girls stick to the mother’s dirt. . .the boys, apparently they break off’ (06).[5]

Although some women had cited the will of God as an explanation in some other contexts, such as having a large family, none of the women referred to their pregnancy loss in this way. Indeed, the only reference made to this kind of explanation was rather critical. A Protestant woman asked: ‘How can anybody go and tell them (women who have lost children) that it was God’s will? You know everybody says, “Oh, there must be a purpose for it”’ (09). Another Protestant woman, whose handicapped infant son had died, reflected on the role which her religious faith had played at that time. Comparing herself to her husband, she observed: ‘I would be, of the two of us, I would say I would be the more religiously inclined person and yet my husband coped far better than I did. . .my faith was sorely tried’(10). Involvement with their church meant, for some women, the difficult experience of attending the baptisms of other children. For two women this occurred on the first occasion that they went to church following the death of their own infant.

On the whole, the women reported the clergy as having had little involvement with them at the time of their pregnancy loss. In the case of those women who miscarried at a relatively early stage of their pregnancy, the clergyman would not have been told, and would not have known, of the event. Some of the women who suffered later losses did refer to their clergyman visiting, and one woman explained how her clergyman had helped her in a way that her family could not. Speaking of the funeral of her premature son, which had taken place while she was still in hospital, she said ‘The Reverend --- came to see me afterwards and told me a little about it and I was grateful, for it meant that I hadn’t to ask whenever I went home. You can talk to strangers sometimes better than you can talk to your own’ (09).

‘Just one of those things’: Pregnancy Loss in Context

The women spoke of and displayed a range of reactions when recalling their experiences of pregnancy loss after many years, from a very matter-of-fact approach, through gentle regret to considerable distress. The reasons for the diversity of their emotional reactions to the events are not immediately clear. Common-sense assumptions regarding the nature and impact of pregnancy loss suggest that the later the loss (i.e.

the greater the gestational age) the more distressing the experience would have been for the woman, and that if a woman had already had children then the loss would have been experienced as rather less significant than if she had none. These assumptions were not, however, reflected in the responses of the women interviewed, nor are they supported by recent studies into the predictive value of different factors in causing psychological distress following pregnancy loss. Indeed, the findings regarding factors which may predict whether or not a woman is likely to suffer psychological distress following such an event are rather equivocal (see Slade, 1994 for a review of recent studies in this area). Peppers and Knapp (1980) reported that the grief following a pregnancy loss was not associated with gestational age, and that grief following a miscarriage could be as great as that following a stillbirth or neonatal death. From her study of women who had had a late miscarriage, a stillbirth or an early neonatal death, Lovell (1983) found that those women whose babies had lived, even though for a very short time, were better able to make sense of their loss than those whose loss had occurred at an earlier stage. Jackman McGee and Turner (1991) found that there was no significant association between levels of psychological distress and whether or not the woman already had children.

The degree of acceptance of their loss appeared to derive from the whole context of the lives of the women. Factors such as gestational age and the existence of other children were embedded within the individual complexity of each woman's unique situation. Thus a woman who already had six living children (and went on to have four more) told of how sad she had been at the date on which her miscarried baby would have been due and said that she would still think about the baby on that date: 'I said I will always remember this. I says it would have been born in September. If everything would have gone well I would have had another baby. . .. Near the date I think about that baby because it would have been eleven' (that is, she would have had eleven babies). She then goes on to say, tellingly, 'but that was the only unfortunate thing ever happened to me' (07). For most of the women, however, the material hardship of their lives, during their child-bearing years, provided a context against which to judge the impact of the pregnancy loss. The following observations are fairly typical of the remarks made: 'Times were hard then and you didn't think so much about it. You got on with your work as best you could and that was it' (03); and: 'I just thought it was one of those things' (04). In addition, the generally high fertility rate at that time produced, for some women, feelings of ambivalence to the loss: 'I don't remember being *terribly* upset. I suppose a bit disappointed but you were pregnant again and that was it. In another six months you were pregnant again' (03).

The awareness of the dangers, to the mother, of pregnancy and childbirth influenced the attitudes of both women and men. They compared their situation favourably to that of other people, particularly to women who had died in childbirth (this had happened to the mothers of two informants). The women were grateful for the return of their own health and strength, although a number made remarks such as 'the "miss" took a lot out of me. I bled a lot and wasn't able to go up the old stairs' (04) and 'the miscarriages are far sorer on you than the births, believe it or not' (06). The dangers of pregnancy, pregnancy loss and childbirth were, at that period, not insignificant. Two women lost so much blood following their miscarriage that they needed a blood transfusion, which for one of them resulted in the dangerous development of a clot in the lung.

In a number of cases other losses were felt by women to be of greater significance than the pregnancy loss, thus diminishing its impact. So, for example, the loss of a much loved two-year-old child far outshadowed the impact of two early miscarriages. The losses sustained in the distant past and the emotions experienced at that time form part of an individual's biography which may be superseded, in terms of intensity, by any number of other events in the intervening years. For some of these women, most of whom were widows, the loss of a husband was of much greater significance. In addition, current incapacities and disabilities formed the backdrop to some of these women's perspectives on their lives.

Regrets and Comparisons with Today

A recurring theme throughout a number of these recollections has been that 'if only' something had been done differently at the time, their loss might not have occurred. Even those women who had seemed most stoical over their loss expressed this feeling. A woman who had had two stillborn babies felt that, on both occasions, the child might had lived if different actions had been taken. Recalling the birth of the first child and the actions of the local handywoman, she said:

> The child was born in the bed. There was a woman here, a very good woman she was. . .she came in (and she had attended Mrs --- down the road with all her children born) and she came in and she never lifted the child. She said, 'I must get a taste of Holy Water and baptize it.' So she never lifted it out. But maybe if she had have lifted it out, but then it didn't strike me at the time. I didn't know the child was dead. But then the nurse came and said, 'Was that child really dead?' She said, 'I think if it had got a shake. . ..' But I said I didn't know.

The second stillbirth, in hospital, was attended by a nurse: 'I mind the nurse sitting knitting at the foot of the bed. She never looked up.' The following morning, when the doctor came in, she heard him say, '"if that head had been turned that child could have. . ."; I heard this! I suppose they didn't think I heard it. I mean it could have been born. But there was nobody to bother' (05).

For a number of women the theme of 'if only' was inextricably linked to their knowledge that the care given to pregnant and labouring women today is of a higher standard than that which they had received. 'If only' they had been in their child-bearing years now, instead of thirty, forty or fifty years earlier, then maybe their child would have had a greater chance. One woman, whose son was born at seven months and only lived for a very short time, observed that, 'they used to say a seven-months' birth wouldn't live, but you can read now in magazines where they do, you know' (11). A woman who lost four babies and had one miscarriage missed being helped by the advances of science by only a few years: 'But then they discovered it was my blood, Rhesus negative. When they discovered that it was too late. . .. They must have discovered it when I was forty-two, I hadn't any more after that' (12).

Conclusion

In this small study of elderly rural women's recollections of their experiences of pregnancy loss, one of the major themes which emerged was the significance attached to their loss by the women themselves and by others. The lack of ritual associated with the loss of a pregnancy or an infant stands in stark contrast to the display of ritualized behaviour which is still associated with the death of an adult in rural Ireland. For some women, their memories were made more poignant by the awareness that their loss had occurred at a time when the nature of what was lost was considered to be of little or no value. A pertinent issue in the study of miscarriage, stillbirth and neonatal death is the developmental stage at which human status is attributed. Within the United Kingdom, there has been little concensus in this matter. Legal definitions, clerical pronouncements and lay views incorporate a wide and diverse range of perspectives. Nevertheless, it seems that over the last century, the attribution of human status has been made progressively earlier in the pregnancy. Recent developments in reproductive medicine have meant that some very small premature babies can now survive. Little can be done, however, to help women who threaten to miscarry early in a pregnancy. Nevertheless, over their lifetime, this group of women have witnessed a radical change in the way in which the infant and the unborn child have been viewed. Their memories of their own pregnancy losses exist alongside their present awareness and knowledge of the changes which have taken place since their child-bearing years.

Acknowledgements

My thanks are due to a number of my colleagues, especially Hazel Bland, Eileen Martin, Noel McGuigan, Fionnuala Nic Suibhne and Amanda Shanks at the Queen's University of Belfast; Simon Harrison at the University of Ulster; and Colum Linden for his translation of Ó Súilleabháin's paper (1939). A series of ESRC-funded seminars on Memory and Social Transmission, organized by Elizabeth Tonkin and Harvey Whitehouse in the Department of Social Anthropology at the Queen's University of Belfast, were timely and useful. My special thanks go to the women who participated in the study for sharing their often painful memories.

Notes

1. In her study of the Banshee, Lysaght (1986), commenting on a small number of reports that the death messenger was a child who had died unbaptized, wrote: 'Obviously it is because the rite which would include them in Christian society has been denied them that these beings cannot find rest' (p. 47).
2. The numbers in brackets refer to the code numbers given to the women. See Appendix, Tables 9.1 and 9.2 for data on the women's age and religion and their reproductive histories respectively.
3. '. . .the time lag since an event, while important, had a less powerful effect on recall than the salience or importance of the event, and the degree of emotional involvement' (Ashcraft, 1994, p. 243).
4. Cf. Harris (1961, p. 141): 'Church attendance. . .is not merely a religious act but is also a statement of political affiliation'.
5. The term 'dirt' for womb was used only by this one informant. I am grateful to Dr Simon Harrison for raising the question as to whether

'dirt' is used here to express the view that women's bodies, or particularly their reproductive organs, are dirty and possibly polluting. Alternatively 'dirt' may be used in the sense of soil, in which case the womb is perhaps being likened metaphorically to a field in which the planted seed grows.

References

Ashcraft, M.H., *Human Memory and Cognition*, New York, Harper Collins, 1994

Ballard, L., '"Just Whatever they had Handy": Aspects of Childbirth and Early Child-care in Northern Ireland, Prior to 1948', *Ulster Folklife*, vol. 31, 1985, pp. 59–72

Barclay, C.R., 'Truth and Accuracy in Autobiographical Memory', in M.M. Gruneberg, P.E. Morris and R.N. Sykes (eds), *Practical Aspects of Memory: Current Research and Issues, Vol. 1, Memory in Everyday Life*, Chichester, John Wiley and Sons, 1988

Cohen, G. and Faulkner, D., 'Life Span Changes in Autobiographical Memory', in M.M. Gruneberg, P.E. Morris and R.N. Sykes (eds), *Practical Aspects of Memory: Current Research and Issues, Vol. 1, Memory in Everyday Life*, Chichester, John Wiley and Sons, 1988

Connerton, P, *How Societies Remember*, Cambridge, Cambridge University Press, 1989

Cooper Foster, J., *Ulster Folklore*, Belfast, H.R. Carter Publications, 1951

Crozier, M., '"Powerful Wakes": Perfect Hospitality', in C. Curtin and T. Wilson (eds), *Ireland from Below*, Galway, Galway University Press, 1989

Day, A. and McWilliams, P. (eds), *Ordnance Survey Memoirs of Ireland: Parishes of County Antrim V, 1830–5, 1837–8: Giant's Causeway and Ballymoney*, Belfast, Institute of Irish Studies, The Queen's University of Belfast, 1992

Harris, R., 'The Selection of Leaders in Ballybeg, Northern Ireland', *Sociological Review*, vol. 9, 1961, pp. 137–49

Jackman, C., McGee, H.M. and Turner, M., 'The Experience and Impact of Early Miscarriage', *Irish Journal of Psychology*, vol. 12, 1991, pp. 108–20

Lovell, A., 'Some Questions of Identity: Late Miscarriage, Stillbirth and

Perinatal Loss', *Social Science and Medicine*, vol. 17, 1983, pp. 755–61

Lysaght, P., *The Banshee: The Irish Supernatural Death- Messenger*, Dublin, The Glendale Press, 1986

Mytum, H., *The Origins of Early Christian Ireland*, London, Routledge, 1992

Nic Suibhne, F., '"On the Straw" and Other Aspects of Pregnancy and Childbirth from the Oral Tradition of Women', *Ulster Folklife*, vol. 38, 1992, pp. 12–38

Ó Crualaoich, G., 'Contest in the Cosmology and Ritual of the Irish "Merry Wake"', in A. Duff-Cooper (ed.), *Cosmos*, The Yearbook of the Traditional Cosmology Society, vol. 6, Edinburgh, Edinburgh University Press, 1990

——, 'The Production and Consumption of Sacred Substances in Irish Funerary Tradition', in H. Huttunen and R. Latvio (eds), *Entering the Arena*, Turku, Department of Cultural Studies, University of Turku, and the Finnish Society for Celtic Studies, 1993

Ó Súilleabháin, S., 'Adhlacadh Leanbhai', *The Journal of the Royal Society of Antiquaries of Ireland*, vol. 69, 1939, pp. 143–51

——, *Irish Wake Amusements*, Dublin, Mercier, 1967

Peppers, L.G. and Knapp, R.J., 'Maternal Reactions to Involuntary Fetal/Infant Death', *Psychiatry*, vol. 43, 1980, pp. 155–9

Prior, L., *The Social Organization of Death: Medical Discourse and Social Practices in Belfast*, London, Macmillan, 1989

Rabbitt, P. and Winthorpe, C., 'What do Old People Remember? The Galton Paradigm Reconsidered', in M.M. Gruneberg, P.E. Morris and R.N. Sykes (eds), *Practical Aspects of Memory: Current Research and Issues, Vol. 1, Memory in Everyday Life*, 1988

Scheper-Hughes, N., *Saints, Scholars and Schizophrenics*, Berkeley and Los Angeles, University of California Press, 1979

Sheehy, N., 'Talk about being Irish: Death Ritual as a Cultural Forum', *The Irish Journal of Psychology*, vol. 15, 1994, pp. 494–507

Slade, P., 'Predicting the Psychological Impact of Miscarriage', *Journal of Reproductive and Infant Psychology*, vol. 12, 1994, pp. 5–16

Sugrue, D., 'An Examination of Aspects of Tradition Relating to Some *Ceallunaigh* in Uibh Rathach', unpublished M.A. thesis, National University of Ireland, Cork, 1993

White, L., 'Memorial to Loved Babies', *Belfast Telegraph* 8 September 1994, p. 4

Appendix

Table 9.1. Age and religion

Code Number	Age	Religion
01	73	Protestant (Gospel Hall)
02	83	Catholic
03	77	Catholic
04	89	Catholic
05	84	Catholic
06	72	Catholic
07	73	Protestant (Church of Ireland)
08	71	Catholic
09	65	Protestant (Presbyterian)
10	69	Protestant (Presbyterian)
11	73	Protestant (Presbyterian)
12	82	Catholic

Table 9.2. Reproductive history

Code Number	Number of children who lived to adulthood	Pregnancy losses and infant and child deaths
01	9	one miscarriage
02	5	one stillbirth
03	5	two miscarriages and one child death
04	6	one miscarriage
05	9	one miscarriage and two stillbirths
06	10	eight miscarriages
07	10	one miscarriage
08	2	one miscarriage
09	2	one infant death
10	3	one miscarriage and one infant death
11	1	one infant death
12	0	one miscarriage and four infant deaths

–10–

'Something More Than Blood': Conflicting Accounts of Pregnancy Loss in Eighteenth-Century England[1]

Mark Jackson

Introduction

In May 1799, a number of Susanna Staniforth's neighbours in Sheffield became suspicious that she had given birth to, and subsequently disposed of, an illegitimate child. In order to substantiate their suspicions, Susanna's neighbours immediately informed the parish officers, who called in a surgeon to examine the suspect. In his evidence before the coroner on 10 May, John Moorhouse, the surgeon instructed to perform the examination, described Susanna's response to his questioning in the following words:

> 'Well Sir the Neighbours say I've bore a Child which is a lie. I'll go up Stairs and convince you its a lie' – this Witness went up Stairs with her, she clapped her hand on his Shoulder and said to him, 'to tell you the truth I've miscarried' – Witness asked her to produce the matter of which she had miscarried – she said she was only five months gone, that she had buried it – that it was a false Conception, that it was only Blood – that she had burnt it.[2]

Undeterred by her account of her pregnancy and its outcome, John Moorhouse proceeded to examine Susanna's breasts and, convinced 'that they had the appearance usual with Women about the time of Child Birth', asked the parish officers to search Susanna's father's house for the child. Later that evening, Moorhouse was again summoned by the parish officers, this time to examine the body of a child that had been discovered locked in a box in the house. His evidence at the inquest strongly challenged Susanna's testimony that she had been miscarried of something other than a full-grown child:

> Being asked by the Coroner and Jury if the Child produced is at the full Period of Gestation, saith, 'Yes' – If it is his opinion that Child was born alive – saith 'Yes' – Saith that he can discover no marks of violence upon the Body excepting that the Navel String has been separated by some sharp Instrument and was not afterwards tied up, the want of which wou'd in his opinion produce the death of the Child by Bleeding.[3]

The form and content, and the social and medico-legal implications, of this conflict between Susanna Staniforth and her accusers were reproduced elsewhere in eighteenth-century courts. Throughout the century, unmarried women refuted suspicions that they had murdered new-born children by insisting that they had been miscarried either of a premature stillborn child or of little more than a quantity of blood.

In this chapter, I shall use the unpublished Northern Circuit assize court records of the prosecutions of these women to explore the terms and implications of these conflicting accounts of pregnancy and pregnancy loss in detail. These court records comprise the depositions of witnesses and suspects taken before magistrates and coroners, indictments and inquisitions, and gaol calendars and court minute books.[4] In the present context, the most interesting records are the depositions, the form and content of which were determined not only by the accounts provided by witnesses and suspects but also by the formal language and procedures adopted by the examining official and his clerk. The written depositions on which this chapter is based should thus be seen as the product of the conflicting attempts of suspects, witnesses, coroners and magistrates to make clear their own accounts of events.

In the first section of the chapter, I shall examine the manner in which disputes about the outcome of pregnancy were constructed within a particular social context, and the extent to which they drew heavily on a number of historically and socially contingent debates. These debates concerned the role and status of unmarried women, the concealment of illicit sexual relations, and the relationship between bastardy levels and the poor rates. In the second section, I shall examine alternative accounts of pregnancy loss in detail. These accounts, provided by the suspects, their accusers and medical witnesses, can be understood not only as part of the broad social context outlined in the first section but also as articulations of particular and often contradictory perceptions of the body and its functions. In the final section of the chapter, I will explore how medical evidence was used by the courts to provide a narrative and language of pregnancy loss that mediated between the accounts of suspects and their accusers.

Social Context and the Generation of Conflict

The overwhelming majority of women accused of murdering their newborn children in the eighteenth century were unmarried women, that is single women or, more rarely, widows (Malcolmson, 1977; Hoffer and Hull, 1981; Beattie, 1986; Jackson 1992). This contemporary preoccupation with the pregnancies of single women profoundly influenced the form and content of debates about the outcome of pregnancy in these cases and can be traced to a number of factors.

Throughout the eighteenth century, women were 'understood either married or to be married' (Hill, 1989, p. 221). From this perspective, both single women and widows were regarded with suspicion (Hill, 1989; Staves, 1980/1). In some instances, an unmarried woman servant was clearly identified as a sexual threat to the stability of the family in which she served.[5] In more general terms, during a period when an increasing population was viewed by a multiplicity of commentators as a means of improving the nation's wealth, marriage and the family were regarded as both essential components of social order and prerequisites for national prosperity (Andrew, 1989). Accordingly, women 'who through motherhood were the central figures in the family' (Jordanova, 1980, p. 49) were thought to serve society best by marrying and producing children in wedlock (Mandeville, 1724; Defoe, 1727). Perhaps surprisingly, given that they may already have produced children, widows were seen as particularly marginal. According to William Alexander, in his lengthy *History of Women* (1779, vol. II, p. 287): 'As the state of matrimony is of all others the most honourable, and the most desired by women, so that of widowhood is generally the most deplorable, and consequently the object of their greatest aversion.'

Single women and widows, who remained outside the family, threatened both familial and national stability, and their behaviour was routinely subjected to greater scrutiny than that of their married counterparts. The force and focus of this scrutiny is particularly evident in parochial efforts to regulate what was perceived as illicit sexual behaviour. Although some historians, notably Lawrence Stone, have suggested that there was a dramatic shift in accepted standards of sexual behaviour in the late seventeenth and eighteenth centuries and that a growing reluctance to police it was associated with an increase in premarital sex, pre-nuptual conceptions and bastardy levels (Stone, 1977), it is clear that in certain circumstances the sexual activity of unmarried women in particular was not tolerated.

In general terms, this intolerance can be seen as one expression of a double standard of sexual morality, according to which a greater premium was placed on female than on male chastity (Thomas, 1959).

More particularly, in the eighteenth century the obsession with female chastity was couched in terms of property and possessions. The loss of a young unmarried woman's chastity was regarded as depriving fathers of their daughters and masters of their servants. The double standard was, however, to some extent increasingly double-edged, since the loss incurred by such sexual activity was both recognized by, and recoverable in, the law. As Susan Staves has argued (1980/1, p. 110), in the late seventeenth and eighteenth centuries, 'the courts began to allow a variety of new civil actions that permitted women or their fathers to recover damages from seducers, including both the notorious action for breach of promise of marriage and several less well-known actions permitting fathers to collect for a species of trespass and/or the loss of their daughters' domestic services'. Significantly, as Staves suggests (ibid.), the 'rise of new civil litigation reflects a willingness to understand seduction as secular rather than religious experience'.

This preoccupation with the secular aspects of sex before marriage is evident elsewhere, particularly in discussions of bastardy and the poor rates. Thus, while concern about the moral implications of pre-marital sex may have declined along with the decline in ecclesiastical jurisdiction after the Restoration, the practical consequences of illicit sex remained problematic. Pre-marital sex became a clear cause for parochial concern (that is it became 'illicit') once a woman became pregnant and threatened to burden the parish with a bastard. In these circumstances, a woman's family and neighbours made every effort to indemnify the parish against the charge of maintaining a child by encouraging the woman to identify the child's father and by pressuring the man identified to marry the woman or at least to maintain the child. Eighteenth-century assize and quarter-session records, the diaries of parish officers and magistrates, and a variety of printed ballads and plays testify to the extreme measures that parishioners would adopt in order to avoid supporting another bastard child on the poor rates. It is clear, for example, that parish officers were prepared to expend enormous amounts of time, money and effort ensuring that couples were married (Varsey, 1984). Court records also make clear the legal redress (in terms of punishment and seizure of goods) available to a parish confronted by the economic burden of a woman and her chargeable bastard.

Anxieties about the financial burden of bastards stemmed from late sixteenth- and early seventeenth-century fears about (and legislation dealing with)[6] both the moral and financial implications of a rising population of wandering poor. Significantly, however, by the turn of the eighteenth century, central legislative initiatives and local measures focused exclusively on the potential economic burden associated with pre-marital sex. Further legislative measures introduced in 1662 and 1733 no longer described the bearing of bastards as against God's law, nor referred to the women concerned as 'lewd' (as earlier legislation had done) and restricted their terms of reference to indemnifying parishes against the financial cost of supporting bastards.[7] Both the new civil actions available to wronged fathers and legislative and parochial interest in chargeable bastardy testify to the secularization of attitudes to pre-marital sex.

Together with the statutory system of poor relief through taxation, seventeenth- and eighteenth-century bastardy laws exposed the mothers of bastards to the scrutiny and accusations of rate-paying neighbours. The punitive framework within which such accusations were assessed encouraged single-pregnant women to conceal their pregnancies from their families and neighbours. Although in many cases it was extremely difficult for women to conceal their pregnancies from the people with whom they lived and worked, often in close proximity,[8] this subterfuge enabled unmarried pregnant women to preserve their reputation for a little while longer, sometimes avoiding instant dismissal from service[9] and eluding the punitive clutches of hostile rate-paying parishioners.

In many cases, however, the advantages conferred by concealment were short-lived. If a woman gave birth to a child that lived, it became impossible for her behaviour to pass unnoticed any further and she would be harassed until the child had been filiated and arrangements made for its maintenance. Moreover, if a child died before, during or shortly after birth, its mother remained open to suspicions that she was in some way responsible for the child's death. Such suspicions found support in the law. According to a statute of 1624, enacted in response to fears that some single women were murdering their new-born children in order to avoid the shame and punishment associated with bearing an illegitimate child, any woman that concealed the death of a bastard child was presumed to have murdered that child unless she could prove that it had been born dead.[10]

Although women were rarely convicted for murder under this statute in the eighteenth century (Jackson, 1992), the legal presumption created by the 1624 statute provided rate-paying parishioners with further ammunition in their struggle to reduce the financial load on their rates. Although a dead bastard child no longer posed a threat to the rate-paying community, the anxiety aroused by local suspicions that a single woman had become pregnant with a potentially chargeable bastard, combined with the irritation generated by the woman's efforts to thwart local inquiries by concealing her condition, provided the momentum for prosecuting her for murder. The prosecution of single women for the murder of their illegitimate children can thus be accounted for in two ways: as a suitable vehicle for the expression of local anxieties about the consequences of the sexual activities of single women; and as a means of providing a deterrent to other single women at risk of burdening the parish in the future (Jackson, 1992).

This social framework, and in particular its legal parameters, exerted a profound influence on the structure of the narrative accounts of the pregnancies of single women whose children had been found dead. In the first instance, rate-paying parishioners mobilized a number of prominent social anxieties when they claimed that women who had concealed their pregnancies and deliveries had given birth to mature live-born children and had subsequently murdered them. In response, suspects defended themselves against both local accusations and the rigours of the 1624 statute by adopting the strategy offered in the terms of that statute and declaring either that their children had been born prematurely and dead or that they had been delivered of nothing more than a certain quantity of blood.

Conflicting Accounts of Pregnancy Loss

Concerns about the character and conduct of single women, anxieties about the contribution of bastardy to the rising poor rates, frustration at the deceptive strategy of concealment and the need to provide examples of the sanctions that could be inflicted on those women that thwarted conventional attempts at social control formed the context in which contradictory accounts of pregnancy and pregnancy loss were generated and assessed. Within this setting, how did women accused of murder account for pregnancy loss?

The depositions of suspects before magistrates and coroners suggest that suspects' efforts to dispel suspicions of murder involved several strategies. In the first instance, a number of women provided their accusers and the courts with a chronological narrative of pregnancy which made explicit the premature and accidental nature of the loss of that pregnancy. A suspect's claim that she had been delivered of only a quantity of blood or had been miscarried of a premature child was thus consolidated by reference to the precise times at which sexual intercourse and delivery had occurred. In 1790, for example, Hannah Pullen testified that 'she had connections with a person who had carnal knowledge of her Body for once which to the best of her recollection was about eighteen Weeks before her delivery'.[11] Similarly, on 24 July 1762, Elizabeth Eltoft testified that 'on or about the Twenty Fourth day of December last past. . . Robert Wilks. . . had carnal knowledge of this Examinants body only once and did then beget her with Child'.[12] In these and other cases, factual details of this nature were used to reinforce suspects' claims that they had been prematurely 'delivered of or Miscarried of' little more than blood and to deny responsibility for a child's death.

As I shall discuss later, both lawyers and medical practitioners acknowledged that premature births were likely to be stillbirths. The inclusion of details supporting claims of prematurity therefore constituted an important element of suspects' attempts to refute allegations that they had given birth to and murdered a live-born fully developed child. Suspects' efforts to defend themselves against allegations of maternal neglect or murder at birth were also bolstered by the inclusion in their accounts of those circumstances that might have caused them to be delivered prematurely. In 1756, for example, Grace Furnace indicated that her child had been born prematurely and dead because she had injured herself lifting 'a Load of Coals'.[13] A recognized association between mechanical injuries of this nature and what were referred to as 'miscarriages' or 'spontaneous abortions', evident in obstetrical texts throughout the eighteenth century (Smellie, n.d., pp. 53–4), rendered this component of suspects' accounts critical to the process of assessing maternal responsibility.

The terms in which suspects presented their accounts of pregnancy loss also make evident a significant slippage between constructions of menstruation and early pregnancy loss. This slippage functioned at several levels. First, some women claimed that the presence of blood on clothes and bed-clothes, usually interpreted by a woman's neighbours as indicative of recent delivery, was, on the contrary, a mark of normal menstruation. Thus in 1797, Ann Stephenson was reported to have pointed to blood on the floor of her chamber and said to her mistress: 'now Mistress you see how you have blamed me wrongfully'.[14] Blood, suspects were implying, could be misleading as a sign of recent delivery and murder.

This conflation of menstrual blood and the products of early pregnancy loss appeared in other guises. Some suspects claimed to have been delivered only of a quantity of blood. In 1730, Prudence Newsome testified that she had been delivered 'of something like bloud of the bigness of her Hand'.[15] And, in 1799, Susanna Staniforth testified that she had been delivered of 'only Blood'.[16] On other occasions, suspects acknowledged that the substance of which they had been delivered possessed more form and substance than blood, but nevertheless denied that that substance constituted a child. Thus, Elizabeth Eltoft admitted that she had been 'delivered of or Miscarried of. . .a hard substance', but insisted that this substance 'had not the form of a Child'.[17] Likewise, Hannah Pullen testified that she had been 'delivered of a Substance which appeared to be like a lump of Flesh but there was not any appearance of the shape of a Child'.[18] In this context, it is significant that when suspects in these circumstances did admit to having conceived, it was sometimes referred to as 'a false Conception' unworthy of further attention.[19]

In calling to mind the blood loss of menstruation, referring to the unformed nature of the substance of which they had been delivered, and emphasizing the false nature of conception, suspects were reproducing accounts of female physiology, and in particular of menstruation, conception and pregnancy, evident elsewhere. The slippage between constructions of menstruation and early pregnancy loss, for example, is embodied in at least two other locations: in the availability of proprietary medicines ostensibly produced for 'bringing on the menses', but almost certainly serving the alternative function of terminating unwanted pregnancies (Crawford, 1981; McLaren, 1984); and in the belief that menstrual blood yielded 'Nourishment to the Embrio, when suppressed by Conception' (Freind, 1729, pp. 4–8).

The conflation of menstrual blood loss and early pregnancy loss, reinforced in this way by wider cultural conceptions of female physiology, enabled suspects to produce a coherent account of pregnancy loss that stressed the accidental and premature nature of the loss and emphasized their own lack of responsibility for it. In their depositions before magistrates and coroners, suspects portrayed themselves as the innocent dupes of male deceit and seduction, a portrayal sustained by their depiction of themselves as the hapless victims of a further 'sad misfortune',[20] that of miscarriage. Suspects' use of such phrases to portray themselves as the passive sufferers of tragedy (a portrayal also evident in contemporary ballads and broadsheets) was aimed at deflecting a contemporary presumption that unmarried women were likely to nurse deliberate malevolence towards their unborn children on account of the shame associated with bearing an illegitimate child (Hale, 1736, vol. I). This strategy was reinforced by the manner in which terms such as miscarriage and abortion (both of which were used to describe the loss of an unformed mass of blood or the birth of a premature stillborn child) were incorporated into suspects' accounts of events. Miscarriage was something that happened *to* women rather than something done *by* women.

It is likely that many of the witnesses in these cases, particularly those drawn from the suspects' circle of immediate family and friends or from her fellow servants, shared many of the suspects' cultural perceptions of menstruation, conception and pregnancy. However, most witnesses and those responsible for pursuing the accusations into the courts adopted interpretations of the evidence that differed significantly from those of the suspects. Thus, witnesses insisted that the presence of blood on a woman's clothes or bed-clothes indicated something more sinister than menstruation or miscarriage. Their suspicions, both of the suspects' behaviour and of their explanations of their circumstances, clearly informed their actions. In 1797, Ann Maycock was reported to have said to Sarah Ward, who was accused of giving birth to and murdering a bastard child: 'I suspect there is something more than Blood and I shall seek for it'. The subsequent search of the house in which Sarah Ward lived revealed 'a Male Child lying in a large Earthen Pot. . .and dead.'[21]

In addition to rejecting suspects' explanations for the presence of blood, witnesses strongly challenged their accounts of accidental and premature delivery. Such accounts were regarded simply as defensive strategies employed by women keen to escape both the rigours of local animosity and the severity of the law. Evidence derived from the examination of the women under suspicion or of the products of delivery (discussed below) was presumed to reinforce suspicions that certain women had given birth in secret to live-born children. Moreover, witnesses disputed the picture of a hapless, passive victim implicit in many of the suspects' accounts, particularly if the suspect had given birth to bastard children previously.[22] Fuelled by concerns about bastardy levels and poor rates and about the activities of single women, the testimony of prosecutors and witnesses emphasized the malevolent agency of suspects, who were thought to have contributed to the deaths of their new-born children in one or more of a number of ways: by neglecting to ensure that assistants would be present at the birth; by failing to tie the navel string or umbilical cord; or, in some cases, by wilfully inflicting violence on the child. In this construction of events, women who claimed to have been miscarried through no fault of their own were, on the contrary, clearly to be held culpable for their children's deaths.

Medical Evidence and the Mediation of Conflict

The adversarial nature of proceedings in court threw these opposing accounts of pregnancy loss into further relief. In reaching verdicts, jurors therefore had to decide between substantially different accounts of events. Since most women tried for this offence in the north of England were acquitted, it would appear, at least superficially, that suspects' accounts of events were privileged by the courts, a conclusion reinforced by evidence of emphatic humanitarian pronouncements in support of these women. In an address published in 1784, for example, William Hunter (1784, p. 267) publicly sustained the claims of suspects by exposing cases in which, he believed, innocent women were falling victim to the 'prejudice and blind zeal' of their neighbours.

On closer inspection, however, the significance of acquittals is more complex. By the time they were discharged or acquitted at the assize sessions, suspects had already lost their jobs, had spent several months in gaol awaiting trial, and in some cases, had been forced to leave their homes after the trial as a result of the scandal (Brockbank and Kenworthy, 1968). The fact that such women continued to be tried for murder even in the face of a high acquittal rate suggests that coroners, magistrates, judges and jurors were prepared to countenance some form of retribution for their behaviour. Since the aim of this retribution was to provide a deterrent, acquittals should be seen not as unqualified support for suspects, but as a practical means of moderating the harsh presumptions of the 1624 statute while at the same time acknowledging the claims of a woman's neighbours to protect their own interests. In this section, I shall argue that the courts legitimated this compromise between, on the one hand, the parochial need to deter women from threatening the parish, and on the other hand, the need to dispense merciful justice in individual cases by acknowledging the uncertainties in the evidence provided by medical practitioners.

On the face of it, much medical evidence presented in both pre-trial inquiries and the trial courts supported the account of events given by a womans' neighbours. In particular, medical witnesses were often reluctant to accept suspects' claims that they had been delivered prematurely of 'only Blood', 'a false Conception', or, indeed, of a premature child. Such claims were routinely disputed on the basis of careful examination of the suspect for signs of recent childbirth and the products of delivery for evidence of a viable child.

Proof of recent delivery depended almost exclusively upon the demonstration of milk in a suspect's breasts. Thus in April 1788 John Heslop, a constable in the parish of East Rownton in Yorkshire, testified that on directions from the surgeon, he 'ordered a Woman then present to Draw or suck her [Ann Benison's] Brests [sic] and findeing Milk it was put into a Tea Cup and the Milk so taken out of Ann Benison Breast was sufficient to certify she had had a Child'.[23] Significantly in the present context, the demonstration of milk in a suspect's breasts was taken to indicate that the woman had given birth to a *full-term* child. It was therefore used to rebut her claim that she had been miscarried of a premature, and by implication, stillborn child. As we have seen, in 1790 Hannah Pullen testified to a magistrate that she had been delivered of a substance 'like a lump of Flesh' only eighteen weeks after she had had 'connections with a person who had carnal knowledge of her Body'. William Tindall, the surgeon called in to examine her, refused to accept Hannah's account of her pregnancy. According to his deposition:

> he was sent for to examine Hannah Pullen who it was said had Miscarried that on examining her from milk being in her breasts and thus full and distended and from having the Discharges usual with lying in women he has been led by experience to believe that she was at or near her full term nor does her situation agree with the account she gives of the period of pregnancy.[24]

Even in the absence of the child or its dead body, therefore, evidence derived from the examination of a suspect provided medical practitioners and the courts with a preliminary means of assessing suspects' and witnesses' accounts of pregnancy and its likely outcome.

Evidence derived from examining the suspect was reinforced by inspection of the products of delivery. In particular, when a child's body was discovered (as was usually the case in those cases that reached the trial court), it was rigorously inspected for evidence of maturity and viability. The presence or absence of hair and nails were regarded as particularly significant. While a new-born child with hair and nails was presumed to have been born at full term, the absence of hair and nails was accepted by medical witnesses and usually by the courts as evidence of the child's prematurity. Significantly, with the influential approval of Matthew Hale, such evidence of prematurity was 'taken as proof by one witness, that the child was born dead', thereby exempting the woman from the presumption of the 1624 statute (Hale, 1736, vol. II, p. 289).

In practice, in the courts, medical opinion rarely supported the accounts of miscarriage proferred by suspects. In those cases that reached trial (and in many others in which the mother was not identified at the inquest), medical witnesses contradicted the testimony of suspects by concluding that the child had been born at full term.[25] When taken in conjunction with evidence of milk in a suspect's breasts, evidence of a mature full term child served to undermine suspects' accounts of the outcome of pregnancy and to substantiate local suspicions of murder.

However, the force of medical opinion on this issue, ostensibly in support of the prosecution's case, was blunted by the uncertainty inherent in the rest of the medical evidence. Although medical evidence could establish that a child had been born sufficiently mature to have been viable, they could not establish with any certainty that the child had in fact been born alive. Uncertainty on this issue is particularly evident in discussions of the hydrostatic lung test, a test which was introduced into English courts in the early eighteenth century in an attempt to distinguish between live and stillbirths (Brittain, 1963; Jackson, 1994). The test involved removing the lungs of a new-born child to see if they floated in water. In theory, if the lungs floated, it was assumed that the child had breathed and had, therefore, been born alive;

if they sank, it was supposed that the child had been stillborn. In practice, doubts both about the procedure and about the implications of the test served to undermine its use as a reliable indicator of live or stillbirth (Jackson, 1992, 1994). In the absence of proof of live birth, it consequently proved impossible for the prosecution to establish that the child had been murdered. Significantly, this weakness in the prosecution's case also severely reduced the evidential impact of marks of violence on a child's body (Jackson, 1992, 1994).

The uncertainty in medical testimony, exposed in court discussions about live birth and violence and openly acknowledged by William Hunter (1784) in the title of his work on this topic, can be seen as the product of a number of factors. First, medical practitioners differed considerably in their assessment of the lung test's validity. Secondly, reservations about the conclusiveness of the lung test and evidence of violence were generated by legal problems inherent in establishing guilt at common law. In particular, equivocal legal definitions of birth and live birth and increasing legal concerns about standards of proof restricted the extent to which medical witnesses could contribute to the courts' attempts to develop a coherent account of pregnancy, birth and death (Jackson, 1994).

Reservations about the certainty of medical evidence can also be attributed to the equivocal social and professional position of medical practitioners in the eighteenth century. In giving evidence, and in discussing the outcome of pregnancy in medical texts, medical practitioners had to balance a number of competing interests. As rate-paying members of a local community, they were sympathetic to the suspicions and prejudices of their neighbours, many of whom constituted the practitioners' current or prospective clientele. Significantly, in the local courts, medical evidence almost invariably refuted the accounts of pregnancy and its outcome offered by suspects in favour of accounts provided by the suspects' accusers.

However, medical practitioners were aware not only of their reputation in the local community but also of their professional standing *vis-à-vis* the law. Efforts to establish a professional status comparable with that of lawyers in the eighteenth century encouraged medical practitioners to demonstrate their medico-legal knowledge in the courts. In doing so, however, they were obliged to accept the constraints of the legal system. In particular, they had to acknowledge legal deliberations about the weight of certain types of evidence and the standard of proof. The scrutiny of the evidence entailed by these deliberations diluted the force of local prejudice and greatly diminished the capacity of medical witnesses to develop their own account of pregnancy and its outcome with any certainty.

The ambiguous nature of medical evidence was accentuated by a further strategy adopted by medical practitioners to boost their professional status. As Thomas Laqueur has suggested (1989, pp. 187–8), one of the ways in which eighteenth-century medical practitioners strove to stake out 'professional turf against the laity in general, against ignorant magistrates, and against the legal profession' was to develop a particular narrative account of people's lives and deaths that linked social commentary with forensic medicine. In the present context, what Laqueur refers to as the 'humanitarian narrative' involved reconstructing the behaviour of women accused of murdering their new-born children on the basis of detailed and supposedly objective medical knowledge of female physiology and pathology. The aim of this reconstruction was humanitarian in that its objective was to elicit sympathy for 'innocent women' in order to save them from execution (Hunter, 1784, p. 290; Laqueur, 1989).

As Laqueur suggests (1989, p. 184), the adoption of this narrative strategy was not entirely altruistic, since it formed part of a process in which medical practitioners attempted to define themselves as subscribers to the 'party of humanity'. More importantly in the present context, their adoption of a humanitarian approach influenced the weight and direction of their evidence in court. Thus, reservations about the results of the lung test represented an extension of humanitarian arguments encouraging the more lenient treatment of pregnant single women in general, arguments that (through their rejection of the terms of the 1624 statute) had, ironically, encouraged the use of the lung test in the first instance.

Inconsistencies in medical procedure, legal constraints and medical practitioners' alignment with ostensibly humanitarian opposition to the conviction of women under the 1624 statute all served to limit the extent to which medical testimony could accurately distinguish between live and stillbirths or reliably determine the cause of death. Perhaps paradoxically, it was this uncertainty in the medical evidence that most assisted judges and juries in their commitment to tempering the harshness of statute law with what was regarded as an appropriate measure of mercy. Uncertainties raised by discussions of the medical evidence worked in two ways. First, they served to undermine the strength of neighbours' accounts of maternal negligence and murder. Secondly, they provided a legitimating rationale for acquitting women accused of this crime. In this way, the courts could mitigate the severity of the law by steering a middle course not only between the conflicting accounts of events offered by suspects and their accusers, but also between the rigours of the law and emerging humanitarian concerns. Thus, while persistent prosecutions and occasional convictions satisfied the neighbourhood's demands for the public expression of local anxieties, frequent acquittals, legitimated by medical opinion, satisfied humanitarian concerns (and the claims of the accused women themselves) that suspects were guilty of little more than concealing their pregnancies. The admission of expert forensic medical opinion therefore provided the courts with the necessary evidential and interpretive flexibility to accommodate conflicting accounts of the same events.

Conclusion

Throughout the eighteenth century, single women were accused by their neighbours, relatives and friends of concealing their pregnancies and murdering their new-born children. Such accusations were driven by anxieties about the conduct of single women and the potential burden of increasing numbers of bastard children. In response to these accusations, many suspects claimed that they had been miscarried of little more than blood or, at the worst, that they had given birth to a premature stillborn child. In this way, they attempted to convince both their accusers and the courts that they should not be held responsible for the outcome of their pregnancies.

In the courts, these alternative constructions of pregnancy loss were thrown into sharper relief. In attempting to decide between these conflicting accounts, judges and juries sought the opinion of a further group of witnesses, medical practitioners. This strategy enabled the courts to mediate not only between the accounts of events offered by suspects and their accusers, but also between the severity of statute law and increasingly prominent humanitarian sensibilities. Thus, while the courts generally agreed with suspects' neighbours that accused women had been delivered of 'something more than Blood', they disagreed with the neighbourhood's construction of events and acknowledged the validity of the defence offered by suspects by conceding that there was insufficient evidence to sustain a charge of murder.

Notes

1. The phrase 'something more than Blood' is taken from the evidence of Sarah Morris 'touching the death of a Male Child born of the Body of Sarah Ward Singlewoman' in 1797. The depositions are in

the Northern Circuit assize records in the Public Record Office, class-mark ASSI 45/39/2/121–2. A version of this chapter was presented at an informal Departmental Seminar in the Wellcome Unit for the History of Medicine, University of Manchester, on 26th April 1994. I am grateful to Mark Jenner and John Pickstone in particular for their comments on that occasion.

2. The depositions from this case are in the Public Record Office, in ASSI 45/40/1/118.
3. Ibid.
4. These records are housed in the Public Record Office in Chancery Lane: ASSI 41 (minute books); ASSI 42 (gaol books); ASSI 44 (indictments, inquisitions, gaol calendars); and ASSI 45 (depositions).
5. See the comments of Ann Dent about 'a Report of too great an Intimacy between the Witnesses Husband and Jane [Jackson]', in Jane Jackson, 1785, ASSI 45/35/2/90–1.
6. See in particular 18 Eliz.c.3., 1576; and 'An Act for the due Execution of divers Laws and Statutes made against Rogues, Vagabonds and sturdy Beggars, and other lewd and idle Persons', 7 Jac.I c.4, 1610.
7. See 'An Act for the better Relief of the Poor of this Kingdom', 13 & 14 Car.II c.12 s.19, 1662; and 'An Act for the Relief of Parishes and other Places from such Charges as may arise from Bastard Children born within the same', 6 Geo.II c.31, 1733.
8. Efforts at concealment, including wearing loose clothes and passing off their increased size as 'dropsy' or some other complaint, only delayed recognition of the signs of pregnancy. Jane Barnes (1745, ASSI 45/23/1/3A–E) was one of the few women later accused of murder who successfully eluded discovery during pregnancy.
9. Although servants were in theory protected by law from summary dismissal, there are numerous examples in the court records and in contemporary diaries of women being dismissed from service after their pregnancies had been discovered. In 1782, for example, Elizabeth Leake, suspecting that Ann Goodair was pregnant, 'insisted on her leaving her Service directly which Ann did so accordingly that Day'; Ann Goodair, 1782, ASSI 45/34/3/51–2.
10. 'An Act to prevent the Destroying and Murthering of Bastard Children', 21 Jac.I c.27, 1624.
11. Hannah Pullen, 1790, ASSI 45/37/1/176–8.
12. Elizabeth Eltoft, 1762, ASSI 45/26/6/19a.
13. Grace Furnace, 1756, ASSI 45/25/4/58–9.
14. Ann Stephenson, 1797, ASSI 45/39/2/100. See also Mary Windas, 1786, ASSI 45/35/3/223–4; Mary Wigfield, 1792, ASSI 45/37/3/

221–3; Hannah Leighton, 1793, ASSI 45/38/1/114–17.

15. Prudence Newsome, 1730, ASSI 45/18/7/47–50.
16. Susanna Staniforth, 1799, ASSI 45/40/1/118.
17. Elizabeth Eltoft, 1762, ASSI 45/26/6/19a.
18. Hannah Pullen, 1790, ASSI 45/37/1/176–8.
19. See the evidence in Margaret Baker, 1771, ASSI 45/30/1/22–26; Ann Hollingworth and Robert Bradbury, 1799, ASSI 45/40/1/6–17; Susanna Staniforth, 1799, ASSI 45/40/1/118.
20. The words by which Ann Atley is reported to have described her pregnancy loss to Mary Hebden in 1746; ASSI 45/23/2/12–13.
21. Sarah Ward, 1797, ASSI 45/39/2/121–2.
22. As Elizabeth Ryals put it, in response to neighbourhood suspicions that she was pregnant again: 'When one has once done amiss it is common for people to reflect'. Elizabeth had given birth to two bastard children who were still alive in 1770 when she was prosecuted for murdering her third bastard child at birth. See Elizabeth Ryals, ASSI 45/29/3/174–5.
23. See the depositions in Ann Benison, 1788, ASSI 45/36/2/10–12.
24. Hannah Pullen, 1790, ASSI 45/37/1/176–8.
25. It is also worth noting that even medical evidence in support of a suspect's claims could be overruled by a jury. Thus, some inquest juries were prepared to ignore both a suspect's account of events and corroborating medical evidence of prematurity if they felt that the circumstances merited a verdict of murder. For example, in 1789, an inquest jury investigating the death of Dorothy Henderson's bastard child ignored medical evidence that the child had been born three months prematurely, preferring instead to interpret marks of violence on the child's body as evidence of live birth and murder; see Dorothy Henderson, 1789, ASSI 45/36/3/85 and ASSI 44/104ii.

References

Alexander, W., *The History of Women*, London, 1779

Andrew, D.T, *Philanthropy and Police: London Charity in the Eighteenth Century*, Princeton, Princeton University Press, 1989

Beattie, J.M., *Crime and the Courts in England 1660–1800*, Oxford, Clarendon Press, 1986

Brittain, R.P., 'The Hydrostatic and Similar Tests of Live Birth: A Historical Review', *Medico-Legal Journal*, vol. 31, 1963, pp. 189–94

Brockbank, Dr. W. and Kenworthy, The Rev. F., (eds), *The Diary of Richard Kay, 1716–51*, Manchester, Chetham Society, 1968

Crawford, P., 'Attitudes to Menstruation in Seventeenth-century England', *Past and Present*, vol. 91, 1981, pp. 47–73

Defoe, D., *Conjugal Lewdness, or Matrimonial Whoredom*, London, 1727

Freind, Dr. J., *Emmenologia*, translated by Thomas Dale, London, 1729

Hale, M., *History of the Pleas of the Crown*, London, 1736

Hill, B., *Women, Work and Sexual Politics in Eighteenth-Century England*, Oxford, Basil Blackwell, 1989

Hoffer, P.C. and Hull, N.E.H., *Murdering Mothers: Infanticide in England and New England 1558–1803*, New York, New York University Press, 1981

Hunter, W., 'On the Uncertainty of the Signs of Murder, in the Case of Bastard Children', *Medical Observations and Inquiries*, vol. 6, 1784, pp. 266–90

Jackson, M., 'New-born Child Murder: A Study of Suspicion, Evidence and Proof in Eighteenth-Century England', Leeds, unpublished Ph.D. thesis, 1992

——, 'Suspicious Infant Deaths: The Statute of 1624 and Medical Evidence at Coroners' Inquests', in M. Clark and C. Crawford (eds), *Legal Medicine in History*, Cambridge, Cambridge University Press, 1994

Jordanova, L.J., 'Natural Facts: A Historical Perspective on Science and Sexuality', in C.P. MacCormack and M. Strathern (eds), *Nature, Culture and Gender*, Cambridge, Cambridge University Press, 1980

Laqueur, T., 'Bodies, Details, and the Humanitarian Narrative', in L. Hunt (ed.), *The New Cultural History*, California, University of California Press, 1989

McLaren, A., *Reproductive Rituals: The Perception of Fertility in England from the Sixteenth to the Nineteenth Century*, London, Methuen, 1984

Malcolmson, R.W., 'Infanticide in the Eighteenth Century', in J.S. Cockburn (ed.), *Crime in England 1550–1800*, London, Methuen, 1977

Mandeville, B., *A Modest Defence of Publick Stews: or, an Essay upon Whoring, As it is now practis'd in these Kingdoms*, London, 1724

Smellie, W., *A Treatise on the Theory and Practice of Midwifery. To which is now added, A Set of Anatomical Plates*, London, n.d.

Staves, S., 'British Seduced Maidens', *Eighteenth-Century Studies*, vol.

14, 1980/1, pp. 109–34

Stone, L., *The Family, Sex and Marriage in England 1500–1800*, London, Weidenfeld and Nicolson, 1977

Thomas, K., 'The Double Standard', *Journal of the History of Ideas*, vol. 20, 1959, pp. 195–216

Varsey, D. (ed.), *The Diary of Thomas Turner 1754–1765*, Oxford, Oxford University Press, 1984.

Author Index

Subject Index

Index

Index